On the Edge of Certainty

On the Edge of Certainty

Philosophical Explorations

Raymond Tallis

First published in Great Britain 1999 by
MACMILLAN PRESS LTD
Houndmills, Basingstoke, Hampshire RG21 6XS and London
Companies and representatives throughout the world

A catalogue record for this book is available from the British Library.

ISBN 0–333–76323–8 hardcover
ISBN 0–333–80022–2 paperback

First published in the United States of America 1999 by
ST. MARTIN'S PRESS, INC.,
Scholarly and Reference Division,
175 Fifth Avenue, New York, N.Y. 10010

ISBN 0–312–22416–8

Library of Congress Cataloging-in-Publication Data
Tallis, Raymond.
On the edge of certainty : philosophical explorations / Raymond
Tallis.
    p.   cm.
Includes bibliographical references and index.
ISBN 0–312–22416–8
1. Philosophy of mind.   I. Title.
BD418.3.T355   1999
128'.2—dc21   99–22107
                                                         CIP

This book is printed on paper suitable for recycling and made from fully managed
and sustained forest sources.

10   9   8   7   6   5   4   3   2   1
08   07   06   05   04   03   02   01   00   99

Printed and bound in Great Britain by
Antony Rowe Ltd, Chippenham, Wiltshire

For Robert Boyd and Les Turnberg in friendship, admiration and gratitude

Contents

Note

A Critical Dictionary of Neuromythology was previously published as *Psycho-Electronics: a Guide in the Form of a Lexicon to the Pseudo-Science of Cognitive Mechanics*. Ferrington, the publisher, unfortunately ceased trading shortly after publication. I am grateful to Mark Rogers for his comments on the text and for permission to reprint the *Dictionary*. 'The Poverty of Neurophilosophy' was originally written in response to a request to address the Conciousness Club at the Institute of Neurosciences, Queen Square Hospital. It is a pleasure to thank Professor Richard Frackowieck for the invitation and for the generosity with which he and his colleagues at the Institute of Cognitive Neurology attended to arguments which were somewhat at odds with their own views. The title piece, 'On the Edge of Certainty', has had a rather complex history. An early version, written in the late 1970s, and titled 'Tell them I have had a wonderful life...', was part of a still unpublished collection (*Strings*) of explorations of language conducted through a series of meditations on twenty or so utterances chosen almost at random. In the early 1980s, I expanded the piece to its present form. It gathered dust until I sent it to David Perry of the BBC who saw its potential as a piece of radio drama. We worked together on it and it was broadcast, to very positive reviews, in 1989. I recently revisited the original version and felt that it had sufficient merit to publish.

Acknowledgement

It is a pleasure to acknowledge the continuing support and kindness of Charmian Hearne and Tim Farmiloe of Macmillan. Without them, this book, like most of its predecessors, would not have seen the light of day.

Preface

The phenomenon of human knowledge is no doubt the greatest miracle in our universe.[1]

The books I have published over the last decade have for the most part been critiques: of post-Saussurean theory and all its satellite-isms; of cultural criticism with its hostility to modernity, to science and to the idea of progress driven to a significant degree by the deliberate activity of rational, conscious agents; and of biological and computational theories of the mind. Although the arguments of these books were for the most part devoted to countering the widely received views with which I was, and am, in profound disagreement, they also provided opportunities to advance positive ideas of my own on issues I felt had been seriously misunderstood by others. Among these ideas is one that is more important to me than any other: it is fundamental to my way of seeing things; it lies at the root of the astonishment that is both the origin and target of my philosophical activity; and again and again (sometimes to my surprise) it turns out to be the goal towards which my arguments are directed. This is the idea that man is, above all, an explicit animal and that it is the capacity for making things explicit which lies at the heart of all that human beings are and do. This capacity is, moreover, utterly mysterious, being underivable from anything else. It has no place, for example, in the world as described by the physicist or the biologist. And from this originates much of my dissent from the scientism that has taken such a hold on much philosophical thought.

This seemingly obvious, even banal, idea, which is argued for and expounded at length in the book to which it gives the title, *The Explicit Animal*,[2] is so simple that it is very difficult to express in a way that makes it other than an empty truism. And yet it feeds into the views I have advanced on the nature of language – and in particular my dissent from structuralism and its successors; on the nature of human culture; on the hope of progress; and, most obviously, on the nature of the mind. It is, admittedly, an idea that has relatively little content and yet, as I have already implied, overlooking explicitness is central to many of the fashionable misconceptions that have assumed a dominant place in twentieth-century thought. Indeed, it is most visible in its absence: as that which is missing from many contemporary accounts of the most distinctively human activities and the thoughts, feelings and ideas that underpin them. Explicitness is the cardinal characteristic of (to expropriate Marx's term) 'the species being' of humanity.

The five essays in this collection had their own occasions and were written entirely independently of one another. And yet they do have one thing in common, beyond not having being fully aired before and being capable of being described, in perhaps a slightly extended sense of the term, as 'philosophical': they are all preoccupied to different degrees with the notion of man, the explicit animal.

This is most evident in the opening essay, 'Explicitness and Truth (and Falsehood)', which argues that theories of truth do not 'start far enough back' because they focus too narrowly upon the criteria for differentiating truth from falsehood while overlooking the conditions that are necessary for truth and falsehood to emerge. Truth and falsehood both depend upon an act of making-explicit and any account of truth that does not include this is incomplete and consequently liable – as in the case of Tarski's Semantic Theory of Truth – to shrink towards a truism or even a tautology. I argue for an expansion of the concept of truth-conditions to encompass the conditions under which both truth and falsehood emerge, as well as the conditions that distinguish truth from falsehood. Truth and falsehood share *existence conditions*: the explicitness that creates possibilities and makes the actual, the existent into truth-conditions, the possibilities that are actualised. It is by transforming the existent into a realised possibility – and so distancing it from itself – that explicitness creates the conditions for the emergence of truth. (This essay, incidentally, is the hardest read of the pieces in the book and the reader may wish to leave it to the end.)

The central argument of *The Explicit Animal* was that computational, biological and other materialist theories of mind traduced the nature of human consciousness. In such theories, the mind is animalised and/or mechanised and effectively eliminated, if not in fact, at least as a problem or entity utterly different from those that are currently being fruitfully addressed by science. During the course of writing *The Explicit Animal* it occurred to me that the key to the scientistic approach to mind and human consciousness – which enabled mind to be eliminated even as the distinctive mystery of the mental was being apparently addressed – lay in the persistent misuse of certain pivotal terms and concepts. I therefore considered that it would be useful to collect these terms in a small *Critical Dictionary of Neuromythology*. I imagined that this would put paid once and for all to the credibility of writers who purport to describe the human mind while leaving out what is essential to humanity – self-consciousness and deliberative, chosen action; in short, explicitness. Unfortunately, the Dictionary, like *The Explicit Animal*, has not stemmed the flow of Bluffers' Guides, which enable scientistic thinkers such as Daniel Dennett (*Consciousness Explained*[3]) and Stephen Pinker (*How the Mind Works*[4]) to persuade the general public that it is possible to find the human mind in the mechanisms that have been – or would one day be – observed in the human brain. This failure of the *Critical Dictionary* to make an impact may have had something to do with the fact that its small, idealistic publisher went out of business shortly after the book was issued and it had received only a single (though very favourable) review in *The Journal of Consciousness Studies*. For this reason, I felt it would be worth republishing this little book here: the 200 copies in a cardboard box in my attic are not best placed to join that wider conversation in which writers aspire to participate.

The third piece, 'The Poverty of Neurophilosophy', continues the critique of neurological or quasi-neurological accounts of consciousness, in particular those wedded to the informationalist and evolutionist models prominent in a certain strain of cognitive psychology. Its main focus, however, is upon a particular feature of human consciousness that seems to be unlikely to yield to a neurological explanation: its highly structured, highly organised, open complexity. Compared with the richness of ordinary human consciousness, neurophilosophy seems poverty-stricken indeed. Although this essay is concerned with the inadequacy of neural accounts of consciousness, it also recognises the achievements of the neurosciences in helping us to understand how the brain works and, more particularly, the ways in which it does not work. Any critique of 'neuromythology' must try to reconcile the poverty of neurophilosophy with the richness of basic neuroscience and the therapeutic potential of the clinical neurosciences. The essay ends with one, rather unsatisfactory, suggestion as to how this might be achieved.

One of the most compelling arguments against materialist theories of mind was advanced in a famous essay by Thomas Nagel, 'What is it like to be a bat?'[5] in which he pointed out that, however complete our scientific knowledge about an organism, we should still not know *what it is like to be that organism*: even if I knew everything there was to know about the nervous system of a bat, I still would not have the slightest notion of what it is like to be a bat. This argument lay at the heart of a broader vision, which Nagel expounded at greater length about a decade after his 'bat' article, in *The View from Nowhere*.[6] In the latter, one of the most important contributions to the philosophical literature of the last few decades, he pointed out the mutual irreducibility of the objective view (which culminates in science) and the subjective view of the individual human being. Nagel acknowledged that his argument was closely allied to a profound idea that T.L.S. Sprigge had put forward independently a few years before Nagel's 'bat' article: that there is something corresponding to *what it is like to be* the body that I am and that this something does not correspond to the body's physical characteristics – those properties, for example, that are revealed to scientific investigation or even to the ordinary objective or third-person gaze. This insight of Sprigge's seemed to me to cast light on the elusive notion of explicitness and to enable it to be approached from a particular angle; from that indicated by the 'fact' that I am explicitly this thing, as in part expressed in the fact that this body is what I *have* to be, in the sense of my being compelled or obliged to be it. 'That I am This (Thing): Reflections on Deixis, Explicitness and the Tautology of the Self' is a slightly Heideggerian exploration of a network of thoughts around this peculiar ('even embarrassing', as Valéry's M. Teste noted) notion of my being explicitly a particular thing.

This fourth essay is more 'literary' than the other two, mixing a bit of gossip with the metaphysics; at any rate, giving the thoughts a more personal occasion. For a long time, it has been my ambition to close two kinds of gap: between so-called 'Continental Philosophy' and the so-called 'Anglo-American analytical tradition'; and, more radically, between fiction and philosophy. In 'Philosophies of Consciousness and Philosophies of the Concept, Or: Is There Any Point in Studying the Headache I Have Now?' (in *Enemies of Hope*[7]) I argued that both Anglo-American analytical and continental phenomenological traditions had strengths and weaknesses and that neither was adequate by itself. (I also pointed out the important cross-over between the traditions.) In 'Metaphysics and Gossip Notes Towards a Manifesto for the Fiction of the Future' (in *Theorrhoea and After*[8]) I postulated a new genre of writing which would combine the abstract rigour and the universalising ambitions of philosophy with the narrative power of fiction, and would avoid the deficiencies of both: philosophy's tendency to seem unoccasioned, uprooted from the passions and concerns of everyday life; and fiction's tendency to be of too local or focal an interest; in short to be trivial. 'That I am This (Thing): Reflections on Deixis, Explicitness and the Tautology of the Self' is a modest advance in the direction indicated by 'Philosophies of Consciousness and Philosophies of the Concept'. The final essay is a move in the direction indicated by 'Metaphysics and Gossip'. 'On the Edge of Certainty' interweaves biographical facts about Wittgenstein with reflections on the thoughts he committed to paper in the final weeks of his life.

On the very last day of his thinking life, Wittgenstein touched on the mystery that is close to my own preoccupations and that haunts this present book. Although it was written over a decade ago, 'On the Edge of Certainty' seems to represent a way forward for my own thinking and, in this sense, may indicate an ending of one approach to philosophical enquiry and the beginning of another. Not that there is anything particularly novel about the convergence between philosophy and fiction. Since its very beginning, philosophers have resorted to dramatisation, at least in the form of dialogues, to present their arguments. And it is only comparatively recently that narrowly focused technical papers – which address issues whose palpable context is other philosophy papers written by professional philosophers who keep their own personal preoccupations in the background – have become a kind of philosophical norm. The commitment to the piecemeal approaches to specific, clearly defined, technical problems is not dishonourable; indeed, when one encounters certain other modes of philosophising (in particular, what I have elsewhere called 'guru goo'), one is grateful for the rigour and honesty of technical philosophy. But there comes a point at which it seems necessary to find alternative modes of expression of philosophical curiosity and wonder that are more explicitly in touch with fundamental concerns and that address the hungers of the thinking mind in a more rounded way.

The first and last essays have something else in common. They both concern themselves with a particular entry from Wittgenstein's *On Certainty*,[9] his last work:

> It is so difficult to find the *beginning*. Or, better: it is difficult to begin at the beginning. And not to try to go further back.

'On the Edge of Certainty' discusses how this thought reaches to the very heart of Wittgenstein's vision. 'Explicitness and Truth (and Falsehood)' argues, however, that the problem with most theories of truth is not that they start too far back, but that they don't start far back enough. The philosophical debate, at least of late, has been entered too far downstream. Discussion of the nature of truth overlooks the extraordinariness of the fact that, for us humans, there *is* something called the truth and that this, just as the existence of something called falsehood, requires thinking about before one engages in the business of establishing criteria for differentiating the true from the false. The problem is, as Wittgenstein well knew, that if one does go far enough back to make truth fully visible, in a manner that also makes falsehood visible, so that one truly *notices* that there is such a thing as asserting what is the case and postulating possibilities, one quite quickly runs into the unsayable.

Perhaps my inclination to try a different approach to philosophy from that exemplified in the rather conventional style and organisation of *The Explicit Animal* originates from the feeling that it is necessary to drama-tise, or fictionalise, philosophical ideas in order to *exhibit* the things they are talking about. At bottom, I am conscious of a frustration at my own inability fully to express the idea that lies at the heart of both my positive vision and my dissent from much contemporary thought about mind, language and the place of humanity in the order of things. 'Explicitness' sometimes seems to boil down simply to the 'that' in 'That X is the case'. The 'that' seems to promise immense riches, especially when the X that is the case is 'the X that *I* am'. Properly attended to, 'that' opens on to indexicality and deixis, which are fundamental features of our selved existences. They have been displaced by the dominant 'third-person' theories of consciousness – both theories that dwell on the varieties of the unconscious that are supposed to decentre us, and theories that derive from the materialist world picture of science from which indexicality and deixis are signally absent; from which, indeed, they have been banished.

Most essentially, we are creatures who are able to experience, and hence to say, 'That...'; and yet we cannot fully articulate what it is that this 'That' – in virtue of which the world is explicit and we live our lives explicitly – is. That we are such creatures is the thought which, more than any other, I want one day to *express*, rather than merely refer to. The suspicion that making explicitness central to the unique nature of humankind is the key to a new way of thinking about some of the most fundamental problems of philosophy may be a delusion, but it is this above all that keeps alive my impulse to philosophise.

Notes

1. Karl R. Popper, Preface to *Objective Knowledge: an Evolutionary Approach* (Oxford University Press, 1972).
2. Raymond Tallis, *The Explicit Animal: a Defence of Human Consciousness* (London: Macmillan, 1991).

3. Daniel Dennett, *Consciousness Explained* (London: Penguin, 1993).
4. Stephen Pinker, *How the Mind Works* (London: Penguin, 1997).
5. Thomas Nagel 'What is it like to be a bat?', *Philosophical Review*, 83 (1974), 435–50.
6. Thomas Nagel, *The View from Nowhere* (Oxford: Oxford University Press, 1986).
7. Raymond Tallis, *Enemies of Hope: a Critique of Contemporary Pessimism* (London: Macmillan, 1997).
8. Raymond Tallis, *Theorrhoea and After* (London: Macmillan, 1999).
9. Ludwig Wittgenstein, *On Certainty*, edited by G.E.M. Anscombe and G.H. von Wright. Translated by Denis Paul and G.E.M. Anscombe (Oxford: Blackwell, 1974).

1
Explicitness and Truth (and Falsehood)

Introduction

On 5 April 1951, just over three weeks before his death, Wittgenstein recorded this thought in his notebook:

> It is so difficult to find the *beginning*. Or, better: it is difficult to begin at the beginning. And not to try to go further back.[1]

This captures in a nutshell much of what he had tried to say during his forty years as a philosopher. Philosophers, he had argued, ran into trouble when their arguments, questions and thought-experiments went so far back as to remove the very context in which philosophy, or philosophical discussion, is possible. For example, an argument about the reality or otherwise of an external world or of other minds cannot truly be had because such arguments presuppose the existence of a real external world and of other minds. More generally, the systematic doubt, from which philosophy since Descartes was supposed to start, cannot be sincere because we can express and argue over our doubts only if we stand on the firm ground of many things that have to be taken for granted; worse, such doubts cannot even be intelligible because they have to be expressed in words whose meaning conditions would be suspended by systematic doubt. Much philosophical discourse ran the risk, therefore, of being either pragmatically self-refuting or nonsensical or both, and consequently of being vacuous and insincere.

While I agree that philosophers do frequently run the danger of beginning too far back, the starting point for this essay is a concern that much recent discussion of the philosophical notion of truth has been damaged by the opposite fault: that of beginning too far down the track. I shall argue that we shall not understand the notion of truth, or ask the right questions about it, or develop the right kinds of theories, unless we step back from preoccupation with what it is that makes statements and propositions true or false and consider the conditions, or the context, which *both* truth and falsehood presuppose: the necessary background from which the notions of truth and falsehood and the categories of the true and the false emerge. The extent to which this background, these preconditions, are overlooked will become clear when in due course we consider the so-called 'deflationary' theories of truth, in accordance with which the concept of truth is more or less empty.

The approach to the notion of truth that I shall argue for here builds upon and to some extent presupposes arguments and ideas put forward in my book *The Explicit Animal*[2] and the discussion of the Correspondence Theory of Truth that occupies the final chapter of my critique of post-Saussurean literary theory, *Not Saussure*.[3] It will, therefore, be useful to begin by reiterating some of the points made in those two books.

Explicitness and truth

The concept of explicitness is central to the 'defence' of human consciousness advanced in the *The Explicit Animal*: human beings are, above all, *explicit* animals. The emphasis in the book on explicitness – and its numerous, perhaps too numerous, reminders of the ways in which human beings are explicit in what they do and think, while material objects and non-human animals are not – was intended as a corrective to certain influential trends in contemporary philosophy. Notable among these were biological materialism – which assimilated humanity to animality and the mind to the activity of the brain – and functionalism which, in so far as it tolerated such 'folk psychology' notions as 'consciousness', 'beliefs' and 'thoughts' at all, attempted to reduce them to input–output relations of the brain or of the whole organism understood in computational terms. My quarrel was with those who, by dint of biologising or computerising the mind, marginalised a distinctively human consciousness, both in respect of its status as a something in itself and in respect of its role in human life: human action, human experience, human affairs seemed to be delegated to a coalition of automata. By emphasising the place of explicitness in human life – one aspect of which can be expressed by saying that we do things deliberately and consciously and frequently with express reference to enormously complex rules and to often strikingly abstract categories that we humans have brought into existence – I wanted to make it impossible to overlook consciousness in the way that present-day computer-besotted and scientistic thinking encourages us to do.

If I were to pull out one thread from the interwoven arguments of *The Explicit Animal* and describe it as fundamental it would be this: we cannot assimilate human beings to the materialist, physicalist, biologist, computationalist world pictures because those world pictures are confined to descriptions of automatic mechanisms, perhaps rooted ultimately in the laws of physics, while human beings are not, ultimately, mechanisms. (Which is not to deny that we are dependent upon mechanisms in order to live our ordinary lives; the most important among these are, of course, the multitudinous mechanisms of the human body.) If we *are* animals (and it would be very difficult – indeed daft – to deny this), then we are very distinctive animals in virtue of the fact that we do things deliberately with, as I have said, explicit reference to complex rules which are mobilised by often highly abstract considerations. We are aware of our actions and reactions in a way that no other animal is aware of its actions and reactions. We are aware not only of the immediate occasion, the sensory content and of the proximate consequences of our actions, but of the wider – indeed limitless – framework through which they make explicit sense to us, and to others like ourselves.

This fundamental difference between ourselves and the other animals – and, indeed, all other material beings – may be illustrated readily by considering certain behaviours that we may at first sight think of as common to both human beings and non-human animals. (See *Explicit Animal*, especially Chapter 6.)

Compare, for example, feeding behaviour in non-human animals and human beings. Animals typically eat simply as a result of bumping into food. The bumping may be guided subconsciously through a response to various cues or by highly programmed hunting (or seeking) routines, but these routines are unknown to the animals themselves, or at least not expressly present to, even less explicitly formulated by, them. At its most sophisticated in non-human animals, eating is the result of a successful hunting or gathering expedition. By contrast, in human beings eating is a highly complex socialised ritual, and both the food and the resources used to obtain it are the product of a multitude of actions that are carried out in conscious obedience to a vast number of rules and other explicit considerations. It is perfectly normal for a human being to eat as a guest or another human being and for, say, the guest to mobilise her awareness of the host's financial situation – precipitated, perhaps, by a rise in the mortgage interest rate which she had heard about on the radio on the way to the lunch engagement – to choose a less expensive dish than the one she would have chosen on the basis of spontaneous preference. This complex awareness is capped by another crucial and telling difference: she is able to give an account of the meal and the reasons for the choice of dish afterwards, and may do so in order to present herself in a certain favourable light to her interlocutor.

The distance between human and non-human animals is even more dramatically illustrated in the case of 'learning behaviour'. Nothing could be more remote from the 'bump-into-and-know' (or 'bump-into-and-experience') of animal learning than the typical activities by which human beings consciously extend their knowledge. The mother who calculates that, by increasing her contributions to the baby-sitting circle this year, she will have enough tickets in the bank to be able to attend an evening class next year in order to study for a degree in law with the ultimate aim of becoming a solicitor, is a perfectly ordinary example of an adult (human) learner. It would be inconceivable to think of an adult non-human primate behaving in this way. The difference is so great that it seems absurd to use the same terms – 'learning' or 'learning behaviour' – to encompass the acquisition of experience in both non-human animals and human beings.

This, then, was the role the notion of 'explicitness' played in *The Explicit Animal*: as the key difference between humans and non-human organisms; and as a something, easier to illustrate by example than to capture in a definition, that sets humans off from the rest of nature – from the universe that is described by physicists and biologists – and from the world of machines. Human beings have highly developed, exquisitely elaborated, consciousness of what they are about. The extent to which that consciousness is collective or individual, the degree to which it has an unconscious core and misreads and misunderstands itself, and the validity of its feeling that it is an autonomous point of origin have all been hotly disputed.[4] Modernist and postmodernist attempts to 'marginalise consciousness' by claiming that human consciousness is more enmired than it imagines in things that it is unconscious of would not, even if they were well founded, gainsay the truth that human beings do things for explicit and explicitly avowed reasons, rooted in complex rules and predicated upon equally complex abstract notions.

In *The Explicit Animal*, I largely left explicitness to take care of itself: I invoked it repeatedly to indicate the distances between humanity and animality and humanity and materiality. I made only a token gesture towards determining the place of explicitness in the world at large. It was as if to assert it as a distinct *sui generis* category was sufficient in itself. This assumption of the self-evident meaning of the term is a serious deficiency in *The Explicit Animal*, although I did attempt to capture it other than by means of illustration. Let me summarise that attempt here, because, as I have already indicated, the notion of explicitness is central to the interpretation of the concept of truth that I wish to put forward in this essay.

In the Overture to *The Explicit Animal*, I asserted that explicitness was '*underivable*, least of all from matter' (p. 3). I envisaged a hierarchy of increasing explicitness as follows:

Increasing Explicitness	Object/Content
?	—
Discrete existents	Whatever there is in the absence of consciousness
Explicit existents	Objects of perception
Explicit awareness of existents	Explicit objects of perception
Explicit explicitness	Discourse about perception; information
Explicit explicit explicitness	Metalanguage; discourse about discourse

The hierarchy, I must emphasise, was not intended to indicate an ontogenetic sequence. The terms were chosen to leave open any questions about the relationship between the increasingly explicit layers of consciousness and the rest of the world, a relationship that we usually find most convenient, but perhaps ultimately rather unhelpfully, to cast in the narrow form of the relationship between mind and matter.[5]

One way of making explicitness 'visible' is to imagine the difference between a world with and a world without it. This is a potentially messy approach because it raises all sorts of questions, not the least of which is what it is that explicitness makes explicit; or to put it another way, whether what is made explicit is simply whatever was there in the first place or whether there is a divergence between the appearings disclosed to explicitness and the beings that explicitness makes be explicitly there.[6] It is, however, useful to consider the difference between the following:

  i) X;
 ii) that there is X;
iii) Mary: 'There is X';
 iv) John: 'Mary said that there is X.'
  v) Fred: 'I have examined John's claim that Mary said "There is X".'

We might image X standing for the existence of an object or a state of affairs or the occurrence of an event.[7] Explicitness is, then, what is added when we move from i) in the direction of v). As we move from i) to v), something else – extremely important – is added: truth and falsehood. The central argument of this essay is that we cannot understand truth without referring to explicitness. Nor can we understand falsehood: truth and falsehood are born twins, the condition of the possibility of one being the condition of the possibility of the other.

To bring this idea into focus, it might be useful to recall a couple of passages from Wittgenstein's *Tractatus*:[8]

> One could say that the sole logical constant was what *all* propositions, by their very nature, had in common with one another. But that is the general propositional form. (5.47)

> The general propositional form is: This is how things are. (4.5)

The passage from i) to v) is also the passage towards propositions – 'This is how things are' – which are then able to carry truth-values. A proposition is best captured in the form of a statement when it has the status of a possibility that may or may not be realised; there may or or may not be an existing state of affairs corresponding to this possibility. If there is no such state of affairs, the proposition is false; if there is such a state of affairs, the proposition is true. The general propositional form is '*That* X is the case'; its explicitness carries the transformation of X from plain X to '*That* X [is the case]'; or the transition from one to the other.

In the course of drawing out this relationship between explicitness and truth, I am straying a little into the territory of the next section, though this is inevitable in view of the special relationship between truth and propositions and, consequently, between truth and statements. I will return to this matter presently but will first consider the question that inevitably arises when it is argued that explicitness is the difference between i) and v) and that truth (falsehood) emerges in parallel with the emergence of explicitness: at what point between

i) and v) does truth (and falsehood) emerge as a fully fledged category? This is a mostly, but not entirely, empty question. Let us give it some focus by substituting for X an object such as 'a pebble on the ground' in i) to v):

  i) a pebble on the ground;
 ii) that there is a pebble on the ground;
iii) Mary: 'There is a pebble on the ground';
 iv) John: 'Mary said that there is a pebble on the ground.'
  v) Fred: 'I have examined John's claim that Mary said "There is a pebble on the ground".'

It is evident that truth has emerged by the time we reach iii). It is equally evident that i) – a pebble on the ground – is not in itself a truth (even less a falsehood). The difficult (and not uninteresting) question is where, between i) and iii), truth emerges. Pebbles *per se* are not true or false; assertions about them made by human beings are. We may imagine the categories of truth and falsehood as being embryonic or inchoate in ii) – 'that there is a pebble on the ground'. How well developed the embryo is will depend upon how we interpret the 'that'; or what it is in virtue of which the 'that' can prefix the existence of the pebble on the ground so that its being on the ground itself has existence.

The obvious candidates are:

i)   unfocused awareness;
ii) more focused sensations which in some dim sense refer back to the pebble;
iii) and yet more focused and intelligible (and even, in some sense, classifying) perceptions which are manifestly 'of' the pebble.

It is not easy to apply the concept of 'truth' ('falsehood') to something as vague as awareness. What seems to be missing is an element which, even if it is not actually asserted, believed, inferred, can at least be in some sense *wrong*. While explicitness is necessary for the emergence of truth, 'thatness' is not of itself sufficient to count as truth – or as knowledge. The old argument that sensations are incorrigible and do not, for this very reason, amount to genuine knowledge seems to be relevant here: a particular sensation in isolation cannot be true or false, or a bearer of truth or falsehood, or amount to a truth or a falsehood. If we think of the increasing explicitness that is expressed in the passage from unreflective, unformed experience to fully-formed knowledge, the category of truth and falsehood emerges somewhere around perception – as the level at which it is possible to misinterpret things; that is, to get them wrong. It will be evident from this that the possibility of getting things right and of getting them wrong have the same general conditions: in short, that truth and falsehood have the same general possibility conditions.[9] (For this reason, I shall speak henceforth not of truth or falsehood separately, but of the two together: TF.)

Exactly where TF appears is either an empirical matter or (more likely) a matter of definition; not, at any rate, something to be established by an uncovering of *a priori* essences. The purpose of the present discussion, however, is served sufficiently if it accepted that explicitness is the necessary condition of TF, even if the exact point in the development and elaboration of explicitness at which TF emerges is left open. The connection between TF and explicitness may seem so obvious as to seem hardly worth labouring. A couple of examples may indicate otherwise and underline the point of this essay, which lies not only, or even chiefly, in the position it is putting forward but also in the positions from which it is dissenting.

The first is a complex set of misunderstandings that result in the separation of the notions of truth and falsehood from consciousness.[10] These anti-psychologistic views lie at the heart of computational theories of the mind, but they go all the way back to George Boole for whom psychologism was not an explicit issue. Boole's entirely laudable endeavours to bring notational transparency into logic – i.e. the general principles defining the valid connections between propositions – were significantly misdescribed by him in the title of his book *An Investigation of the Laws of Thought, on Which are Founded the Mathematical Theories of Logic and Probabilities*. It was the culminating expression of his belief – immensely influential in the succeeding 150 years – that logic was best understood in mathematical rather than philosophical terms. This in itself was harmless – indeed fruitful; but, combined with the notion that logic was central to the laws of thought, it created the first element of the framework which, via the notion of truth-tables and the mathematical logic of Bertrand Russell and many others, encouraged a consciousness-free notion of truth. From this, it was but a step to the Churchlands' notion of the mind as a logic engine and the popular Syntactic Theory of Mind (discussed in *The Explicit Animal*) in which the logical or grammatical connections between content-free elements of 'mind' are emphasised at the cost of content and meaning in the customary sense. The separation of TF from consciousness is one of the predisposing conditions that have led to the promulgation of computational theories of mind.

A more extreme example of the failure to link truth and explicitness – and the separation of TF from consciousness – comes from a recent article by Derek Parfit.[11] In 'Why Anything? Why This?', he addresses the fundamental philosophical question of why there is anything rather than nothing. He considers the relative probabilities of there being something rather than than there being nothing at all, and argues that even if there were nothing at all – what he calls the Null Possibility – albeit that it is superficially less improbable than other possibilities, this still leaves something to be explained. In formulating the Null Possibility, we might, he says, imagine away living beings, stars and atoms, but we would not be able to imagine away everything. There would still, he argues, 'have been various truths, such as the truth that there were no stars or atoms, or that 9 is divisible by 3'. Parfit is here assuming that *truths may exist in the absence of anything – truth-speakers, languages, consciousnesses or even material objects*.

This is an extreme expression of the belief that truths somehow exist in themselves. It is, of course, somewhat unusual as well as extreme: while many thinkers imagine that truth can exist independently of conscious truth-bearers (in other words, they overlook the explicitness condition), few imagine that there can be many truths existing independently of there being anything for truth to be true of. For Parfit, in the world where there is nothing, there is still the truth *that* there is nothing. In addition there are certain analytical, abstract truths such as that 9 is divisible by 3. Notwithstanding that this view *is* extreme and unusual, it is revealing that a mainstream philosopher such as Parfit may believe that, in a universe of nothing, the truth *that* there is nothing may still in some sense exist. Parfit's argument shows how truth is often thought of: as something that can be obtained free, as a gift bundled up with the state of affairs that it is true of. When, as in Parfit's example, that state of affairs is [the existence of] nothing, the universe gets, free of charge, the truth 'That there is nothing'.

The absurdity of this is sufficiently evident, but it is worth spelling out in order to extract from it the insights that, by default, it illuminates. If the existence of certain beings were sufficient to generate the truths that describe those beings, then whatever existed would count as a standing assertion that it – that existent being or state of affairs – was the case: the universe would be a sustained, albeit implicit, declaration of itself. This is absurd enough, but it becomes even more absurd when we consider what truths could be unpacked from, or mapped upon, this self-declaring universe. There would be truths about total, subtotals, parts, elements, etc. The list of 'free' truths would be endless for there is, of course, an infinite number of ways of describing the universe or, indeed, any part of it.[12]

This consideration should make sufficiently obvious the fact that none of the descriptions – and consequently the truths corresponding to them – has a discrete existence prior to the existence of human consciousness(es) making them explicit. To reiterate: what Parfit's argument amounts to is an extreme example of a very widespread tendency: that of assuming that truth comes free; that things include 'the truth of those things' as a free gift. So a universe in which there is nothing still contains the truth '*that there is nothing*'.

Parfit's example is helpful because very few people will want to argue that Nothing can contain anything at all, not even the truth *That there is nothing*, or *There is a universe but it contains nothing*, or *The universe contains nothing*. The example serves the Wittgensteinian philosophical purpose of making a piece of disguised nonsense into patent nonsense. Even those who feel that truths can exist among things without the need for there to be truth-bearers, explicit animals who make existents explicit as truths or things about which there are truths, will draw back at the suggestion that such truths can exist, even if there is nothing for truths to be true about. However, it is important not to lose sight of the fundamental problem which affects those who claim that there are truths in a world without truth-bearing consciousnesses. One way of bringing this problem into focus is to consider why or how it could happened that someone as intelligent as Parfit could have been persuaded of the belief that there are still truths in an entirely empty universe.

Parfit, I want to argue, is a victim (in common with those who overlook the need for truth-bearing explicitness) of what I will describe in the next chapter as the Fallacy of Misplaced Explicitness. In Parfit's case, explicitness, which belongs to the actual universe containing human beings, is displaced to the Null Possibility universe. The truth 'That there are no stars or atoms' in reality belongs to the actual universe (in which there *are* stars and atoms and, alongside these, explicit animals to turn these existent into facts), but Parfit has displaced it to the Null Possibility universe, where there is nothing at all. In a world where there is nothing, there is no truth either, not even the truth *that* there is nothing. That truth can exist only in a world where there is something; specifically in the consciousness of those who postulate, and think about, a possible world where there is nothing. The latter world is the truth-condition of the truth 'There is nothing', while the former is the existence condition of that truth.

The notion of 'existence conditions' is central to my argument about the nature of truth. An existence condition of TF is a necessary prerequisite of there being either truths or falsehoods. *That* there is nothing is a truth *about*, a truth *of*, the Null Possibility universe, not a truth *in* it. The kind of entity that is necessary to make the truth '*That* there is nothing' exist is a conscious being and one able to make things explicit at a very high level; in short, an articulate explicitness. Any other view, which holds that there can be truths among material things (or, in the case of Parfit's universe, truth in nothingness), is sheer animism and opens the way to absurdity.

To put it crudely, in Parfit's essay, Nothing is given the credit for truths that only Something – and indeed a very special something – can bear. And there is no limit to the amount of credit that Nothing may be given according to Parfit's way of thinking; for example, in his Null Possibility universe, there are yet other truths – such as that '9 is divisible by 3' – which apparently don't require the existence of anything to be true. Indeed, one might imagine that the entire menagerie of analytical truths – which do not, after all, depend upon the existence of any particular states of affairs, or any states of affairs at all (including the state of affairs that there is nothing) – living their revenue-free and capital-free lives in total contentment in a universe of non-existence – in a non-universe. In addition, there would be an infinite number of truths about the universe itself, such as: that it is composed of nothing at all; that it is not composed of something; that it is not composed of not-nothing; that it is not not composed of not-something; etc. There would be more; for example, that it is not a universe that can or could sustain human life.

The crowded nothingness of the Null Possibility universe is a dramatic illustration of what happens when one forgets that one needs truth-bearers as a precondition of truths, or more generally of TF. Why are philosophers inclined to do this? It may be because they have not thought sufficiently about the ontological status of truths. Or, if they have, have tended to think of truths as things in a world, existing in their own right. For Parfit, it seems the truth that '9 is divisible by 3' must exist in its own right, so it can go anywhere; it can exist even in a world where there are no minds and there are no material things either.

The position for which I am arguing is that truths do not have this kind of aseity. Truths (and falsehoods) are *of* the world but they are not *in* it – except in so far as they are given linguistic expression or other material embodiment by TF-bearers. They are not stand-alones; they have to be borne by truth-bearers able to make the world (or part of the world, or state of affairs) of which they are true explicit. The belief that truths can stand alone – so that they can exist even in a universe consisting of nothing – is the ultimate expression of the Fallacy of Misplaced Explicitness, which displaces explicitness from one place to another. In the example drawn from Parfit, explicitness is displaced from the universe of existents, our universe, which contains conscious beings who can see that the Null Possibility universe would have no stars or and who make the truth 'That there are no stars and atoms' explicit, to the Null Possibility universe itself. Truths *about* the Null Possibility universe, which are made explicit and so exist in our universe, are fallaciously seen as truths *in* the Null Possibility universe.[13]

Explicitness and theories of truth

The tendency to overlook explicitness as a necessary precondition of TF eases the passage from traditional theories of truth (such as Correspondence and Coherence Theories) to certain contemporary theories – usually described as 'deflationary' – that evacuate the notion of truth of specific characteristics and threaten to make it either trivially analytic or empty. It is an important consequence of my argument that truth will seem to be empty so long as it is not recognised that it is is founded, as is falsehood, in explicitness.

Tarski's Semantic Theory of Truth[14] is an example of a potentially deflationary account of truth. If we accept his theory, there is indeed a risk that the notion of truth *per se* will seem redundant. Tarski captured the notion of truth in this formula:

'Snow is white' is true if and only if snow is white.
Or, more generally,
   'p' is true, if and only if p

Tarski himself did not intend that this should capture the entirety of the notion of truth. His formula was intended to specify a consequence of any adequate definition of truth and his aim was a narrowly technical one: that of defining the notion of truth for the sentences of formal languages in terms of the referents of their primitive names and predicates. In short, Tarski was concerned specifically with sentences (rather than, say, propositions). However, his notions were close to those of the deflationary theorists for whom the very notion of truth – understood as a property of propositions – was redundant. While, for Tarski,

'p' is true if and only if p

was a technical observation, it was a formula that might have seemed to writers such as Ramsay to have captured all there was to be said about truth itself. Ramsay, who died before Tarski published his theory but who, like Tarski, was influenced by Frege and the latter's hostility to psychologism, argued that since 'p' and 'p' is true' have the same truth-conditions, the predicate 'is true' adds nothing to the informational content or the meaning of any proposition. The concept of truth is, therefore, redundant; to assert that 'p is true' is the same as to assert 'p'.

The emptiness of the notion of truth is, I submit, not inherent in the nature of truth itself; rather, it is an inevitable consequence of starting too far down the track and overlooking all that has been necessary to get to the point where there are such things as discrete propositions and sentences that express them. If this is overlooked, the notion of truth is in danger of being evacuated of content – as Ramsay thought it should be. 'p' and 'p is true' have the same truth-conditions (and in verificationist terms the same meaning). They do not, however, have the same *existence* conditions – and this is the crucial point. The propositions and their related sentences correspond to different noticings and they make explicit something different. To put this another way, the conditions that will lead to the one being picked out (in the case of a proposition) or asserted (where 'p' and 'p is true' are sentences) will be different from the conditions that will lead to the other's being picked out. Let us examine this claim in relation to Tarski's famous example.

I may say 'Snow is white' in order to inform someone who has never seen snow what colour it is or to add to a list someone is trying to compile of things that are white (linen, clouds, etc.) for a poem. In contrast, I will typically say '"Snow is white" is true' or 'It is true that snow is white' in response to a challenge to my own or someone else's assertion that snow is white. It is not too tendentious a reading to unpack from Tarski's formula:

'"Snow is white is true" if and only if snow is white'

the following:

'If anyone said/asserted that 'Snow is white", this would be true if and only if snow were white.'

In order to obtain a full understanding of the notion of truth, one has not only to specify the truth-conditions, in the narrow technical sense, of true utterances but also to specify their existence conditions – the conditions under which they are possible and the conditions that would lead truths to being picked out as propositions, or asserted in sentential form. Any theory of truth that omits these existence conditions of TF will threaten to empty the notion of truth and reduce it to a trivial tautology such as is seemingly expressed by Tarski's Semantic Theory. And once one overlooks existence conditions, the route to the kind of absurdities discussed earlier in relation to the Null Possibility universe is short and straight.

The Semantic Theory seems trivial – truistic, tautologous – because the elements on both sides of the definition of truth are, inescapably, expressed as sentences, as in:

'Snow is white' is true if and only if snow is white.

In Tarski's system, the sentences are different, inasmuch as the second sentence refers to the outside world (it is an object sentence) and the first sentence (in quotations) refers to, by citing, the second sentence and so is metalinguistic. So Tarski is not quite saying A is A; but he seems to run close to this. And the concept of truth – in one reading a version of the Correspondence Theory, in another a version of the Coherence Theory – seems thereby almost to be reduced to 'A is A' because the TF-making work that underpins the generation of propositions that may be true or false has been presupposed on both sides of the definition and therefore seems to factor out.

Once it is accepted that any theory of truth has to include an account of the existence conditions of TF as well as the truth-conditions of true statements, it will be recognised that, whatever their differences, Correspondence, Coherence and other theories of truth have much in common; that what they have in common may be more important, and central to the characterisation of the nature of TF, than what separates them. In fact, it is possible to read into Tarski's definition inchoate forms of both Correspondence and Coherence Theories.

It is most readily seen as a version of the Correspondence Theory, inasmuch as it asserts that truth resides in the correspondence between the state of affairs asserted in a sentence 'Snow is white' and a state of affairs in the real (or at least extra-linguistic) world – that snow is white. If, however, the relationship asserted in a metalinguistic sentence defining the nature of truth – '"Snow is white" if and only if snow is white' – is seen to be between the two component sentences within the compound sentence – the metalinguistic 'Snow is white' and the object-linguistic 'snow is white' – then it could be argued that Tarski is defining truth in terms of the coherence between sentences within a particular system of discourse, a system (for example, English) that encompasses both object- and metalanguages.

If Tarski really were trying to capture the whole nature of truth (and it is not clear that he was), he would, according to the position being developed in this essay, have to incorporate into his account the essential precondition of truth, the overarching (or underpinning) emergence-condition of truth (and falsehood): explicitness. Truth has to be made to exist through explicitness: its content is that which is made explicit. We may think of that which is made explicit as a *possibility*. Those possibilities to which there are corresponding existents are truths; and those to which there are no corresponding existents are false-hoods.[15] One possible connection (others will be explored later) between Correspondence and Coherence Theories is as follows: possibilities are linked – empirically, probabilistically – with other possibilities – hence the Coherence Theory (which will include the coherence between states of affairs that fall under the same laws); and possibilities are linked with actualities (the expressions asserting them are true) in a relationship of correspondence.[16]

TF requires a state of affairs to be made explicit. That is to say, it requires two things: a) the state of affairs, and b) the explicitness (the noticing, etc.) that carves it out, picks it out, encircles it. Explicitness is the forgotten condition of the emergence of TF. A theory of truth (or of TF) that places this at its centre is not easy either to make entirely visible or to defend. For a start, it is difficult to specify separately and with sufficient precision both what it is that is made explicit and what it is like after it has been expressed linguistically; what it is before and after it has been made explicit; what, in short, explicitness does. This problem of separate specification of that which is made explicit before and after it has been made explicit is why explicitness, making explicit, is easy to overlook when theories of truth are being formulated. The reason for this is obvious: the only way of specifying what it is that is made explicit is by expressing it linguistically. The possibility of picking it out extra-linguistically – e.g. by 'pointing' to it in some way – was ruled out for very good reasons by Wittgenstein in the early pages of *Philosophical*

Investigations:[17] even in the case of a particular concrete object such as a cat, seemingly the kind of entity most amenable to alinguistic ostension, to specification unmediated by language, it is difficult to know what is being pointed to (the cat? the colour of its fur? the presence of an alien body in the room? an instantiation of sleekness?) without using the linguistic descriptors to pick them out.

This difficulty in picking out what it is that is made explicit, separately from the language in which that which has been made explicit is expressed, encapsulated, in some sense embodied, accounts for the apparently tautologous – even empty – nature of Tarski's Semantic Theory of Truth. This difficulty also lay behind the rather tortuous discussion in *Not Saussure* (see Chapter 4 and, especially, Chapter 7) in which I tried to point separately at what was made explicit and the expressions in which that explicitness was captured. In the end, I settled for a notation intended to capture one version of the Correspondence Theory in which the symbol 'S^r' stands for a statement in and through which it is asserted that there is a state of affairs denoted by the symbol 'R^s' – the reality expressed in and through S^r. The notation was intended to take account of the fact that there was a kind of internality in the relation between statements and the states of affairs they point out, inasmuch as the latter can be demarcated, circumscribed only by being captured in statements, while not at the same time giving credence to the idea that the states of affairs were internal to language. While language was essential as the means by which states of affairs, aspects of the world, were made explicit, given aseity, it was not that by virtue of which the state of affairs existed.

This relationship between statements (understood as typical existence conditions of truth and falsehoods, of TF) and the states of affairs (pieces or aspects of – extra-linguistic – reality) which make statements true or false is captured in the notion of a *fact*. Facts are neither internal to language, since assertions *per se* do not make facts truths; nor are they entirely independent of language, since bits of reality do not naturally divide into a determinate number of facts that can be counted. Facts (F) are the fusion of S^rs and R^ss:

$$F = \boxed{\begin{array}{c} S^r \\ R^s \end{array}}$$

The R^s owes its explicitness, or its stable, embodied explicitness, but not its existence, to the S^r.[18]

Any theory of truth that aims to be complete, therefore, must take account of the existence conditions of TF before it looks for criteria to differentiate truth from falsehood. This recognition of the existence conditions of TF is, I argue, something all adequate theories would have in common, through which they would be deeply connected. If Coherence, Correspondence and Pragmatist Theories seem quite disconnected from one another, this is only because they are addressed to different questions about truth, respond to a discussion that begins too far down the track, by which time they have parted company. My argument is that the theories have parted company not because they represent mutually exclusive accounts of the same thing, but because they illuminate different aspects of something whose fundamental essence lies upstream of their main focus of concern. Deflationary and redundancy theories of truth, in particular, are inadequate because they neglect the *existence condition* of TF. If we denote the element necessary to bring TF into being – explicitness – as E, then the deflationary theories of Frege, Ramsay, Strawson and others are seen to fail by missing out E.[19]

I should like to illustrate the common roots of theories of truth first by examining the relationship between the Correspondence and Coherence Theories and showing how they are not as entirely opposed as they seem to be and then examining the pragmatic theories favoured by 'hardliners' inclined to biologism and a variety of others who would like to relativise truth and knowledge to organic need (as do Darwinians) and social pressures (as do postmodernists who relativise truth to discursive formations and communities of discourse) while all the time leaving out E.

Correspondence and Coherence Theories of Truth

As already noted, in *Not Saussure* I defended a version of the Correspondence Theory of Truth. The context of this defence was a rebuttal of so-called 'post-Saussurean' thinkers who (erroneously) claimed that Saussure's theoretical linguistics provided a basis for denying the extra-linguistic reality of the objects, states of affairs, etc., referred to in discourse. I argued that Saussure's ideas did not license the notion that the referents of language as used in ordinary discourse were themselves intra-linguistic; on the contrary, there was a real (external) correspondence between declarative statements and things 'out there' in an extra-linguistic world. I emphasised, however, that the correspondence was *not* between discourse and extra-linguistic *facts*, since the latter were themselves the products of the interaction between discourse and extra-discursive reality. In other words, although I argued against the post-Saussurean notion that the 'truth' of discourses is an internal affair of language, I was not unaware of the difficulty of defining the status of 'facts'. Facts are neither purely intra- nor purely extra-linguistic: so the truth of declarative utterances is not grounded in a simple external relationship between the intra-linguistic meaning of strings of symbols and facts understood as entities existing independently of language. In the present discussion, I want to modify my support of the Correspondence Theory of truth further by emphasising how correspondence is possible only within the context of explicitness; that is to say, within a consciousness which has transformed the contents of physical and not-so-physical reality into truth-conditions of statements. Explicitness is the condition of the emergence of truth-conditions, elevating what exists (objects, states of affairs, etc.) to the status of being the truth-conditions of an assertion that such-and-such is the case. It follows from this that, in supporting the Correspondence Theory of truth against the assault of the post-Saussureans, I am not suggesting that the correspondences are entirely external to consciousness: there cannot be truths(s) or falsehood(s) without subjects. Consciousness is the explicitness condition that makes truth-conditions possible. It is the condition of there being truth-conditions: there is no truth (or falsehood) without explicitness. It does not, however, follow from this that truth-conditions are entirely internal to consciousness, any more than they are internal to language: idealism, linguistic or otherwise, is not permitted. What explicit consciousness does is transform that which exists (either as part of consciousness or as that which it intuits as outside of it) into the truth-condition of an assertion that it exists.

Even so, I want to argue that the opposition between the Correspondence and Coherence – or between externalist and internalist – Theories of truth is not as sharp as I previously suggested when my primary concern was to challenge the post-Saussurean claim that statements do not refer to realities outside of language. More specifically, I would like to argue that the explicitness condition for truth (correspondent or any other variety) surrounds the latter with coherence. Correspondence is real, but it exists within a framework whose truth-feel is at least in part founded in coherence: the coherent world experienced and expected by the conscious being living in an intelligible universe, a universe in which it has found coherent sense. This idea is most easy to grasp in the context of scientific theories.

Modern philosophy of science increasingly favours a sceptical attitude towards claims of absolute truth for scientific discourse and the notion that its articulated laws, etc. are an undistorted mirroring of the objective, pre-human, extra-conscious nature of things. This has been prompted by reflection upon the tendency for theories, with increasingly impressive claims to being the final say on the matters with which they deal certainly, to be displaced by other theories with even more impressive claims to be the final say on things. For Popper, who has done more than anyone else to foster this more reflective, even sceptical attitude, the crucial event was the displacement of classical by relativistic physics. If even Newton's laws were open to correction, then nothing any more was safe. With the rapid development of particle physics and the increasing pace of theoretical change in the sciences as a whole, there has been a widening consensus amongst philosophers of science that, despite what some scientists may claim, in their work and, more particularly in their pronouncements to the general public, the final say is no longer at hand. The advance of science does not bring us any nearer to the objective truth of things. Theories are replaced by better theories and, according to Popper, 'better' does not mean 'closer to objective/ absolute/final/eternal truth'. Rather, it means: able to accommodate more observations; and (more important, since even 'degenerate' theories such as those associated with psychoanalysis may be modified *ad hoc* to take account of new observations) able to predict new observations. The better theory predicts novel facts. A further feature of the better theory – a kind of 'cash value' test of its validity – is that, through its superior predictive power, it increases our ability to control the world in accordance with our needs and desires.[20]

Popper has argued against the claim that the inaccessibility of final truth opens the way to relativism. Granted that, if all theories have an infinitely small probability of being true, then all are at an infinite distance from absolute truth and are consequently equidistant from absolute truth. It does not follow from this, however, that one theory is as good as another. For Popper, the criteria by which one theory is displaced by another provide a basis for preferring one to the other and grounds for eschewing relativism. These criteria have already been mentioned: they include the ability to accommodate the known facts and the power to predict novel facts which are subsequently discovered. Using these criteria, we can anticipate an endless succession of increasingly powerful theories without having to yield to the claims of relativism.

Popper's philosophy of science includes a version of Tarski's Correspondence Theory of Truth. Although it is very much part of his conception of science that observations would not be made without theories to guide our investigations (and, more widely, our conscious-nesses are searchlights rather than buckets), observations are, ultimately, independent of theories. How else would they support or (more impor-tantly) refute them? The theories drive us to unearth the facts but they do not determine them. To express this in terms that connect more closely with the present preoccupations, facts are made explicit, are uncovered, by theories, but they are not internal to them. When an uncovered fact refutes a theory, this is a matter not only of mere non-coherence but also of non-correspondence. It is fundamental to Popper's philosophy that facts are not only not internal to theories but that they are also not internal to discourse. Accordingly, he has attacked those whose philosophical theorising has taken the form of investigating the meanings of words or 'the logical geography' of concept terms. (His hostility to the 'linguistic turn' in philosophy and to the later Wittgenstein, whom he regarded as inspiring it, was legendary.) Nothing is less interesting, he held, than the question of the meanings of words; what matters are the states of affairs that do or do not correspond to the assertions we make when we are using them.

Popper, then, denies that science gives access to absolute truth or that it is progressing towards it while, at the same time, he rebuts relativism; in particular, the view that the truth of science is internal to scientific discourse or to the theories that drive and direct scientific observation. Despite the failure of science to touch, or increasingly to correspond to, absolute truth, its progress is not merely towards increasing coherence within itself. So much for Popper. To take the discussion about the nature of truth further, let us begin by (a) re-examining relativism, and (b) making one or two observations relating to particle physics – the queen, or at least the *ultra ne plus*, of the sciences.

It would be absurd to deny the relativity of the ordinary truths that are perceived or experienced. Different people experience different things at different times; consequently, observations, beliefs, etc. may be relative to the viewpoint of the individual human being or, even, a particular moment of a particular individual. At this level, the influence of subjectivity is clearly evident: what I see in a specific situation, or what I see in that situation at different times, will depend upon many things, ranging from my physical position to my desires, current interests, personal history, etc. At a higher level, observations – and the theories that bring them together, explain and predict them – may be relative to cultural norms, historical epochs and to prevailing paradigms and models of explanation and understanding. At a higher level still, they may be relative to the discursive norms of the particular discipline within which the observations are made and the theories advanced. Observation and theory-making in physics after Einstein, and even more after Planck and Bohr, was rather different from observation and theory-making before them. Kuhn, emphasising discontinuity at the expense of continuity (though the latter is, in fact, less marked than the former), emphasised the influence of prevailing paradigms. Finally, and at the highest level, we may speak of the relativity of theory and observation to collective human consciousness – to the totality of human experience.

One may, however, accept the reality of lower-level relativities without (as Popper pointed out) succumbing to the belief that one theory is as good as another; but one may also accept the highest level dependency of truth ultimately on the totality of human consciousness without conceding that truth is rendered 'merely' relative in any substantive or disabling sense. Relativity of truth to the totality of actual and of possible experience is not relativity in any invalidating sense; for outside of experience there is no such thing as truth. This point connects with the argument at the heart of the present essay and it derives from my position that explicitness is uniquely the home of truth and falsehood – of TF. The truth cannot lie beyond consciousness, outside of explicitness; and, since this is the case, the collective human grasp of the truth cannot 'fall short' – of objectivity or whatever – in any meaningful sense; in particular, it cannot be merely relative. This position will shortly be invoked to support a 'final level' Coherence Theory of Truth.

Before I address this and argue for a 'highest level' Coherence Theory of Truth, based upon the notion of explicitness as the necessary existence condition of truth, let me return briefly to contemporary physics and the relationship within it between correspondence and coherence. Two developments are relevant to the present discussion. The first is the increasing recognition of the role of the observer in the nature of the observations made, even (or especially) at a sub-atomic level. Relativity theory relativised states of motion and of rest to that of the observer and abolished absolute positions in and distances of space and time. Heisenberg's Uncertainty Principle identified what had been regarded as an insuperable obstacle to objectivity by emphasising the way in which the process of measurement affects the observations made through measurement. The significance of Heisenberg's Uncertainty Principle has been at once both understated and exaggerated. It has been understated inasmuch as it has been taken to mean merely that the location and momentum of an elementary particle cannot both be measured precisely at the same time. There is measurement-related 'quantum smearing' which has been incorrectly read as merely reflecting the fact that the very process of observation interferes with the system that is being observed. According to the Copenhagen interpretation, the implication of the Uncertainty Principle goes deeper than this: an elementary particle does not actually *have* a location and a momentum at the same time. This mutual exclusiveness is replicated with respect to other dualities, most notably the complementarity of the wave and particle forms of elementary entities. In this case, measurement causes wave-packet collapse: one sort of measurement reveals particle-like properties; another wave-like properties. Without measurement (or without observation – and there is an important difference here), the wave-packet is uncommitted either to wave or to particle form. This seems deeply relativising – apparently undermining the claim of fundamental physical laws to be 'about' anything other than physical measurements and highly artificial human observations – until one recognises that notions such as 'position' (taken in isolation) and 'momentum' (taken in isolation) are artefacts. The problem at the microphysical level applies also in ordinary life, at the level of macroscopic objects and was, in fact, first identified by Zeno in relation to the flying arrow. Zeno argued that, since an arrow either occupied a position (and so was still) or was in motion (and so could not be thought of as having a point location), movement was unreal. Anxiety around this Copenhagen interpretation of Heisenberg's Uncertainty Principle – like Zeno's anxieties – is based on a failure to appreciate that isolating one dimension of movement (position, velocity, momentum) is a useful ploy but an artificial one. What science usefully separates cannot be regarded as necessarily existing in isolation: a particle does not have a position alone (without, for example, also having velocity) any more than an arrow has length alone without width, or size without position. The Copenhagen interpretation of quantum physics, therefore, no more undermines the notion that the facts of physics correspond to external objective reality than do our ordinary observations of ordinary objects such as flying arrows or falling stones.

The second threat to an open, correspondent understanding of physics is the increasing divergence of physical theory from common sense and its increasing disconnection from the deliverances of sense perception. Orthodox particle physics – which now holds that empty space is a seething cauldron of virtual neutrinos, that space itself has ten dimensions, of which seven are curled up or in some other way hidden and that every particle/event in the universe acts on every other particle/event, however distant – seems to have only the slightest toe-hold on imaginable, never mind everyday, experience.

Even if the Uncertainty Principle can be tamed, these other developments would suggest that truth in physics has ceased to be a matter of correspondence to experience outside the discourse of physicists. This seems to be reflected in the fact that the most recent modifications in advanced physical theory have been prompted only by observations that could not have been made outside the very special situations of physics research laboratories. Virtual neutrinos are not required to account for our everyday experience, to build bridges or even to send rockets into outer space. At the very least, we would seem to be confronted in physics with one form of relativism: the truths of physics are true only within physics; they are relative to the discourses of physics. This scepticism seems especially justified in relation to very recent developments in superstring theory which have generated notions and claims that are not only currently untestable but which no imaginable experiment could test. Superstring theory will live – or die – on the basis of its ability to formalise and bring together other higher-level theories of physics. Its truth seems to reside in its *coherence* with other truths of physics.

Against this, and in favour of the claim that such physical theories really are about the extra-discursive material world, that they are about the physical world rather than the physics world – despite their total divorce from common sense and sense experience and the inescapable role of the subject – is the predictive power of such theories. Admittedly, this power is restricted to predicting rather extraordinary phenomena – rather than the deliverances of the senses or the fact that a particular bridge will or will not fall down. Most typically, and most spectacularly, they predict new particles, which are subsequently discovered. For example, esoteric theories in particle physics predicted the existence of two particles – W and Z – that would emerge under certain, very highly specialised circumstances and would have certain, rather extraordinary properties.[21] These were subsequently produced and under precisely the circumstances anticipated by the theorists. This suggests an impressive correspondence between the theory and extra-theoretic reality. But are the W and Z particles genuine extra-theoretic entities? Are they any more extra-theoretically real than the indivisible atoms that had earlier served physical science so well – indeed until the atom was split and the indivisible atom was shown in some sense to be a theoretical entity rather than an extra-theoretic reality? For the observations that support the existence of the W and Z particles are even more remote from those of ordinary experience than the observations that sustained atomic theory; and the very process of 'observing' consists of placing a complex mathematical interpretation upon a few extraordinarily esoteric events occurring in a so-called Higgs field. The particles have never been seen or, strictly, observed; they have been inferred from observations remote from them. There is good reason, therefore, for thinking of them as theoretic entities, as constructs. The correspondence between their being predicted by the theory and their being shown to exist is, arguably, not a correspondence at all; rather, it is an instance of coherence between one part of physical theory and another.

This is not an entirely eccentric interpretation. On the contrary, it is very much in line with the present overall ambition of physics, which is to arrive at a Grand Unified Theory. There is currently much more talk of unification than of arriving at 'the final truth' about the nature of things. Behind this is the intuition that the truth about the universe will be rather simple and that the present complexity of mathematical physics is only a transitional phase.

So much for fundamental physics – which, collectively, must count as the most ambitious and wide-ranging attempt to arrive at the most general truths about the extra-mental world. It would seem that the predictive power of its highest level, or most fundamental, theories does not support a correspondence account of its truths. We are left, at the highest level, with coherence. And yet, at the lower levels of physical theory – and even more so in lower-level sciences such as neurobiology or geology – we have a clear correspondence between discourse and the things they are about. There is no question of a 'neuron' being a theoretical entity; even less of a brain being a purely theoretical construct. And this suggest that the Correspondence and Coherence Theories of Truth may not be simple alternatives; rather that 'coherent' and 'correspondent' truths may be observed at different levels. We may see this within particular sciences. To continue with the earlier example, the W and Z particles may be theoretical entities, rather than extra-theoretic ones; nevertheless, they are external to the theories that predicted them. After all, the prediction could have turned out to have been wrong: in this sense, the truths about them are correspondent rather than coherent.

To simplify grossly, we could say that there is a correspondence between predicting theory and predicted entity; but both are internal to the larger theoretical framework of contemporary mathematical physics: they are evidence of its coherence. This may be illustrated diagrammatically:

The correspondences form the basis for a gradual convergence of physical theory towards Grand Unified (or coherent) Theory. At a lower level, the basis of truth is more directly one of correspondence between an observation predicted on the basis of a theory and a predicted observation actually observed:

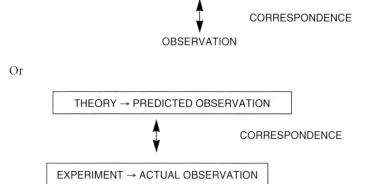

Or

As we move from the lower to the higher level, so we move from correspondence between theory and observation, to correspondence between higher- and lower-level theories and, ultimately, to coherence between higher-level theories. Even at the highest level, however, we should be able to follow an 'audit trail' down to observations of 'extra-discursive' elements (events, entities) that are not internal to physics.

The intra-theoretic nature of the observations or entities predicted by, or triggering, a theory will be evident to a greater or lesser degree. A wolf observed by an ethologist is clearly not a theoretical entity in the way that a Z particle 'observed' by a physicist is. Nevertheless, the naturalist's observations of the wolf will not be totally undirected or even utterly unprejudiced sense perception: they will be of a certain character, a character that will stamp them as being a legitimate part of the discipline of ethology. Scientific observations take place within a more or less conscious theoretical framework and in relation to a more or less explicit theory. Scientific observations are strikingly less free range than everyday observations; compared with science, everyday observation is unfocused gawping. This distance from ordinary observation will vary with different sciences; and it is obvious that ethology is less remote from everyday perception than is particle physics. In the latter, correspondence seems to dominate over coherence (and observations seem outnumbered by formulae and equations) though large-scale ethological theory will tend more explicitly to coherence.

We may think of correspondence and coherence as two different movements or modes of the truth-seeking consciousness. Which is the more fundamental? If I had to choose between one and the other, I would be inclined to believe that, at the highest or deepest level, coherence is the ultimate standard of truth. This is not merely because human consciousness is inescapably theory-ridden so that, in a sense, the entities it is conscious of are theoretical entities. That in itself would not be sufficient to give coherence an edge over correspondence. For the entities are rooted – as they have to be – in things that are not themselves contents of consciousness: this is a necessary condition of survival, given that consciousness is dependent upon an extra-conscious body to survive. The more compelling reason for suggesting that coherence is a more fundamental facet of truth than correspondence is that the higher the order of truth, the more convergence there is; at the higher levels, the pursuit of truth is the pursuit of a unified account of things.

In support of this, I would cite the facts that a) the aim in science is always towards developing larger, more encompassing theories; and b) that explanation usually takes the form of relating smaller groups of observations to larger ones, smaller theories to bigger ones. Thus explanation in biology tends towards reduction of biological entities to instances of physical ones acting in accordance with the laws of physics. And the trend in physics is towards increasingly grand, more tightly unified theories. And at the level of ordinary, everyday observation there is a tendency towards coherence within a framework which is much more loosely defined (to the point where it is almost unchallengeably invisible) but which may be unearthed by descriptive metaphysics. Amongst its theories (the matrix from which all reflection and conscious theorising starts) are: the belief that there are external, enduring objects independent of ourselves; that there are other minds constituting the public to which those objects are exposed; and so on. The movement towards truth is towards coherence within that framework. The unified field theory of physics is a step towards the unified mind-and-body theory of metaphysics. This in turn, perhaps, has as its subconscious target the unification of consciousness within and across the theoretical framework of its ordinary observations. The unification of science, in other words, is part of the greater move towards unification of reflective consciousness – indeed of consciousness *tout court*. At the heart of explicitness is the sense that the sense of the world is coherent and that the world that consciousness is conscious of is intelligible. The intuition that 'the real is rational' is that the world we are conscious of makes coherent sense; that truths will converge in mutually consistent principles, which will in turn converge in an overriding principle, or in the Truth.

Before I wind up this part of the discussion, I shall try to outline a theory of truth that comprehends both correspondence and coherence accounts. Truth (and falsehood) are specific, emergent attributes of the world that a uniquely explicit animal, the human animal, posits itself as being located in. Explicitness is the existence-condition of TF. Specific truths (and falsehoods) are seen as corresponding to the states of affairs they are 'about'. Truths and falsehoods have different levels of generality: the transition between one level of generality and another is marked by coherence between the truths relevant to the higher level of generality. At the lower levels of generality, individual truths are correspondent truths: they are truths about, corresponding to, particular states of affairs. At the highest level of generality the mass of truth is seen to be entirely underpinned by coherence with other truths rather than correspondence with an extra-verifical world. To put this another way: correspondence becomes increasingly indirect and mediated by other theories. For example, as physics aspires to become a theory of everything, so its truth criteria become increasingly based on coherence rather than correspondence.

As for the entirety of the collective conscious experience, there is no 'outside' for truths to correspond to: ultimately, perception corresponds with itself rather than corresponding to an extra-perceptual, material reality. To say this is not to relativise human truth overall: there is nothing to relativise the *totality* of truth to because humanity is the exclusive home of the kind of explicitness which makes TF possible. There is no absolute, outside of consciousness, which would relativise it. The fact that the totality of human perception has 'only' coherent rather than correspondent truth is not, therefore, a limitation, for there is no truth outside the totality of human perception. There cannot be a correspondence theory of truth when that for which correspondence is sought is everything that exists in so far as it is actually or possibly experienced: so an entire theory of the universe will have coherence (and, indeed, when one relates upwards from a lower to a higher level of generality, coherence is the issue) as it cannot be checked against anything outside of it; and the entire perceptual experience adds up to a coherent universe which cannot be checked against anything outside of it, because this would be outside of experience. Of course, while the Theory of Everything may not be checked against an object or perception equalling its scope, it can be checked against its entailments, its instantiations.

The figure below sets out the relationships envisaged in this theory of truth:

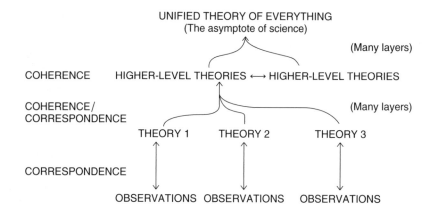

Before taking comfort in convergence of correspondent and coherent truth, and the warding off of the threat of relativism seeming to emanate from the domination of coherence over correspondence in the higher reaches of science, however, it is necessary to address a concern, emanating from a wholly different direction which suggests that our truths are not truths at all but useful fictions. I am referring here to the more 'hard-headed' pragmatic theories, in which truth is seen as a guide to action; more specifically, that a truth is a belief that is useful, and a falsehood is a belief that is useless or worse; that ur-truths have nothing to do with 'objective reality' and everything to do with survival.

Pragmatic theories of truth

Pragmatic theories of truth seem hard-headed because they separate the notion of truth from traditional philosophical and rather sentimental ideas connecting truth with disinterested inquiry as its method and disinterested understanding of reality-in-itself as its goal and reward. For the pragmatist, interest lies at the heart of truth: knowledge is instrumental and truth is intertwined with value, which is in turn rooted in need. Such theories ultimately take their rise from a post-Darwinian perspective which assumes that truth-bearers are first and foremost organisms whose continuous, overriding, fundamental concern in their natural state must be with survival in a hostile world. The truth-bearer is embodied and the criteria for what counts as true bears directly or indirectly on the issue of ensuring continuing existence. The true is what works and this is the case not only for truths that have immediate practical importance but also for seemingly abstract, higher-order beliefs; for example, the belief that there is a God who has certain properties and certain expectations of mankind is true if it provides strength and consolation; the way a worm classifies the objects of the world is true if it assists the worm's survival. The convergence of interest with truth is vividly expressed in William James's classifying beliefs as true or false according to their 'cash value' and in Nietzsche's profoundly cynical rejection of the notion of disinterested inquiry and his seeing truth as the servant of the will-to-power, an essential instrument to drive behaviours that will promote survival.[22] This latter is of particular interest.

In 'On Truth and Lie in an Extra-Moral Sense',[23] Nietzsche begins from the assertion that the human intellect has a small, fragile place in the order of things, in the natural world: it is aimless and arbitrary, shadowy and flighty: 'There have been eternities when it did not exist; and when it is done, nothing will have happened.' The fact that it seems to its owner to have a fix on the great frame of nature is only because its owner gives it such importance. This is hardly proof of the objective validity of truth: 'If we could communicate with the mosquito, then we would learn that it floats through the air with the same self-importance, feeling within itself the flying centre of the universe.' In fact, the intellect is merely 'an aid given to the most unfortunate, the most delicate, most evanescent beings in order to hold them for a minute in existence' and, as a means of preservation, its chief power is simulation – 'for this is the means by which the weaker, less robust individuals preserve themselves' since they lack weapons such as the horns and fangs of beasts of prey.

For this reason, it is astonishing that philosophers should believe in the idea of a disinterested understanding, of an honest and pure urge for truth. The truths necessary for survival – which have nothing to do with truth understood *sub specie aeternatis*, objective knowledge of how things really are – may, however, be generalised beyond the individual: a version of the truth is agreed upon. In order that society shall be possible, what is called the truth is fixed by agreement: 'a regularly valid and obligatory designation of things is invented, and this linguistic legislation also furnishes the first laws of truth.' It is at this point that the contrast between truth and lies originates. The truth is not to be contrasted with deception but with those deceptions which are damaging: truth is the sub-group of deceptions that support our physical and social survival. Even individual concepts entrain illusions; for example, the concept 'leaf' effaces all the differences there are between individual leaves. Truth, in the end is

> A mobile army of metaphors, metonyms and anthropomorphisms – in short a sum of human relations, which have been enhanced, transposed and embellished poetically and rhetorically, and which after long use seem firm, canonical and obligatory to a people: truths are illusions about which one has forgotten that this is what they are; metaphors which are worn out and without sensuous power; coins which have lost their pictures and now matter only as metal, no longer as coins...
> ... to be truthful means using the customary metaphors – in moral terms: the obligation to lie according to a fixed convention, to lie herd-like in a style obligatory for all...

This essay (a posthumously published fragment) must be one of the most influential pieces of writing published over the last century. It captures three aspects of the pragmatic notion of truth: a quasi-Darwinian notion of the value of knowledge; connected with this, a biological relativisation of knowledge to need and survival; and, finally, arising out of the need for social concordance, the relativisation of truth (and lies) to social groups or (to use a term favoured by post-modernists such as Richard Rorty) to communities of discourse. Truth, in short, has nothing to do with what is really out there and everything to do with biological survival and to do with social survival – in the twin senses of the survival of individuals within society by compliance and the survival of societies by ensuring that they have compliant members.

As in the case of all fundamental relativisations of the notion of truth and the connected refusal to accept either degrees of untruth, of robustness of truth, or of the distortion by interests, Nietzsche's views are in the grip of pragmatic self-refutation. If there is no such thing as objective truth, then there is no such thing as the objective truth about truth. There is no more reason for accepting what Nietzsche says about truth than there is for accepting what Plato says about truth or what Hitler says or what ordinary people usually believe about the status of truth and of the difference between lies and falsehood. Nietzsche's beliefs about the nature of truth rely heavily on a picture of the place of human beings in nature and, consequently, upon large, objective, scientific truths; for example, the truth that there have been eternities when the human intellect did not exist. There are other profound problems with Nietzsche's cynical account of the nature of truth, notably that of determining what level of truths (and lies) it refers to.

It may be that Nietzsche was referring only to the kind of higher-order truths that philosophers since the pre-Socratics have pursued and cherished – such as truths about the nature of the human spirit, about the scope of the human intellect or about the existence or nonexistence of God. In which case, there would have to be some point at which Nietzsche's scepticism would cease to apply and objective truths suddenly appear on the scene. It may be a customary metaphor to believe that mothers love their children or that those in power ever govern fairly or for the sake of the people as a whole. The truth that there is a cat in this room, however, is clearly not merely metaphorically true; the difference between 'There is a cat in this room' and 'There is not a cat in this room' is not based upon social agreement. The problem for Nietzsche's position is that of determining at what level one is supposed to move from particular or general empirical or objective truths – which are not subordinate to interests, are not merely convenient, adaptive, lies – to truths that are established as true merely on the basis of social agreement. This difficulty is compounded by Nietzsche's famous assertion that 'there are no such things as facts, only interpretations' – and the modification of that claim – which is that facts are mobilised only in response to interpretations, so that 'the facts of the case' are interest-driven. And also by Nietzsche's claim, in 'On Truth and Lie in an Extra-Moral Sense', that even isolated concepts are artefacts given natural status by social agreement ('Every concept originates through our equating what is unequal') so that there are no objective or natural kinds – not even seemingly indisputable ones such as 'leaves'. The socially stipulated, as opposed to the disinterested non-metaphorical, truth thus reaches down even to the isolated fact.

The most profound and telling objection to a pragmatism which argues that truth is merely a convenient metaphor, or that truths are merely convenient metaphors, and neither has anything to do with any kind of external reality, is that it opens the way to an idealism – if only one of the collective consciousness rather than the individual mind – that is remote from the hard-headed quasi-Darwinian naturalism from which it begins. For it isolates and insulates truth, right down to individual facts (and presumably the experiences that relate to them), from anything outside of the social consensus. As a corollary of this, its adaptionist notion of truth does not explain why some versions of the world are adaptive (and so count as true) while others are not (and so are rejected as false). On the contrary, it seems more likely that beliefs are adaptive because they are true than that they seem to be true because they are adaptive. But this opens up a larger argument about the nature of truth, in particular, about the status of pragmatic theories, and about the relationship between ourselves as living organisms and our status as knowers and as TF-bearing creatures.

Some observations on evolutionary epistemology

In 'On Truth and Lie in an Extra-Moral Sense', Nietzsche emphasises 'how wretched, how shadowy and flighty, how aimless and arbitrary, the human intellect appears in nature'. He also assumes that the intellect is a part of nature and that it is wholly subordinated to natural processes. The intellect is 'a means for the preservation of the individual' and, as such, it 'unfolds its chief powers in simulation'. Men are 'deeply immersed in illusions and dream images' and their sensibility 'nowhere leads into truth'. Humans not only lack access to the truth; they also have no appetite for it. Nature conceals the truth (even about themselves) from them and the illusion that they have of being in possession of truths is, like the 'truths' they possess, simply an adaptive device. In Nietzsche's ideas, we see the primitive ancestors not only of the Foucauldian neo-Marxist dogma that knowledge is not so much true or false as legitimate or illegitimate for a particular set of power relations, but of the more interesting ideas which may be gathered under the title 'evolutionary epistemology'.

For evolutionary epistemologists,[24] as for Nietzsche, man is a piece of nature and everything about human beings has to be understood in terms of the need to survive. Nature is intrinsically so hostile that humanity could not afford the luxury of being endowed with characteristics that are not designed specifically to deal with that hostility. There is nothing in nature – and hence in human nature (which is a piece of nature) – to indicate that objective truth, either as a given, provided free with sense experience, or as the goal of a long, disinterested search, would ever arise. Indeed, since disinterestedness (except as a mask to conceal the grossest self-interest, allowing it a freer run) could possibly have any basis, it must be an illusion. Nor is there any reason why mankind – a mere shimmer of weak flesh over the order of things, a minute corner of creation – should be able to penetrate to the truth about the universe or even about part of it. There are reasons for assuming the opposite. Humankind, as Nietzsche says, is in the same position as the mosquito which, feeling within itself 'the flying centre of the world', believes that it enjoys privileged access to the truth about the universe around it. In the case of all living creatures, the universe is refracted through their living bodies: the universe that I know is the universe known to and through my body. Moreover, what is known to and through my body is not only coloured by the properties of the body and, more particularly, the characteristics ('bandwidths' in the most general sense) of my sense organs, but also filtered by built-in considerations of what is of interest to my body, in terms of its survival.

Most evolutionary epistemologists accept at least one half of the Nietzschean story: that knowledge is relative to our bodies and their needs, and that it does not afford us an objective view of nature as she is in herself.[25] Evolutionary epistemology seems to enable us to see how three things are linked: the survival of the organism; the nature of the universe; and the content and structure of experience and of thought.[26] The survival of the organism would not require knowledge that truly reflected the universe as it really is: the organism's 'knowledge' is simply a mode of securing effective responses to the opportunities and threats around it. This would be embodied and expressed in the very structure of the organism, which by incorporating modes of reaction to the environment around the organism, effectively embodies those 'truths' about the nature of the world that are essential to the organism's survival.

Peter Munz,[27] for example, has expressed the relationship between the physical character of the knowing organism and the world it knows in Popperian terms, as follows:

> Every evolved organism is a sort of trial-and-error experiment with the environment. If it survives, its structure must embody at least some correct information about the environment. If it does not embody such information, it is an 'error' and will soon disappear. In

that sense one can say that in biological evolution every organism is an embodied or incarnated theory about the world. In the same sense, one can say that in the world of human culture all hypotheses about the world are disembodied organisms. (p. 74)

'Correct' here merely means 'supportive of survival'. This may actually be incorrect from another point of view; or at least only partly correct. For example, it suits a robin to see every object which has the colour pattern of a red blob against a brown background as if it were another robin. This will usually be true, though it will cause the robin to be deceived when it is exposed to a piece of brown sacking daubed with a red mark which it then attacks as if it were a rival robin. The loss in accurate discrimination – between a rival robin and any old surface that shares some of the characteristics of a robin – will be more than offset by a gain in response time due to a simplifying classification system. Likewise the narrow bandwidth of its sense organs will enable an organism to be tuned to what matters to it, rather than what is objectively, comprehensively the case.

Munz, however, argues that the epistemological relativism of this view does not entail a kind of idealism in which the experienced world is solely the product of the perceptual system of the organism. The internal connection between the structure of the organism and the world of its knowledge does not, at any rate, result in an idealism in which worlds are totally relative to knowers and, because the relationship between the knower and the known is effectively an internal one, sealed off from one another. On the contrary, evolutionary theory requires that the organism should *not* be in a prison of solipsism. The perfectly formed mouse has to access a world common to it and the perfectly formed lion, and vice versa, or the one will die deluded between the lion's jaws or the other may perish of starvation. Munz puts this very nicely in his discussion of the ideas of the biologist J. von Uexkull:

[von Uexkull] had advanced the theory that, given the very specific perceptual apparatus possessed by every species, every single species creates through its perception its own environment (*Umwelt*). However Uexkull immediately suggested that this insight could be no comfort to idealists. For since all organisms had evolved successfully on the same planet, the various environments they perceived could not be thought to be their own creations. All parts of the environment had to be compatible with all other parts and that consideration imposes a conceptual constraint upon the singularity of the Umwelt of every single species. (Munz, 1988, p. 75)

The attractions of this version of evolutionary epistemology are very powerful. It seems to guarantee a coupling between our knowledge and reality, to ensure that the former is in some sense 'true' of the latter. If it were not, and the organism were systematically mistaken as to what is out there, it would be unviable, and so would not be.[28] More deeply, we can see evolutionary epistemology as a way of linking the genesis of knowledge with the genesis of the knowing organism. The very process that ensures that the knowing organism comes into being will ensure that its knowledge is, on the whole, and in some sense 'true' – or not, at least, systematically misleading. The very possibility of the organism's existence depends upon the 'accuracy' of its knowledge: nature cannot generate epistemological bum steers because they would not survive.

Of course, accuracy does not have to be absolute or comprehensive. As Antony O'Hear has pointed out, the Darwinian imperative does not require perceptual systems to deliver the whole truth about the world, only to deliver more truths than the competition. The partial truths thus delivered may be only a small part of the truth seen from the point of view of a more richly cognitively endowed species such as man and may be mixed up with quite a bit of untruth. Indeed, the untruth (for example, the untruths frogs 'believe' about flies) may be highly adaptive. It simplifies things and makes situations amenable to rapid reactions. And even man's truths – from the standpoint of which the robin and the frog are sometimes, but not usually, wrong and are hugely uninformed, if not misinformed – may in turn be only a small part of the truth seen *sub specie aeternis* – as Nietzsche pointed out.

It seems as if the biologisation of knowledge can lead to two quite opposite conclusions, although which of the two it seems to support may simply be a matter of emphasis. Evolutionary epistemologists focus on the things we must get right in order to survive; Nietzschean thinkers (and there have been many twentieth-century examples) focus on the things that, in view of the central role of beliefs in ensuring survival, we are likely to get wrong, for example our place in the great order of things. At any rate, there are several problems with the extreme Nietzschean version of evolutionary epistemology according to which human knowledge is not merely inseparable from error but is drowned in it. The first is, by a kind of irony, flagged up by Nietzsche in the opening paragraph of the very fragment we have been discussing:

> In some remote corner of the universe, poured out and glittering in innumerable solar systems, there once was a star on which clever animals invented knowledge.

We are not meant to take this 'fable' seriously but, Nietzsche argues, the position of the intellect in the universe is even worse than it would suggest:

> One might invent such a fable and still not have illustrated sufficiently how wretched, how shadowy and flighty, how aimless and arbitrary, the human intellect appears in nature.

The question we have to ask ourselves is how is it that knowledge – and hence truth and lie (in either the moral or Nietzsche's 'extra-moral' sense) – came to exist in the first place. Nietzsche's ironic vision of the world and his mocking non-account of the origin of knowledge actually demand that that question be asked precisely *because* he has such a low opinion of knowledge and of the intellect's grasp of the truth. I would argue that his position is untenable because, like so many other thinkers, he has started too far down the track. The question we have to ask ourselves is, if knowledge is so unlikely, how did the natural world give rise to it in the first place? More specifically, what could possibly be the evolutionary purpose of consciousness, of truth (and falsehood), of truth (and lie)? The answer, which I have argued at length in *The Explicit Animal*, is that there is no such purpose: most of the things that have to be performed by organisms – including such astonishingly complex achievements as building brains – can be carried out at least as well, and probably better, without consciousness. Unconscious mechanism suffices.[29] And certainly, at the time when specifically human consciousness emerged, and for some time afterwards, it had nothing to commend it. It was more likely to be maladaptive than adaptive. Things done consciously, via the deliberations of human agents, are performed less well than things that happen by mechanisms. Agents are much less reliable than mechanisms. Moreover, with the emergence of specifically human consciousness came all the problems particularly associated with the condition of being a self-conscious animal. These considerations dispose of the simple idea that the first fully conscious human beings had the advantage of possessing both unimpaired mechanisms and, as a bonus, the option of deliberate action; it seems much more likely that, as human consciousness developed, deliberate action – doing things voluntary rather being the site where they happen – was a maladaptive or disadvantageous, but alas now compulsory, alternative to 'letting things happen'. The switch from mechanism to deliberate and purposeful action could presumably not itself be readily reversed – either automatically or deliberately – if the latter proved unsatisfactory.

The attractions of evolutionary epistemology evaporate as soon as anyone asks the fundamental question as to why there should be this mode of coupling of organisms with the material world in the first place; why, in other words, there should be entities, namely conscious organisms, that interact with other entities, with the material world, through the mediation of consciousness, and, more specifically, of knowledge. The idea of clever animals 'inventing knowledge' is absurd; but it is no more absurd than the notion of 'knowledge', of explicit truths (and falsehoods), being requisitioned from within unconscious matter in order to give a few organisms a hand.

In other words, evolutionary epistemology explains only why, if we already access the world through knowledge, that knowledge has on balance to be in some sense true (if we are to be viable); but it does not explain the more fundamental – and in every sense prior – question, why there should be knowledge-mediated access at all. Causal inter-action is sufficient coupling for the rest of the material world: crystals form and endure. And, of course, many organisms are more successful in terms of numbers, geographical range and species-endurance than higher primates, with very little in the way of consciousness. As Mary Midgley points out (in her inimitable way): 'if it's immortality you're after, an amoeba is just the thing to be.'[30]

Evolutionary epistemology explains, in other words, why (to expro-priate Lichtenberg's joke) the cat's eyes are to be found just where the holes in its fur are, but not why there are such things as eyes or cats that possess them and enjoy vision; why there are certain constraints on knowledge – the constraint, above all, to be in crucial respects, true of the material world – but not why there is knowledge, not why there are sentient beings at all – able to get a few things right and everything else wrong. The question has particular force in the context of a neo-Darwinian materialistic world picture; for the latter is precisely the kind of monist world picture into which consciousness does not fit.

Once the priority of this question – why there is consciousness, why there is knowledge – is recognised, then it is possible to turn the problem on its head. Instead of wondering how knowledge fits into the material world, we might wonder how the material world comes out of, or is constructed within, consciousness. In other words, the spectre of idealism returns and von Uexkull's argument cited earlier is no longer available to exorcise it. We are not faced merely with the problem of guaranteeing that there will be a common *Welt* arising out of the different *Umwelts*, or that the *Umwelts* are related to one another in a common world. There is a deeper problem of determining which has priority – consciousness or the material world; and here von Uexkull's argument cannot help us. Neo-Darwinian epistemology, in other words, goes deep enough to raise ontological questions and so to undermine its own foundations which presuppose an unquestioned materialist world picture.

What evolutionary epistemology is unable to explain, then, is why there are these centres of concern and self-concern called organisms – such as mosquitoes that imagine that they are the flying centre of the universe – that have crystallised out of the causal net or the material world. Or, indeed, why, among the different systems that have pre-cipitated out of the soup of causal interactions of inanimate matter – mineral crystals, stones, etc. – there should be a sub-group that cares for itself and relates to its surroundings in a particular way such that its material surroundings amount to an environment in which it lives – counts as 'its environment' – of which it is conscious and in which it acts or reacts and in which it competes with conspecifics and others. Evolutionary epistemology is unable to explain this and yet is obliged to do so because it is implicitly committed to explaining the purpose of knowledge – or, as with all evolutionary explanations, its origin – in terms of its *purpose*. And this, I think, is the real weakness. For, prior to consciousness, there is no such thing as purpose, or even such a thing as a point of view, which sees an organism as environed, or upgrades part of the material field to the status of 'organism' and down-grades the rest to the status of 'environment'. Evolutionary theory is heavily dependent on teleological explanations, but its starting point and continuing frame of reference is that of a materialist monism into which purposes, points of view and the distinction between organism and environment do not fit. (Any purposes that are discerned in the world prior to the emergence of conscious beings and any formu-lated purposes discerned in the world prior to the emergence of human beings have been planted there courtesy of the Fallacy of Misplaced Explicitness.)

The impropriety of the implicit teleology in evolutionary biology becomes obvious when we *explicitly* assume the long view implicit in neo-Darwinian thought and begin with a world of inorganic matter, proceed to organic matter, continue to living matter and then ascend to conscious organisms. The aseptic world picture of true and consistent Darwinian thought should, if it believes its own hard-nosed materialism, eschew terms that seem to assume the viewpoint of an organism consciously or unconsciously in competition to survive. The organism should be subsumed completely under the totality of the material world and absorbed into the boundless causal net. Because this does not happen, evolutionary thinkers take the existence of organisms for granted when, in fact, organisms shouldn't exist at all. When it comes to fitness for survival, objects that are macroscopically in static equilibrium – such as pebbles and crystal – should not have given rise to fragile polyphasic systems in dynamic equilibrium, namely living organisms.

All of this is pretty obvious and yet it is consistently overlooked in hard-line Darwinian thought and, consequently, by pragmatic theorists of truth for whom the final validation of knowledge is cash value, in particular survival value. How does it come to be overlooked? Answering this brings us back to our central theme. It is easy to forget the fact that knowledge of any sort – true, partly true, complete, incomplete, interested, disinterested – has no place in the naturalistic, materialistic Darwinian scheme of things because we take it so much for granted. More particularly, we overlook our peculiar nature, our status as unique sorts of creatures in the material world, specifically, because it is easy to forget the essential role of explicitness in bringing about both truth and falsehood. Such amnesia makes it possible to imagine (as Munz does) that knowledge is the kind of thing that can be embodied in (unconscious) structure; or that an organism is an embodied or incarnate theory. This is yet another case of the Fallacy of Misplaced Explicitness. It is perfectly illustrated in Paul Churchland's *Matter and Consciousness*[31] where he asserts that 'the possession of information can be understood as the possession of some internal physical order that bears some systematic relationship to the environment', and concludes from this that 'the operations of intelligence, abstractly conceived, turn out just to be a high-grade version of the operations characteristic of life, save that they are even more intricately coupled to the environment' (p. 174). The vulnerability of this viewpoint is underlined by what Churchland says next about 'intelligent life':

> Here again, intelligence represents no discontinuity. Intelligent life is just life, with a high thermodynamic intensity, and an especially close coupling between internal order and external circumstance. (ibid., p. 174)

The question this prompts us to ask is why, if 'close coupling' between external circumstance and internal order is the crucial issue, one should resort to intelligence to achieve it. A boringly reliable mechanism would be a much more sensible choice.

Nietzschean scientistic scepticism about the place of knowledge in the world and the inescapable domination of truth over untruth is, as already noted, self-undermining. The minute position that humankind supposedly occupies in the great order of things cannot be a case for doubting the truth of human knowledge because these doubts are predicated on the assumption that the picture of that position in the order of things – a product of our knowledge – is a true one. Likewise, the fact that different organisms experience the world through different perceptual systems cannot be used as the basis either for scepticism or for an extreme epistemological relativism. For both would then have to be based upon several assumptions, firmly, unsceptically and unrelativistically held:

a)   that there are organisms;
b)   that there are different sorts of organisms;
c)   that they gain access to a world outside of themselves;
d)   that they do so via their sensory/perceptual apparatus;
e)   that these apparatuses are different from one another in ways that would lead one to expect significant differences in the manner that the world is perceived.

In short, Nietzschean scepticism assumes the reliability of knowledge upon which it is based; of the very assumptions that scepticism disallows. The sceptical conclusion, here as elsewhere, can be upheld only as the conclusion of an argument whose premisses set aside the sceptical position.

The theory of evolution cannot deliver any kind of epistomological pay-off because it is itself the late product of certain epistemological assumptions: that we have access to an outside world and that that access, and exposure, is knowledge, or the basis of our knowledge.[32] 'Evolutionary epistemology' is therefore a contradiction in terms: an attempt to lay the foundations of a theory of knowledge using a top storey and a roof. Moreover, it does not address valid questions about the nature of the 'knowledge' that interaction with the organisms yields. One aspect of this warrants further reflection.

We may not unreasonably imagine that the world of the conscious organism is a world of colours, smells, sounds, etc.; a world, in short, of secondary qualities. It is not clear, however, whether those secondary qualities are inherent in the objects to which they are attributed. While primary qualities such as length seem inherent in objects in the absence of organisms sensing them, qualities such as colour, taste and smell seem only to come into being as a result of interaction with sentient organisms. Object A would be longer than Object B irrespective of whether there were consciousnesses perceiving the objects. (Setting aside the Einsteinian consideration that makes length dependent upon the relativities of inertial frames of reference.) For Object A to smell nicer than Object B, there would have to be a consciousness making that judgement. And this is probably true for Object A to be brighter than Object B. This well-accepted difference between primary qualities inherent in the material world and secondary qualities which are inherent only in the experiences of organisms experiencing the material world is a marker of the extent to which the world of the sentient organism deviates from the physical world which environs it. The fact of this deviation in turn may seem to raise doubts about the veridical nature of experience – understood as experience of what is 'objectively' there. At first these doubts, although a matter of concern for an evolutionary epistemology committed to the notion that truth is about being embedded in the material world in order to ensure successful interaction with it, would seem to support a Nietzschean scepticism. Actually, it undermines Nietzschean as well as other brands of evolutionary epistemology; for it sets off experiences, and hence the knowledge, of conscious organisms from nature. Secondary qualities – which, after all, account for most of our experiences – seem to intervene between the conscious organism and physical reality. At any rate, if you were designing a conscious organism, you wouldn't presumably have it experience things that are not there. If one wanted evidence of the superfluousness of consciousness *per se* from an evolutionary point of view, the fact that its contents are composed largely of secondary qualities provides such evidence in abundance. If, as seems to be the case, secondary qualities are imported into the world by conscious animals, they can hardly support survival.

The superfluousness – or worse – of secondary qualities, not to speak of tertiary ones (such as being painful, unpleasant or repulsive), is an aspect of the wider superfluousness of consciousness. It is easy to imagine the organism's behaviour being perfectly effectively shaped by the objective properties of the environment – for example, the wavelengths of light – rather than by subjective truths – for example, that the light is red rather than blue. The epistemological weakness of evolutionary epistemology, in other words, is underlined by the fact that the theory of evolution does not require that there should be such a thing as knowledge in order that the environment should elicit the appropriate (i.e. life-supporting) response from the organism. That secondary qualities have no place in the materialist world picture of neo-Darwinism is a facet of the wider truth that consciousness itself has no place in that world picture. It is not an inherent truth of the physical world that it is bright, that it is red, that it is tasty or that it is painful. It cannot, therefore, be an additional benefit that behaviour (or the reaction of the organism) should be mediated through these things. The argument that shows secondary qualities and conscious-ness to be superfluous applies *a fortiori* to propositional knowledge or to truths mediated through explicit entertainment of possibilities. The fact that such knowledge is useful *now* and has been useful over the last few thousand – or perhaps the last few hundred – years cuts no evolutionary ice because the bodily form that is assumed to make this possible has been in place for many more years than that.

Ultimately, the theory of evolution cannot deliver the epistemo-logical pay-off some philosophers seem to find in it – the constraint that our perceptual knowledge should be true – because it cannot deliver the underlying ontology; namely the assumption that there are material beings and that they fall into two kinds – unconscious material beings (that constitute most of the environment) and the con-scious material beings that are environed, struggle to exist, etc. It cannot deliver the ontology simply because it *assumes* the ontology. This has been well put by David Kelly defending his own position (as advanced in *The Evidence of the Senses*) against Peter Munz's criticism and, in particular, the latter's assertion that 'Without a real world, there would have been nothing to do the selecting and evolution would not have taken place':

> This approach is a complete epistemological inversion: it treats as self-evident a complex scientific theory, and tries to use the theory to validate its own perceptual bias. The theory of evolution is a hypothesis concerning a global mechanism operating over eons, on populations of organisms some of which, according to the theory itself, no longer exist – a hypothesis which, since we cannot see the mechanism itself in operation, must be verified by integrating a huge amount of evidence from countless observations. Munz's state-ment assumes that we can be sure natural selection occurs before we can be sure our senses are valid. How then did he learn about

natural selection if not by relying on his perceptual awareness of such things as animals, books and biology professors? The statement assumes that our knowledge of natural selection precedes our knowledge of a real world. In what nonreal realm did we first establish the occurrence of this mechanism?[33]

It is not necessary to agree with all of this to accept the charge, laid against evolutionary epistemology, of putting the cart before the horse when it is argued that evolutionary theory requires that perception should be true.

The essential point is this: evolutionary theory cannot be seen as a guarantee of the validity (or truth) of perception because it is itself based upon the assumption of the validity of vast numbers of perceptions synthesised into an overarching hypothesis. At the very least, it helps itself to the assumption that perception is rooted in the interaction between material entities – the organism and its environment. And that, ontologically speaking, is a rather lavish free lunch.

The more general point that I wish to elucidate through a critique of one very influential version of pragmatism, namely evolutionary epistemology, is that cashing out truth into something else – in this case constraints upon behaviour – results in the elimination of the category of truth altogether. True beliefs are reduced without remainder to sets of actions, modes of behaviour, that support survival. This effectively collapses the relations between knower and the known and between TF and things they are true or false of. The distance between the knowing organism and the known world is swallowed up into a coupling of the two in mutually fine-tuned mechanisms; or, looking at it more dispassionately, the organism is downgraded to a corner of the physical world and as such has a status no different from that of a pebble. Evolutionary epistemology undermines the very thing that is the basis of its scepticism: knowledge, consciousness, in brief the making-explicit that gives the organism its (supposedly erroneous) perspective and its tendency (*à la* flying mosquito) to see its perspective as a definitive view on and of the world.[34]

One final point: experience, from the point of view of evolutionary epistemology, is understood as exposure to things that are relevant to the organism's survival. But, of course, experience goes beyond exposure; and knowledge goes beyond experience: factual knowledge goes beyond experience-based knowledge; and knowledge of laws, principles, etc. goes beyond factual knowledge. Among many things that evolutionary theory cannot explain is how experience gives birth to modes of awareness that reach so far beyond biologically significant exposure. We have seen how it cannot account for secondary qualities – which in the hard world of materialism do not count as sources of true knowledge. And we now see how it is limited in a different way: it cannot account for most of what we call knowledge; for the many explicit truths by which we steer our lives. Evolutionary theory demands that species (viewed as survivors) should be effective mechanisms. It does not require of them that they should have knowledge of what they are doing or, indeed, any knowledge at all. Such knowledge is costly and, compared with mechanisms, profoundly unsatisfactory.

Evolutionary theory, if it really were the last word on our nature, would predict that there should be no such thing as knowledge, or behaviour mediated by explicit awareness. It would predict, in short, that there would be no knowledge to have an epistemological theory about. Evolutionary epistemology is, therefore, a contradiction in terms.

Truth/falsehood and explicitness

The fundamental error of evolutionary epistemology is that of embedding human knowledge, and truth and falsehood as humanly understood, in the biological, indeed material, world. This was intended both to guarantee that perception should be at least partly true (an organism whose senses got everything wrong all the time simply would not have survived, or even evolved in the first place) and, at the same time, to put perception and human knowledge in its place – so that the partial truth is, at best, grossly incomplete and at worst distorted or mixed with a good deal of falsehood. In contrast, the idea of truth advanced in this essay emphasises explicitness as the necessary condition of the emergence of TF and thus separates the latter from biological, material reality. Truths are true *of* the material (biological, social) world, but they are not *in* the material (biological) world. The distance is signalled in the *of* – as in 'true of', and 'knowledge of', and the *about* in 'in error about', etc.

The extreme pragmatism of evolutionary epistemology reveals that extent to which all pragmatism – which reduces knowledge to an instrument of survival and subordinates the category of truth to that fundamental imperative – like the Correspondence and Coherence Theories of Truth, starts too far down the track. To see truth (and falsehood) for what they are, we need to make visible the explicitness necessary for them to come into being. Only then does it make sense to think about criteria for differentiating truth from falsehood, and true assertions, statements, beliefs or whatever, from false ones. To see truth as being embodied or expressed in an action that promotes survival – and to do so even in those circumstances where that action is simply a reflex – is to import into behaviour the explicitness that strictly belongs to the agent in so far as he or she is acting deliberately, consciously, with reference to a certain hypothesis, etc. Likewise, correspondence of the kind necessary for the Correspondence Theory of Truth can come into being only when the state of affairs corresponding to, say, an assertion has been made explicit as a possibility. Correspondent truth is not given free with the state of affairs whose existence may at some time be asserted. Neither pragmatic nor correspondent truth is embedded in nature.

Truth (and falsehood) presuppose explicitness and so are inextricably bound up in human consciousness. The particularly intimate relationship between TF and language derives from the power that language has to capture the sense of a possible state of affairs and give it existence in its own right as a string of sounds or written signs. It is worth dwelling a little more on this: on the need for explicitness to create TF; and on the role of language in bringing TF to full birth.

It is clear that assertions such as 'The economic trends are increasingly unfavourable' or 'The behaviour of King John became, over time, unacceptable to his people' do not correspond to natural givens: the states of affairs to which they draw attention are not secreted by the material world. There are several obvious reasons for this: the entities invoked in the statements are abstract and general; the statement about King John refers to the distant past; and so on. But what about a true (or false) statement such as 'The cat is in this room'? The referent of that statement would seem to exist of its own accord without having to be made explicit. Surely the cat's being in this room carves itself out of the nexus of reality without relying on the process of making explicit to give it edges? After all, the elements in it – cat, room – are stand-alones which provide their own aseity and, of their own accord, sustain the relationship between them: 'in', after all, is a natural spatial arrangement that is a feature of the physical world.

So one might think; but this is simply not the case. For a start, the entities in question – 'cat', 'room' – are presented as instances of general types. They could just as well have been presented as instances of other general types; as, for example, in the equally true 'The animal is in my study' (which this room happens to be). Or they could have been presented in the form of descriptions. The cat, for instance, could have been expressed as 'a black-furred creature of medium size'. In

other words, even in the case of simple factual statements about particular physical situations, a state of affairs has been presented in a form
that is the outcome of a vast number of choices. Moreover, the
relationship between its elements, the cat and the room, has been
picked out in but one of many possible ways. Other aspects of the
spatial relationship could have been selected: 'The cat is in the far
corner of the room', 'The cat is in the same spot as last time', etc. Or
the account of the relationship between the cat and the room could
have been embellished in non-spatial ways, beyond the mere 'is in'.
For example: 'The cat has entered the room and stayed in it', 'The cat is
dwelling in the room', 'The cat has chosen to remain in the room',
'The cat has assumed his favourite spot'. These focus on different
aspects of the relationship between the cat and the room.

There is a temptation to suggest that there might be a statement, or
group of statements, which express natural truths – 'unadorned natural
truths' – for example, spatial relationships which nature as it were
secretes herself and which require no making explicit in order to exist in
aseity. For example, one might be inclined to say that 'The cat is in this
room' is a natural truth, while 'The furry animal has entered the room
and is at present dwelling there' is not; as if the former made itself
explicit and the latter required a bit of help; or the former was a self-
manufacturing TF, while the latter required a certain amount of processing by human consciousness. But to think this is to miss the point;
which is that 'The cat is in this room' requires as much processing was
'The furry animal, etc.'. After all, as noted much earlier, no natural
scenario spontaneously breaks up into a definite, finite number of truths
(or falsehoods). As I look at this room, I am faced with an inexhaustible
number of aspects that could be expressed as facts of the kind 'The cat is
in this room'. I could list any number of objects, of patches of light, of
overheard sounds, of spatial relations, and there would be no cut-off
between 'natural', 'self-generating' relations, facts, or whatever and ones
that were regarded as humanly inspired; even less would there be a
natural self-generating cut-off.

The truth is that all the statements require an act of making-explicit,
an act that encircles the particular, discrete state of affairs corresponding
to the statement. That this is so even in the case of a truth that we might
be inclined to regard as plain, unadorned, canonical, such as 'The cat is
in this room', is betrayed by the fact that the sentence that expresses it is
not simply an iconic reflection or a picture of a spatial relationship. It
contains three words that are not nouns or expressive of the spatial
relationships – 'The', 'is', 'this' – which serve specifically to focus upon

and define the state of affairs that is expressed. The definite article, by working upon an assumption of uniqueness – and, at the same time mobilising or even creating that assumption – forecloses on a range of possible cats: it narrows a class to one member. The copula 'is' underlines the spatial state of affairs, places it in italics. Finally, 'this', mobilises either deixis to place the cat in the same room as the actual or implied speaker or anaphora to place the cat in the same room that the actual or implied speaker has referred to earlier – to locate it in the same universe-of-discourse as that referred to in immediately preceding utterances (what Strawson referred to as 'story-relative identification'). All of which is necessary to make the truth (or falsehood) exist. Or – to put it the other way round – to transform a piece of reality into the truth- or falsity-conditions of an assertion.

The crucial (though not exclusive) role of language in bringing TF fully to birth will, I hope, be clear from what has been said so far. The present discussion could open on to a wider investigation of the relationship between language, truth and reality and the expressive function of language in turning what in some pre-linguistic sense is there into a nexus of truths (and what is not there into a nexus of falsehoods). I will not, however, open up this wider discussion partly because it is too large a topic to be tacked on to this discussion of explicitness and truth, and in part because I have already sketched out some of the territory.[35] Nevertheless, one point is worth making.

In *The Explicit Animal*, I emphasised the importance of the *arbitrariness* of linguistic signs in ensuring that they are able to discharge their key role as instruments by which explicitness is exfoliated and itself made explicit. Arbitrariness is not itself arbitrary: it is not an accident, or a result of practical limitations, that linguistic signs are quite different from the things they are employed to refer to. On the contrary: it is precisely because arbitrary signs are not naturally connected with whatever it is that they are used to signify – they are not indices, causally related to their significates; nor are they icons naturally mirroring their significates – that they are best suited to creating and sustaining the distance between human consciousness and the natural and social world to which it relates. Arbitrary signs signify their objects but not as proxy for them; they never lose their status as signs. In addition to signifying their significates, they also signify – or at least betray – that they are signs. No one is going to mistake the word 'cat' for a cat. It is this, more than anything, that makes language suitable for postulating possibilities that may or may not correspond to actualities; for asserting what is (and what is not) the case; for giving birth to

TF. Language is above all the home of the possible, turning the actual into asserted truth and the non-existent into asserted falsehood. It is in language above all that explicit consciousness, the home of the possible, itself has a home outside of the actual.

When thinkers attempt to capture the 'species being' of humanity, and try to define what it is that distinguishes human beings from all other creatures, they most commonly allude to the possession of an extremely complex system of languages. They then run into the difficulty of defining what it is about human language that sets it off definitively from non-human languages. (This difficulty is often compounded by a tendency to read into non-human languages features that actually belong exclusively to human language – another manifestation of the protean Fallacy of Misplaced Explicitness. See *The Explicit Animal*, pp. 118–94). I would argue that what distinguishes human language from animal signalling systems is the user's attitude to the language that is used: the explicit acknowledgement of the signs as having the status of signs. Chains of signs are seen *as* chains of signs, so that what is expressed through them is seen as possibility, not actuality. This is utterly different from the situation where, say, an indexical sign stands for the presence of its significate and awakens the expectation of the latter; where, for example, a particular visual pattern signifies to an animal of type A the presence of an animal of type B and evokes in animal of type A the behaviour appropriate to the presence of animal of type B. Under such circumstances, the sign is not seen as a sign but experienced as the object the sign signifies. The red blob on the background is not seen by the robin as a *sign* of another robin but experienced as the *presence* of another robin. The sign is absorbed into the significate and the signs do not create a world of possibility that is parallel to the world of actual events and objects. Humans, by contrast, recognise signs for what they are: they see signs as signs. This absolutely fundamental difference has numerous consequences; for example, utterances do not typically act upon them as causes invoking immediate reaction – they more usually evoke possibilities for consideration. Another consequence is evident in classification of objects: these are always provisional. Even when an object is classified under a 'canonical' heading – e.g. 'cat', 'robin' – it is there to be reclassified under different headings – e.g. 'that absolute pest', 'that little bird with its sad little song', etc. A particularly telling consequence is that humans *play* with the signs they use: they not only lie, but also pun, quote, mimic, etc. Moreover, humans have developed a system of second-order signs, of signs of signs – letters, written numbers, etc.

Nothing could be more remote from the symptoms triggering reactions, calls evoking instinctive responses, etc. that we see in the animal kingdom.[36] All of this underlines how a sign, seen as a sign, is regarded as standing for a possibility, for something that may or may not be the case. Animal calls, their signs, do not assert things, nor do they deny them: they cannot do either because both assertion and denial depend upon the postulation of possibilities and only human sign systems can achieve this. Human discourse, precisely because it explicitly and self-consciously postulates *possible* states of affairs – only some of which will have been extracted from the surrounding actuality – is able to assert such states of affairs and so to make true and false assertions: the possibility of the state of affairs can exist side by side with that state of affairs (or, in the case of a false statement, with its absence) so that the latter can be asserted. While explicitness gives birth to TF, it is language that enables truth and falsehood to grow up into fully formed categories.

The accessibility of the truth

The ambition of this essay has not been to solve the ancient question of 'What is truth?', even less the yet more ancient, even pre-philosophical question of what is The Truth. Rather, it has been to emphasise that it is not possible to see truth for what it is, or to found an adequate theory of truth, without taking into account the explicitness that is a necessary condition of the emergence of truth, as it is of the emergence of false-hood. Theories of truth, I have argued, should begin further back than conventional theories; the latter start at a point where most of what is required to generate TF has been put in place. Correspondence between statements and states of affairs is only part of the basis of the truth – the final step – though it may provide the criterion for separating truth from falsehood. Likewise, coherence between statements at different levels is only one aspect of the nature of truth. The pragmatist's notion of truth as the basis for actions that directly or indirectly assist survival, or are in some other way beneficial, captures another aspect of truth: it is a hard-headed attempt to connect truth to practical need but runs the danger of embedding notions of truth in useful action to the point where truth is effectively eliminated. This eliminativist tendency is concealed by ploys such as, for example, reading explicit truths into adaptive behaviour; for example, seeing a tropism such as the tendency of a micro-organism to swim in the direction of certain pH gradients and to swim away from others as action in accordance with a true belief. If this is temporarily plausible, it is only because elimination of the cognitive content of the truths asserted and believed by The Explicit Animal is offset by reinserting, as it were by hand, analogous cognitive content even into primitive behaviour: what the intelligent human observer sees in the tropism – its general patterns and even its purpose – is donated to the tropism by a process of misplacing explicitness. (This is a reminder of how putting explicitness where it shouldn't be is connected with the tendency to remove it from places where it should be.)

The question of the nature of truth cannot be separated from that of the nature of falsehood. And we cannot complete the discussion of the manner in which truth is distinguished from falsehood without asking how it is there is truth and falsehood in the first place. The question of determining the criterion for distinguishing T from F must be secondary to that of giving an account of how it is that there is TF. The consequence of not recognising this is to espouse either quasi-tautological notions of truth (such as Tarski's Semantic Theory) or more explicitly deflationary theories in which the notion of truth is redundant or empty. The difference between 'p' and '"p" is true' is that the latter makes explicit the fact that the possibility expressed in 'p' is actualised. This additional layer of explicitness is the difference that makes the predicate 'is true' non-empty. The explicitness necessary to generate p in the first place is that in virtue of which the category of truth is not redundant. (Which is not, of course, to subscribe to the notion that there is a *substance* called 'The Truth'.) Failure to recognise the centrality and primacy of explicitness will inevitably reduce truth to a contentless boundary.

Putting explicitness at the heart of the concept of truth opens up many new questions; in particular questions about the relationship between the general propensity of human consciousness to make things explicit and the emergence of specific truths. As Heidegger pointed out,[37] the Greek term for truth, *aletheia*, etymologically means 'uncoveredness'. This connection invites us to ask questions about the relationship between truth (and falsehood) and what is in some sense simply 'there' or 'out there' – between, for example, what is asserted and what is pre-explicitly there. In addressing this question, one has to make some kind of judgement as to what it is that is 'out there' or what 'out there' means: extra-linguistic reality? pre-linguistic reality? the pre-social world? the pre-human world? the pre-sentient world? the natural world? the world of material things?

The fundamental question is this: if truth is uncoveredness – the world made explicit, or explicitly postulated possibilities that happen to be realised – what is it that is uncovered, or made explicit? It is natural to think of there being basic truths that are about, true of, the objective given. The latter may be seen as something that is commonly available to all and as therefore being confirmed by all others as being there: the intersubjectively agreed given, where intersubjective agreement would not be confined to a particular community in a particular epoch, but would be confirmed by all subjects at all times. Alternatively, it may be thought of as some material bedrock of the given, belonging to a pre-human, natural world. If the truth is the sum of those expressed possibilities that correspond to the given, the question then arises as to what counts as the given.

The hierarchy presented at the outset of this essay, which begins with '?' and ends with higher-order statements about statements was, as emphasised there, not meant to be ontogenetic. It was not, that is to say, intended to describe a quasi-evolutionary sequence by which matter gave rise to sentience and the latter to ever-increasing levels of self-consciousness. Nevertheless, there is a temptation to think of a sequence in accordance with which there is first a 'primitive' (material) given and that, subsequently, part of this given evolves towards conscious entities which in turn uncover the given in explicitness captured in truthful statements. The most obvious trouble with that schema is that it does not explain how consciousness emerges – it is, therefore, descriptive rather than explanatory. And although the sequence does not commit itself to a temporal order – first there was matter, then there was sentient life, then there were self-conscious beings such as people – and although it does not commit itself to causal connections, it is still speculative: a quasi-empirical theory about emergence for which, by definition, there can be no empirical evidence. For (to capture one aspect of the problem) consciousness cannot say anything about what was present in the absence of consciousness – what was present in the absence of presence. Even less could it have anything useful, illuminating or reliable to say about the steps leading away or upwards from a putative primordial state of a pre-sentient material world to its own world in which sentient beings uncover, among other things, insentient matter. Finally, and most damagingly, the notion of a pre-conscious world, of a world of insentient matter, as the primitive given can be turned on its head if the concept of matter is carefully inquired into. Such an inquiry may lead to the conclusion that 'matter' is itself a construct of consciousness and that, far from being a primitive given, it is a late entry into the order of things.[38]

The central concern therefore of anyone who wishes to develop a theory of truth that reaches back through a theory of knowledge into an ontology is the extent to which explicitness, uncoveredness, makes explicit, uncovers, what is already there and the extent to which it creates or at least in some sense shapes that which it makes explicit. Does explicitness merely make explicit what is there, in itself, prior to explicitness, to consciousness – like a light being switched on in a room, revealing what was already there in the darkness? Or is it inescapably interactive, so that what is made explicit is not the object in itself but the *interaction* between the known object and the knowing subject? This is a question that carries a heavy freight of epistemological anxieties.

There is a benign sense, already alluded to, in which explicitness does create that which is made explicit. When I capture one aspect of what is before me – for example, 'The Yorkshire accent of the speaker on the radio' – I am giving it a separate and independent existence that it does not have hitherto. Moreover, I give it prominence and front-stageness that it does not have in itself. Further, if I am telling you about a scene at which you were not present, in which I noticed the Yorkshire accent of the man talking on the radio, this aspect comes to stand for the entire scene. Nevertheless, although the expressed aspect of the scene has been in a sense manufactured, the act of creation is epistemologically benign inasmuch as the possibility alluded to was in fact actualised. The Yorkshire accent was 'really there' and its presence could be checked by another observer. The difference between making up falsehoods and selecting aspects of state of affairs, therefore, remains real and robust. Since the scene itself does not have fixed boundaries or a predetermined list of contents – not even my room has a finite list of contents: it includes not only the obvious tables and chairs but also the less obvious but no less real things such as the creases on the sleeve of my hanging raincoat and the relationship between an airmail envelope and a glint in the lampshade – it is not misrepresented by reference to the accent of the radio announcer.

Not all creation-through-focused-explicitness is benign. So long as explicitness transforms something into a truth-condition against which the possibilities that are made explicit can be checked for actuality (and hence truth), then the act of creation is not incompatible with truth and does not undermine the distinction between truth and falsehood. The situation is different when we think of the uncovering process, of human making-explicit, the creation of the human world, in its entirety. Then we have, by definition, no outside against which to check the sum total of possibilities. To check one uncovering against another to determine whether the uncovering process is or is not generating truth is rather like (to use Wittgenstein's analogy) buying two copies of the same newspaper to check whether the news is true. It might be argued that the question of whether the sum total of making explicit – the totality of experiences/perceptions/statements – is itself deceptive is an empty question. For the sum total of making explicit must by definition be all we shall ever know and therefore cannot be corrected by future experience. In that sense, the limits placed upon our knowledge, and upon the truths we shall know, are not really limits at all. The reality we shall be confined to knowing is reality *tout court*. There are no rival versions to challenge or correct this one.

I shall have to leave unresolved the issue as to whether there really is an unanswered question here. It is important to note, though, that the idea of a pure making-explicit – a pure, undistorted uncovering of what is there – is itself not entirely transparent, especially since the process of making-explicit seems to be mediated through sentient creatures who are embodied, incarnate in bodies that have their own needs, agenda and intrinsic properties. What is clear is that uncovering is, seemingly inescapably, the result of an interaction between a sentient organism and the uncovered object. What is less clear is the implications of this for our access to truth. Acknowledgement of the fact that knowledge is mediated by the body of the knower, of course, precipitated the tragic epistemology of Kant and his successors and generated the tantalising notion of the inaccessible ideal object of knowledge – the 'thing-in-itself', the object known as it truly, intrinsically, is – an ideal which we are denied because our knowledge is mediated through our body, specifically through our senses. We know what is there through its inter-action with our body; and what we therefore know, it is argued, is the interaction with our bodies.

Russell put this with the clarity and the crudity that characterised some aspects of his philosophising when he said that all we know are the impulses in our brain – triggered off by the exchange of energy between the brain and the objects we directly or indirectly encounter. This view is itself vulnerable for it assumes that there is a privileged object of knowledge: the activity in our brain; or some of it any rate. This assumption that we know our brain processes realises the question of what we know them with. The response that we don't know them with anything, that they are the knowing, only compounds the difficulty. It requires us to accept that the sequence of the (unknown) events passing from the object to the subject suddenly comes to an end at a particular place in nerve impulses which are both knowers and at which is known. These impulses are, that is to say, self-disclosing and, in disclosing themselves, they somehow disclose objects or events a certain way up the causal stream from themselves – the objects and events that triggered them. Even if we were to accept these extraordinary claims, we would be left puzzling over the fact that what they disclose is something rather different from what is seen on the oscilloscope or any other device. And this makes it reasonable to ask the question whether they disclose their essence – their inner reality – to the subject whose brain they are in and only an external appearance to others, including to the subject when he sees his impulses displayed on an oscilloscope.

Behind this question, and behind the anxiety that explicitness may inescapably distort what is made explicit in a systematic way, is a profound – and consequently illuminating – misunderstanding: a misunderstanding based on the assumption that there are certain definite, even absolute, intrinsic properties in what is there that would correspond to, or translate into, distinctive experiences. That, in other words, there is a content of experience, a form of knowledge, perception, truth that would correspond to what would be disclosed if the object disclosed itself. This assumes some kind of internal relationship between the intrinsic properties of the reality out there and the qualities (perceptions, sensations, etc.) disclosed by a non-distorting process of uncovering. Such an assumption – which brings in its wake a despair at knowing how things are because, for the reasons already noted, all disclosure would seem to be interactive and therefore distorting – has only to be made to be exposed as fallacious. (Even the naive analogy that sees making-explicit as being the equivalent of switching on a light that reveals what is already there would not satisfy the ideal that this would suggest. For the light would expose the object in a particular light and the objects would be seen in their interaction with that light, shadowed and highlighted accordingly.)

Consider a pebble.[39] What would count as knowing it as it is in itself? Clearly the sensations we have when we lift or handle a pebble would not count as knowing the pebble as it is in itself. After all, it is only to *us* that the pebble is solid, hard, cold, etc.: it exhibits these properties in relation to our (comparatively) less solid, softer and warmer flesh. And, as already noted, the properties revealed by science are, ultimately, non-qualitative: length, mass, etc. are quantitative measures and – though these may relate to the range of possible uses the pebble may have, the effects it may produce, the sensations it may give rise to – a scientific description in its purest form is void of any qualitative content. There is no third possibility: the pebble as it would be (seem) when it is disclosed to itself or disclosed in itself. To vary

Wittgenstein's remark,[40] if a pebble could express itself, we should not able to recognise its self-image.

The worry that a non-benign or systematic distortion would seem to be an inevitable consequence of explicitness, of the uncoveredness that is the truth revealed to us, is, therefore, baseless. It is founded on the assumption that there is an intrinsic truth, prior to our making-explicit, corresponding to the self-revelation of objects, the self-disclosure of that which it revealed to us, a truth which we are denied and, compared with which, what is revealed to us is distortion. There is no such 'pure' self-disclosure available to a non-perpectival knower, one whose knowing is uncontaminated by his status, position and composition as a knower. The relatively non-perspectival knowledge of science is no closer to things' self-disclosure than the immersedly perspectival knowledge of ordinary perception: the odourless, weight-less, locationless, sizeless, etc. equations of physics, for example, are not evidently closer to the self-disclosure of a pebble than are ordinary looking and lifting. Perspective may have been shed in the passage from ordinary perception to the 'view from nowhere' (Nagel) that is the asymptote of science but so, too, have secondary qualities and the primary qualities of the particular object: equations, in a very funda-mental sense, are contentless and they can scarcely be a means of revelation of the true nature of the particulars of which the world is composed.[41]

We could address this another way. To equate consciousness with explicitness, with the 'that' that prefixes, italicises or shows forth what is in some sense already there, makes consciousness secondary, a latecomer on a scene already occupied by pre-conscious being – presumably matter. But the transformation of a certain material state of affairs into a condition of suffering or delight, into the object of a need, into the intentional object of a value, or the truth of a statement or whatever, is the emergence of something genuinely new; and in this respect explicitness, consciousness, would then be primary.[42] In so far as matter matters, the last word on its mattering lies with the consciousness to whom it matters.

Let me return to an earlier point in the discussion. The pragmatist's position that truths based on human observations and, in many cases, subservient to human will-to-power, fall so short of objectivity or absoluteness that they are no different from falsehoods – truths are merely the accepted lies – is at least in part based upon the assumption that correspondence – between consciousness and that which is outside of it – has greater ultimacy than coherence within consciousness. This is connected with another assumption that 'relative', human truth is only a small, distorted reflection of objective truth. Against this is the richly supported belief, implicit in the endeavours of science, that we can extend knowledge beyond what is served up to the individual consciousness, beyond even collective human perceptions (and the facts to which they give rise), and collective human needs (which lay down the agenda for control and understanding which science and technology aim at). If, however, truth is secondary to explicitness and hence to presence to humans, and therefore arises out of the interaction between conscious beings and the unconscious world with which they are encompassed, it does not make sense to extend the concept of truth outside of human consciousness; to imagine that there is a world of truth uncontaminated by human consciousness; or to entertain, or to be tormented by, the notion of an objective truth existing among unconscious things that exists for ever out of the reach of our consciousness. To think in this way is to imagine truths existing outside of the existence condition for there being truth! The alternative view I would wish to suggest is that the nearest approximation to a home of absolute truth must be the most advanced forms of explicitness arrived at through the collective efforts of thinkers and scientists. These provide the hardest and the highest criteria of truth. The fact that science cannot, finally, shake off its roots in human observation, in human experience and in human need should not itself be seen as a limitation, an insuperable obstacle to its claims to capture a higher, more comprehensive, truth.

Evolutionary epistemology makes objective truth unattainable: if truth is really out there among things (of which we are one, rather atypical, example), the human version of it would be at best eccentric and remain so. This view, as we have already indicated, undermines the very science, the biology, upon which it is based. Moreover, by making science at every stage infinitely distant from objective truth, evolutionary epistemology seems to remove direction from science: there can be no notion of progress from the more to the less untrue.

On the other, restoring the truth of science in the way that I have suggested seems to court the opposite danger of removing direction from science by making absolute truth all-too-attainable. If truth *were* an internal affair of human consciousness – albeit the collective of actual and possible human consciousnesses – there could, equally, be no journey towards the truth as we would be inescapably embedded in it. If embodied consciousness does not have to achieve the impossible task of stirring out of itself in order to arrive at truth, it surely need not stir at all – because it has arrived already. What, therefore, is the basis of the manifest progress of science and of the endless procession of evermore powerful theories? What is science moving towards if it is not aiming at a truth, or truths, external to scientists and humans in general?

In order to deal with this apparent difficulty, it is necessary to appreciate this: the fact that truth is secondary to explicitness relativises not the *contents* but the *emergence* of truth, the condition of the emergence of the category of truth, to humanity (the home of the highest development of explicitness). Truth, therefore, is neither unattainably 'out there' nor inescapably 'in here', but something that emerges consequent upon the interaction between out there and in here. Unreformed perception is not the content of science; rather, it is but the existence condition of there being any kind of truths – ordinary, homely, everyday truths and the larger truths of science.

Emphasising how truth is secondary to explicitness overcomes the opposition between correspondence and coherence theories of truth, between a truth that is 'out there' and one that is 'in here'. Truth is neither purely a matter of correspondence between one type of thing and another type of thing (perceptions and objects, statements and states of affairs, theories and observations) nor simply a matter of coherence between like things (between one observation and another within a closed circle, between one statement and another in a particular discursive formation, between theory-laden observation and the theories they are laden with). Truth is ultimately a matter of correspondence between things that emerge (become explicit, are picked out) in a coherent collective consciousness.

Concluding thoughts: unsolved problems, the new agenda

There still remain some very difficult questions. Any theory of truth that begins with explicitness will need to address the question that has vexed all thinkers who have approached the question of truth from a starting point in individual human consciousness. It is that of accounting for general, mathematical and scientific truths. These do not seem easy to discover within or build up from the subjective experiences of one person or even of a large number of people. If truth is not 'out there', then we seem to be stuck with an already arrived at truth, which allows for no progress in science towards truth. If truth *is* out there, then science seems to be cut off forever from the truth. The question, therefore, is the relationship between the truth in here and the truth out there; truth as something already attained which we inhabit – indeed suffer, and, in the case of bodily truths, in some sense have as our very being – and truth as an objective something towards which we aspire; the truth of subjective experience and the truth of the universe at large.

Unanswered, this question underlines how reconnecting the concept of truth with that of explicitness as its necessary condition is only a start. The image of explicitness as a kind of moving light over the darkness of pre-conscious matter, or even a light 'dawning over the whole' is inadequate. It does not even point in the direction of an explanation of the origin of error or of the relationship of subjective experience to the objective world of knowledge. Nor does it explain the vast accumulated stores of factual knowledge. It does not account for the historical development of knowledge, either in an individual's life or in the history of mankind. Indeed, further clarification is required of what is, additionally, required to turn explicitness into, say, factual knowledge. How does explicitness ascend towards wider and larger truths that transcend individual consciousnesses? In order to be possessed of knowledge – the kind of thing we actively steer our lives by and the kind of thing we assert in propositions – we need, as Kant said, to have both particular intuitions and general concepts. To be made fact explicit experience has to be a) accurately generalised (i.e. made to a apply to a series of cases and/or placed under general categories), and b) cast in propositional form – so that it can be tested and communicated. This needs to be explored anew. How do we move from '*That* this is the case [for me]' to making the '*That* this is the case' available to others and how do these different factual instances, or this continuous explicitness, dovetail within and between consciousnesses to the collective growth of knowledge?

These questions also highlight the distance between mere 'that', unqualified explicitness, and the active conscious life of ordinary human beings with their world of agency, self-care, enquiry and knowledge and responsibility. And this in turn opens up a new seam of inquiry: examination of the relationship between 'That this is the case', 'That I am [the case]' and 'That I am enworlded'; more specifically, the relationship between what I am, what I experience and where I am placed; or between truths about me and truths about the world.

Thus we redefine (and as part of the redefinition, reorder) the philosophical challenge. Yes, to explain explicitness (the origin of 'that [X is the case],) and the relationship between explicitness and truth, explicitness and knowledge, explicitness and agency, and explicitness and the sense of the enduring self, or an insistent me continuing over time with roles, responsibilities, rights, relationships and destinies. But also to go beyond this to try to connect the explicitness implicit in 'my world' and 'me' with the explicitness built upon in the world of knowledge. Introducing 'explicitness' as the forgotten *sine qua non* of all these other things is a beginning, not an end, of a philosophical task; for we have to see how these other things relate to, are rooted in, arise out of, 'that'. The profound difficulty of connecting the explicit-making activity of the individual with the realm of objective knowledge should not be underestimated. The example of Husserl[43] should be sufficient warning to anyone who is proposing to take the question seriously:

> I became more and more disquieted by doubts of principle, as to how to reconcile the objectivity of mathematics, and of all science in general, with a psychological foundation for logic ... and I felt myself more and more pushed towards general critical reflections on the essence of logic, and on the relationship, in particular, between the subjectivity of knowing and the objectivity of the content known. (translated and quoted in Bell, op. cit., p. 83)

> I was tormented by incomprehensible new worlds: the world of pure logic, and the world of act-consciousness ... *I did not know how to unite them*, yet they had to have some relationship to one another, and form an inner unity. (quoted in Bell, ibid., p. 83; emphasis in the original)

> How can experience as consciousness give or contact an object? How can experiences be mutually legitimated or corrected by each other, and not merely replace each other, or confirm each other subjectively? How can the play of consciousness whose logic is empirical make objectively valid statements, valid for all things that exist in and of themselves? ... How is natural science to be comprehensible ... to the extent that it pretends at every step to posit and know a nature that is in itself – in itself, in contrast to the subjective flow of consciousness? (quoted and translated by Bell, ibid., p. 84)[44]

Tracing the transition from the subject making a world explicit to the consensus truths of science is one very important element of the task of developing a theory of truth that takes its rise from an understanding of the fact that explicitness is the necessary condition of TF. Another element is following the passage from the individual making the world explicit to the collective explicit-making actions of mankind over history. And then there is the task of relating both

individual and collective explicitness-making to the critical sense
that Nietzsche (and the many others who have adopted a pessimistic
view of the status of human knowledge) deny that we have. This
critical sense, which is not confined to one or two individuals such as
Nietzsche, is the intuition – evident in ordinary consciousness – that
knows that it knows and knows that its knowledge is dwarfed by
what it doesn't know, and that deliberately uses its sense of its own
ignorance to energise its push to further knowledge and to wind up
'active uncertainty'. It is present in an embryonic form in an hypo-
thesis-driven search for a lost shoe; it is fully developed in the
anguished, concentrated thought of a theoretician seeking a formula to
bind together the observations others have made. Finally, there is
the question of the ultimate destination of our search for truth: is our
goal, after all, a gradual approximation towards an increasing self-
knowledge, towards the asymptote of transparency of the collective
consciousness living itself out among non-transparent things? Or
does this have to be complemented by an attempt to make that in
which we are located as transparent as we are to ourselves? Or will, in
the end, the two endeavours merge into one? At the very least, since
truth is located firmly within the consciousness of the Explicit Animal,
we are permitted to imagine progress towards greater truth being
reflected in increasing coherence of consciousness at the level of
increasingly well-informed and sophisticated reflection.

These then are some of the issues that come to the fore when we
liberate our exploration of the nature of truth from the narrow considerations of verification, of truth-conditions, of truth-tables and truth
calculus and the other constraints within which the philosophical examination of the notion of truth within the analytical tradition was
enclosed as a consequence of salutary reactions from psychologism and
from other accounts of truth that fail to account for the objectivity of
the truths of science and of some truths of daily life. These reactions
must not be allowed to conceal from us the fact that truth cannot be
understood outside of explicitness and, since the most developed regions
of explicitness are within human consciousness, outside of human
consciousness. The recognition that the emergence of TF presupposes
explicitness, and that factual (sentential, propositional) truth presupposes the existence of creatures who are explicit in the way that
humans are, is not to be confused with the currently popular belief that
truth is constructed, that it is relative to discursive communities, etc.
The metaphysical precondition of there being such a thing as truth – the
existence of explicit animals who are able to make explicit what is

the case so that it becomes *that it is the case* – should not be muddled with particular local conditions that may determine which truths are unearthed, valued, emphasised or even invented. The metaphysical requirement is not a relativising one for we all live under the same metaphysical dispensation. (That is perhaps definitional of metaphysics.) The constraint on actual truth is the constraint necessary for truth to emerge and not upon the kinds of truths that do emerge. Because explicitness, and hence consciousness, is necessary for there to be TF, the conditions of consciousness (for example its bodily conditions) cannot be reasonably regarded as either limiting our access to the truth or, indeed, preventing our knowing it. The seeming relativism of my subordinating truth to human explicitness is not a true relativism; and it has nothing to do with the very specific relativisms so popular in contemporary thought: cultural relativism, the relativity of truth to discursive communities, the influence of power relations in determining what counts as truth, and so on.

This also helps to put into perspective the scepticism that is apparently justified by what is discovered about our origins. Evolutionary epistemology seems to suggest that knowledge and our sense of what is true and false should not only be relative to our sensorium (and so, at best, filtered and at worst distorted) but also that what emerges in our consciousness as true will be passed through a further sieve which will ensure that it is favourable to biological and social survival. Once we recognise that truth is a child of explicitness and that such explicitness is unique to mankind, the biological straitjacket constricting our sense of what is true will be loosened. The additional point that survival will be best served by a predominance of truth over falsehood rather than vice versa, and that beliefs supporting survival will do so because they are true rather than counting as true because they support survival, will be able to pack its full weight.

To say this is not, of course, to go any way towards solving any of the many problems in the philosophical exploration of truth that I have indicated a little while back, in particular the puzzling relationship between subjective experience (the truth experienced by a single consciousness) and the objective truth about things: between the former and intersubjective or consensus truth, scientific truth, transcendental truth, and *The* Truth as a notional point-of-convergence for all (important!) true statements. The present essay's function has only been to argue that making progress with such problems requires that we break out of the customary frame of reference triangulated by the conventional theories of truth which start too far down the track. Any theory of truth that is going to do its job must recognise the existence of something – explicit-making consciousness – that is needed to turn a state of affairs into the truth conditions of an assertion or a belief. Truth requires truth-makers: this is what we discover when we start far enough back. It is not impossible that starting this far back will not only help to identify the true problems of truth but indicate the direction in which solutions may be fruitfully sought.

Notes and references

1.   Ludwig Wittgenstein, *On Certainty*, edited by G.E.M. Anscombe and G.H. von Wright, translated by Denis Paul and G.E.M. Anscombe (Oxford: Blackwell, 1974), paragraph 471, p. 62e.
2.   Raymond Tallis, *The Explicit Animal: a Defence of Human Consciousness* (Macmillan: London, 1991).
3.   Raymond Tallis, 'Facts, Statements and the Correspondence Theory of Truth', chapter 7 of *Not Saussure: A Critique of Post-Saussurean Literary Theory* (1st edn, 1988; 2nd edn, 1995).
4.   For an exhaustive discussion of the role of the conscious human agent in human affairs and a reaffirmation of this role against postmodern critiques, see Raymond Tallis, *Enemies of Hope: a Critique of Contemporary Pessimism* (London: Macmillan, 1997).
5.   Nevertheless, the place of explicitness in the wider universe does need to be considered if the appeal to 'explicitness' as a defining – or irreducibly distinctive – feature of humanity is to be truly satisfying and not merely a veto upon a certain line of thought.
6.   This question – to which I return later in the essay – is also glanced at in Chapter 4 'That I am This (Thing): Reflections on Deixis, Explicitness and the Tautology of the Self'.
7.   Because, at this level – in the absence of explicitness – X cannot be understood explicitly either as an object, or as an object at a particular place and time, or as part of, or the central character in, a state of affairs. At this level, the difference between objects and states of affairs – or between objects and 'That objects are/exist' etc. – has not been established. Someone might argue against this as follows: while 'That X' manifestly does not exist before explicitness has, as it were, brought 'That – ' into existence, surely objects and states of affairs exist. In response to this, I would say that there are no such things as 'states of affairs' – discrete, sealed off constellations of entities – in the absence of explicitness, embodied in a description, to ring-fence them. (This must not be taken to suggest that truth is relative to language, or that the truth-conditions of true statements are to be found inside discursive communities – for reasons that will be set out later in this chapter.) If, in the absence of explicitness, there are no such things as states of affairs contrasted with single, bounded material objects, then the latter also do not exist because the notion of a free-standing object acquires its full definition in contrast with states of affairs. (Again, this is not to say that explicitness creates the world of objects – or,

worse, to echo the Lacanian lunacy that 'it is the world of words that creates the world of things'.)

8. *Tractatus Logico-Philosophicus* 5.47 and 4.5. The importance of this passage became clear to me only when it was cited by P.F. Strawson in his illuminating *Introduction to Philosophical Logic* (edited by P.F. Strawson; Oxford Readings in Philosophy, OUP, 1967). Of course, explicitness – that X is the case – is manifested not only in formulated or formulable propositions nor, indeed, solely in the cognitive realm: states of affairs are also made explicit in suffering and delight. But the further we are below propositional consciousness, the less explicit are states of affairs and the more explicitness is absorbed into implicitness.

   Strawson goes on to say:

   > It is a tenable, though more debatable, thesis that the philosophical logician's questions are also inextricably intertwined with others, which are conventionally assigned to other branches of philosophy; that the theory of the proposition cannot really be separated from the theory of knowledge or the theory of being. (p. 2)

   To which I can only say Amen!

9. I am inclined to say that the notion of truth arises when it is possible to say that there was an at least implicit assertion that may be wrong. (As many philosophers would argue that one can lay claim to knowledge only where one could be wrong. Sensations, for this reason would not count as knowledge.) This implicit assertion would, of course, have to be made explicit in order to be tested. There is a point beyond which one cannot safely or at least justifiably refer an explicit assertion backwards to an implicit one; beyond this point, it is rather like referring a snowball back to the drift it came from, asserting that the former was implicit in the latter. This point cannot be determined objectively; it is, however, the point at which TF is born. (Determining this point is rather like determining the point at which a foetus counts as a human being; or the point at which the inchoate and possible turns into the pre-actual.)

   The reason I have placed perceptions on the far side of the TF divide – so that it makes sense to say of them that they can be true or false – is that perceptions can be *wrong*. More precisely, illusions reveal the assumptions or inferences implicit in all perceptions – connected with their classifying and recognition functions. This is, however, a tricky area because the inference is, as Helmholtz first pointed out, unconconscious and is made fully conscious only through the experimental psychologist's interpretations of the basis of perceptual illusions. There is a danger – imply illustrated by the discourses of cognitive psychologists – of succumbing to the Fallacy of Misplaced Explicitness. (For a detailed discussion of Helmholtz's carefully guarded use of 'unconscious inference' and the subsequent misuse of his notion by cognitive psychologists, the reader may wish to consult, 'Unconscious Consciousness' in Raymond Tallis, *Enemies of Hope: a Critique of Contemporary Pessimism* (London: Macmillan, 1997).)

10. This is connected with the error of separating the notion of 'information' (and even knowledge) from consciousness. For a detailed discussion of this,

see the entry on 'Information' in *A Critical Dictionary of Neuromythology*, in this book.

11. Derek Parfit, 'Why Anything, Why This?', *London Review of Books* 22 January 1998.

12. There is an analogy between the natural occurrence of truths and the natural occurrence of facts. We can no more say what intrinsic truths the universe would contain in the absence of truth-bearers than we could say how many facts there are in, say, a landscape in the absence of any description of it. The number of facts will be relative to the manner in which the landscape is made explicit and described. We shall return to this point presently, noting here only that it does *not* license a position of unbounded relativism.

13. It is possible that I have been unfair to Parfit. He might actually agree with me that truths such as 'That there is nothing' do not exist in the putative empty universe of his Null Possibility; that this truth exists in our world, though it is about – true of – the Null Possibility world. Such an argument, however, would run counter to the point, central to his essay, that there are still things which would have to be explained in the Null Possibility universe – namely certain empirical and necessary truths.

14. Alfred Tarski, 'The Semantic Conception of Truth and the Foundations of Semantics', in *Philosophy and Phenomenological Research*, vol. 4 (1944) pp. 341–76.

15. Truth-values are fully developed only in relation to linguistically expressed possibilities – such as possibilities which are *asserted* (or at least seriously entertained) in sentential or quasi-sentential form.

16. Meanings – for example, the meanings of individual words – are, in a sense, general possibilities. They are, however, incomplete in two senses – which becomes evident when the meaning of a word is compared with the referent of a completed sentence asserting a state of affairs. First of all, these meanings are not asserted: they are that through which TF assertions can be made. And secondly, they are not fully specified: they are that through which a fully specified referent can be specified. Compare 'cat' with 'There is a cat in this room'. The passage from the incomplete to complete specification is achieved by a combination of two processes:
    a) multiplying the number of general terms – so that the referent is coned down upon as if by successive Venn overlaps;
    b) the mobilisation of deixis, which abruptly narrows down the number of candidates falling under a single general term, if the universe of discourse is small enough.

17. Ludwig Wittgenstein, *Philosophical Investigations* (translated by G.E.M. Anscombe, 1953). Oxford: Blackwell, The first forty or so paragraphs (pp. 2–19) are particularly relevant. The problem of linguistic and non-linguistic 'picking out' of referents is also discussed in *Not Saussure*, op. cit., pp. 107–11.

18. This notation also captures the definitional *truth* of facts – the sense in which facts are true by definition – the facts are the facts. 'Give me the facts' implies, 'Give me the true facts'. 'It's a fact' implies 'It's a true fact', 'It's true', 'This really is the case'.

19. Tarski's Semantic Theory seemed to some to license a deflationary account of truth. Its quasi-tautological form certainly seems to justify this. From the perspective being developed in this essay, this is merely an illustration of the tendency towards deflation which becomes inevitable once the explicitness that creates the conditions for TF is overlooked. The correspondence and other theories of truth have content but, it will be argued by deflationary theorists, only at the cost of importing into the concept of truth things that don't strictly belong to it. The passage from emptiness to content requires contamination with impurities.

20. I have argued against the notion that science does not progress and that scientific knowledge does not reflect nature – because it is relative either to specific social groups (the scientists themselves or the society that hires or more diffusely influences them) or to the needs of the human organism – in *Newton's Sleep* (London: Macmillan, 1995) and *Enemies of Hope* (London: Macmillan, 1997). This issue is touched on later in the present essay.

21. For an excellent equation- and, indeed, number-free discussion of the W and Z particles and the theories that have predicted its existence, suitable for people who are as subnumerate as myself, see Paul Davies, *The Mind of God: Science and the Search for Ultimate Meaning* (London: Penguin, 1992), pp. 206–9.

22. Pragmatism has two very powerful currents at present, associated respectively with the names of Foucault and Rorty. Foucault, who 'conducted his inquiries in the sun of Nietzsche's great search' asserted that knowledge is not so much true or false as legitimate or illegitimate for a particular set of power relations. For Rorty, who is less paranoid but still profoundly relativistic, and for many other postmodern thinkers, 'truths are ... judged only by interpretive communities on the basis of persuasiveness' (Jeffrey Friedman, 'Postmodernism vs Postlibertarianism', *Critical Review* 5(2) (Spring 1991), 145–58).

23. Friedrich Nietzsche, 'On Truth and Lie in an Extra-Moral Sense', a posthumously published fragment. Available, in a translation by Walter Kaufmann, in *The Portable Nietzsche* (New York: the Viking Press, 1954), pp. 42–7.

24. I do not pretend to be *au fait* with the entire literature which could be reasonably gathered under this heading, but am sufficiently familiar with the two main contributing streams: neo-Darwinian biology (Richard Dawkins et al.); and Darwin-influenced epistemology (Karl Popper et al.).

25. The other half – beloved of nihilists and cynics, whose patron saint is Michel Foucault – is that knowledge is not only mediated by the survival needs of our organic bodies but is subordinated to the will-to-power, in particular as it is collectivised in the dominant groups in society, so that, as noted above, knowledge is not so much true or false as legitimate or illegitimate for a particular set of power relations. This is espoused particularly by (anti-humanist) humanist intellectuals rather than scientists. The latter are less keen on the sociologisation of science because it undermines the status of their own disciplines. (So, too, does Darwinian biological epistemology, but the relativisation of scientific discourse to the rhetoric of a particular dominant power group is too heavy and immediate blow to bear. Scientists may be able to withstand the observation – itself the result

of science – that knowledge is relative to the exigencies of organic existence but they cannot tolerate a further relativisation originating from
society.)

26. I am aware that the concept of 'evolutionary epistemology' has two quite
distinct aspects. The first (which is not addressed here) is the analogy
between the evolution of the organism and the growth of knowledge,
whereby new ideas are seen as mutations and the advance of science is
seen as the result of a Darwinian struggle for survival between ideas. This
is, of course, particularly associated with Karl Popper and is beautifully
expounded in his *Objective Knowledge: an Evolutionary Approach* (Oxford
University Press, 1972). The second, which is relevant to the present argument, is the notion that the *content* of knowledge is to be understood in
evolutionary terms.

27. Peter Munz, 'Sense perception and the reality of the world', *Critical Review*
2(1) (Winter 1988), 65–77.

28. This is analogous to the Weak Anthropic Principle in cosmology according
to which certain properties of the universe, though astonishing and
improbable, are inevitable as they are the necessary conditions for life –
and hence observers, and hence astonished physicists – to have been
possible.

29. See especially Raymond Tallis, *The Explicit Animal*, Chapter 2, 'Biologising
Consciousness: I Evolutionary Theories'.

30. Mary Midgely, *Beast and Man: the Roots of Human Nature* (London:
Methuen, 1980), p. 150.

31. Paul Churchland's *Matter and Consciousness* (Cambridge, Mass: MIT Press,
2nd edn, 1988) is an excellent summary of mainstream thinking about the
relationship between matter and mind and the biologism that informs
much of that thinking.

32. Antony O'Hear has put this beautifully (in 'The Evolution of Knowledge',
Critical Review 2(1) (Winter 1988), 78–91):

> For, in doing epistemology, we are not entitled simply to assume certain
> results of science or any other field of enquiry ... Evolutionary epistemol-
> ogy ... invokes our biological knowledge in order to refute a particular
> brand of skepticism. We are asked to accord the deliverances of the
> senses some positive degree of probability because biology teaches us
> various things about the origins and past development of our sensory
> faculties. But, given that biology itself is a part of our system of knowl-
> edge, and in the end acceptable (if it is) because of its accord with
> sensory evidence, there is a massive circularity in attempting to justify or
> probabilify our sensory data by appeal to biology ... To invoke biology,
> and to see our perceptual apparatus as a biologically constituted device is
> not so much to refute skepticism or idealism as simply to side-step them.

33. David Kelly, 'The Evidence of the Senses', letter in reply to Peter Munz's
review of his 'The Evidence of the Senses', *Critical Review* 2(4) (Fall 1988),
pp. 183–4.

Darwinian theory does not account for the emergence of the kind of
activity that is typically carried out by scientists who devote their lives to
pursuing the truth about our origins. What they – and, more importantly,

sceptical quasi-biological philosophers such as Nietzsche – most notably ignore is our *critical* sense – the sense that has driven the evolution of culture since primitive times. If man is the clever animal who invented knowledge, he is also the even cleverer animal who invented (explicit) ignorance. He is the animal who is aware of what he does not know, who feels impelled to make enquiries of the universe and to do so by means of an elaborate and deliberately elaborated sense of being insufficiently knowledgeable. Human knowledge goes beyond sensing or bumping into or reacting to; and one of the most striking ways in which it goes beyond in this sense is reflected in the transformation of seeking into systematic enquiry, and in the 'active uncertainty' that is thinking and is cultivated in science. It goes sufficiently far beyond bumping into and reacting as to develop a theory of its universe and of its own place within it. Which is precisely what a mosquito does not do: it has no notion of 'the universe' in which to place itself as the flying centre. Nietzsche's attribution of philosophical or cosmological egocentricity to a mosquito is therefore ill-founded.

34. The notion that our knowledge is somehow damaged as to its truth by its being necessarily perspectival is itself flawed. Our perspectival knowledge is *true* – of a perspective, and since reality to a consciousness is inescapably perspectival, this knowledge is true of reality. Moreover, not only is it perspectival but it also shows *that* it is perspectival. When I see an object from behind, I see how it looks from behind and know that I am seeing it as it looks from behind.

We have no conception of knowledge that would count as full, saturated, that would be non-perspectival, i.e. from no perspective. The very phrase 'the view from nowhere' is (as Nagel meant it to be) itself contradictory. The nearest we may get to it is in the higher-level equations of science which, taken in isolation, removed from all application, are virtually empty: at best they say something about the form of reality or the scope of possibility; they do not yield reality itself.

The fact that our knowledge is mediated through our material bodies and that the latter have their own (survival) agenda which influences the structure and function of our sense organs and hence the experience that we have seems to be a kind of limitation on our knowledge. Even more does the fact that experience arises out of our interactions with the material world which is posited not in itself but as our environment: we get neither it, nor our bodies, 'pure' and 'uncontaminated' relative to my existence. It reveals only the important *interactions* between me (this organism) and that which is implicitly or explicitly posited as its environment. We have, however, to ask ourselves against what benchmark our knowledge seems to be limited and impure. The fact that our knowledge is inescapably perspectival is a cause for concern only when we compare it with an idealised scientific understanding which is somehow liberated from its roots in experience and yet, at the same time, not entirely empty. And this, as we have seen, is an impossibility. The fact that it is inescapably interactive is a cause for concern only when it is compared with another ideal: that of experience generated by the pure self-disclosure of objects – another impossibility. The notion of a form of knowledge that transcends both local perspectives and the interactions between knower and known is therefore a chimera.

35. See *Not Saussure*, op. cit., Chapter 4, 'Reference Restored', in particular section 4.3 'Words, Senses, Objects', pp. 107–11, and *The Explicit Animal*, op. cit., Chapter 7, 'Recovering Consciousness'.

36. The system of numbers helps to make the point here. We know from its behaviour that a bird may be able to tell the difference between two small quantities. For example, if there are five men with guns in a field, the birds in the adjacent rookery will be quite calm. If, however, one man disappears, so that only four remain visible, the rooks will be agitated, as they may suspect a surprise assault. This may be interpreted as an ability to count up to 5 – or to tell the difference between 4 and 5 – and, hence, to use abstract symbols. This, however, is an over-interpretation. The birds cannot separate the numbers from the particular group to which they apply. They do not have the concepts of, or the signs for, the class of all classes of 4 (or 5) objects. They do not, in short, have the sign corresponding to the written number. They could not manipulate the signs nor would they be able to make anything of the difference between, say, 42 and 43 or 1,000,000 and 1,000,001 and this is not merely a matter of degree of skill in handling abstract quantities: they do not have abstract quantities. They do not map numbers on to an abstract sense of size, or connect them with measures of duration or distance, or use them to create units – things such as inches and seconds that, unlike men with guns, do not have existence outside of notational schemata.

37. 'We must think *aletheia*, unconcealment, as the opening which first grants Being and thinking and their presenting to and for each other. The quiet heart of opening is the place of stillness from which alone the possibility of the belonging together of Being and thinking, that is, presence and apprehending, can arise at all'. 'The End of Philosophy and the Task of Thinking', translated by Joan Stambaugh, collected in David Farrell Krell, *Martin Heidegger: Basic Writings* (London: Routledge and Kegan Paul, 1978), p. 387. However, it is important to appreciate that Heidegger did not believe that *aletheia* maps exactly on to the notion of truth:

> *Aletheia*, unconcealment thought of as the opening of presence, is not yet truth. Is *aletheia* then less than truth? Or is it more because it first grants truth as *adequatio* and *certitudo*, because there can be no presence and presenting outside of the realm of the opening? (p. 389)

38. The circularity – reminiscent of an Escher staircase – is complex. It is evident that the *concept* of matter is a late entry in the order of things. The question then arises as to whether we can think of matter as existing *per se* independently of the concept required to bring various modes of physical being together under the same heading. Birds exist, clouds exist, rocks exist, but does matter exist? (Cf. There are noises and flashes of light and warmths and electric shocks, but does energy exist? Is there such a stuff as energy that is neither sound nor light nor warmth nor, etc.?) Another circularity threatens when we try to think through the relationship between concepts, experiences and things. G.E. Moore argued against the standard empiricist notion that concepts were abstracted from experiences of indi-

vidual things on the grounds that material things can themselves be thought of as 'a colligation' of concepts.

39. This overlaps with territory also covered in Chapter 4, Section 4.2 and 4.3.

40. 'If a lion could talk, we could not understand him', *Philosophical Investigations*, op. cit., p. 223e.

41. Schopenhauer's solution to the epistemological prison of Kant's *Critique of Pure Reason* is therefore not only fallacious but also unnecessary.

    For Kant, the thing-in-itself was unknowable because our knowledge of whatever was revealed to us was always mediated through our sensory system and, more fundamentally, through the forms of sensible intuition. The phenomenal world of our perceptions could not give us any hint of the noumenal world of the thing-in-itself. Against this, Schopenhauer argued that there was one piece of the world we knew, as it were, from within: that bit of the world which we ourselves were. It was through our being a particular thing – our own body – that we would know noumenal reality. In this way we would access the inner world – the world of the will – and so be liberated from our confinement to the prison house of phenomenal reality.

    From the position developed here and also in Chapter 4, Schopenhauer's solution was unnecessary because there would be no 'what it is like' corresponding to the noumenal world; any what it is like would be merely phenomenal. I would argue that it is also fallacious because it assumes that simply being a thing is a sufficient condition of knowing it; that being is the equivalent of self-disclosure, or self-disclosure enjoyed by that same self. It would follow from this that being a pebble is enough to enjoy 'what it is like to be a pebble'.

    There is an additional problem with Schopenhauer's view, in that it assumes that the thing that we embodied beings are is a single thing. In which case, my being-this-thing would give me privileged self-disclosure of the gut and the spleen as well as all parts of the brain. This is manifestly not the case.

42. What is new? Of course, explicitness makes the actual a fulfilled possibility; two steps: a distance created – the possibility; and a distance crossed – the actual as a fulfilment of a possibility and the basis for the truth of an assertion. But there is more than this that is new. Explicitness makes whatever is there into a world; imbued with values as well as encountered; as something factually known as well as suffered; asserted as well as known.

    This shows, if further evidence were still necessary, that we cannot understand explicitness naturalistically. It is not caused by the material properties of the extra-corporeal world interacting with the material properties of the body: it is not a material effect of material causes. The interactions between object X and my body are not sufficient to cause '*That* there is an object X with such and such properties over there related to my body'. The truths about the physical world are not caused by the physical world. In contrast, living things *are* part of the physical world: organisms and their sensory systems are effects of the physical world.

43. These quotations are taken from David Bell's excellent *Husserl* (Routledge: London and New York, 1980).

44. One could summarise the fundamental problem for Husserl as follows: that
of explaining how there is progression from the immediately given to a
systematic objective account of the universe: the movement from explicitness to truths; from truths to knowledge; and from knowledge towards
forms of absolute certainty and to The Truth. What is the relationship
between the self-evidence of the immediately given and the certainty – less
than that of immediately given, but more than all else in between – of the
well-established notions arrived at through scientific research? How do we
get past the apodeictic certainty of the immediately given? Answering that
question would begin with the observation that the immediately given
becomes uncertain when it is put under a certain category, when it is seen
to be an example of a such-and-such, when, in consequence, expectations
that, by definition, go beyond the immediately given, are raised, assumptions are made; when, that is to say, the immediately given is interpreted
as having a significance that reaches beyond itself; when, in other words
its *meaning* is understood, under generality.

2
A Critical Dictionary of Neuromythology

Prefatory note

This pocket dictionary of neuromythology arose as a by-product – but not, I hope, as a waste product – of the writing of another book, *The Explicit Animal* (London: Macmillan, 1991), a critique of contemporary materialistic accounts of human consciousness. During the course of writing that book, I became conscious that certain terms were used repeatedly and that the use, or more precisely misuse, of these terms lay at the heart not only of the errors in neurobiological and computational theories of the mind, but also of their apparent explanatory force. It seemed to me that a critical dictionary of such terms would be as effective as a more conventionally structured argument as a way of refuting the dreams and fantasies of the artificial intelligentsia and others who would assimilate minds to brains and brains to machines. Although this *Critical Dictionary of Neuromythology* is complementary to *The Explicit Animal* and may be read in conjunction with it, it does stand on its own as the arguments given in the entries are complete.

As in the case of *The Explicit Animal* a handful of texts – notably P.N. Johnson-Laird's *The Computer and the Mind* – has been drawn upon repeatedly as the source of the views criticised here. This is in a sense unfair, as the source texts have been selected mainly because they provide the best expressions of these views. In other words, they have been singled out for their merits – of clarity in particular – rather than for their deficiencies. My dissent from the ideas advanced in these texts in no way diminishes my indebtedness to them.

I remain enormously grateful to Mark Rogers who enabled this Dictionary to see the light of day, when it was first published independently by the now alas defunct Ferrington Press. He read the manuscript with great care and made many useful suggestions which have been incorporated into the text.

Introduction: thinking by transferred epithet

> A *picture* held us captive. And we could not get outside of it for it lay in our language and language seemed to repeat it to us inexorably.
>
> Wittgenstein[1]

Both biological and computational models of consciousness depend for their apparent plausibility upon the use of certain terms that have a multiplicity of meanings. These terms are popular with theorists because, within the shades of their voluminous connotative folds, arguments that would not stand up in broad daylight may seem to carry conviction. The reader or listener, in allowing the use of the terms, does not know what is being assented to. The most important characteristic of these terms is that they have a foot in both camps: they can be applied to machines as well as to human beings and their deployment erodes, or elides, or conjures away, the barriers between man and machine, between consciousness and mechanism. The usual sequence of events is that a term most typically applied to human beings is transferred to machines. This begins as a consciously metaphorical or specialist use but the special, restricted, basis for the anthropomorphic language is soon forgotten: the metaphorical clothes in which thinking is wrapped become its skin. Machines described in human terms are then offered as models for mind (described in slightly machine-like terms).

To see what is wrong with the vast majority of philosophical discourse in the field of cognitive science, and what is amiss with physicalist accounts of the mind generally, we need to look particularly carefully at the first step: the application of human terms to machines. In most cases, as we shall see, the process of epithet transfer is no more valid (or no less metaphorical) than referring to the place used to house candidates for execution as 'a condemned cell'. When we hear of a man who has spent the last year in a condemned cell, we know that it is the man, not the cell, who faces execution. It is the man, not the cell, who should have right of appeal. It is the man, not the cell, on whose behalf we grow indignant. When we are told that a telephone receives information, however, we fail to notice – or at least fail to be alerted by – the fact that it is we, not the telephone, who require, are able to receive, and are glad of, *information. This is not because there is more justification in taking the transferred epithet literally in the case of the telephone than in the case of the prison cell but because '*information' has a multiplicity of meanings which 'condemn' does not. In the case of the telephone, the transferred epithet adopts a protective colouring to suit its new surroundings.

It is not too much of an exaggeration to claim that the greatest advances in breaking down the mind/body, consciousness/mechanism, man/machine barriers have come not from neurobiology or computer science but from the use of such transferred epithets. The engineer's customary courtesy in his dealings with his machines (not qualitatively different from that which prompts sailors to refer to their ships as 'she') has permitted many assertions to pass 'on the nod' that would otherwise be challenged. Indeed, such courtesies have come so to dominate our language that it is almost impossible to look critically at the idea that machines have *memories, that they 'store *information' and do *calculations, or that different parts of the nervous system 'signal' to one another. We are so accustomed to hearing that radar 'sees' an enemy plane or that it 'hunts' a target that we have ceased to notice how we are conferring intentionality upon systems that are themselves only prosthetic extensions of the conscious human body.

Epithet transfer is, I have indicated, two-way: machines are described anthropomorphically and, at the same time, the anthropic terms in which they are described undergo a machine-ward shift. These same terms, modified by their life amongst the machines, can then be reapplied to minds and the impression is then created that minds and machines are one. To cross the machine/mind barrier, it is not sufficient to make the mind machine-like; one must do so using terms that have already unobtrusively mentalised machines. If you make machines into minds by describing them in mental terms, you are already half way to making minds into machines. The awaiting terminology is more friendly. As a result, it is possible to overlook, for example, that seeing a computer as anything other than an unconscious automaton is crude animism.

This journeying of terms between the mental and the physical realms lies at the root of the myth that modern neurological science has somehow explained, or will explain, or has advanced our understanding of, what consciousness truly is. My concern is thus with the

---

* An asterisk indicates that there is an entry corresponding to the term thus marked.

foundations of *neuromythology*, a pseudo-science that exploits the justified prestige of neuroanatomy, neurophysiology, neurochemistry and the other legitimate neurosciences. The terms that I have selected for this critical dictionary of neuromythology seem to me the most important among those that are responsible for carrying discourse painlessly – indeed almost unwittingly – across the man/mechanism divide. They are vital to the illusion that machine models of consciousness – whether wet biological or dry computational – have explanatory force. Indeed Janus-faced words like '*memory' and '*information' – which look in the direction of both man and machines – seem to dissolve the very problems that philosophically are most interesting. In consequence, most neurologically-based biological and computational explanations of consciousness begin beyond the point where the real questions are to be found. The terminology starts, as it were, on the far side of the answers. If this Dictionary serves any purpose at all, I hope that, by showing the hollowness of the answers built into the terminology, it will restore the questions and the sense of the mystery of human consciousness.

One final preliminary point. At the time that this Dictionary was conceived, I had not read Peter Hacker's contribution to *Mindwaves*.[2] On reading Hacker, I discovered that I was not unique in my critical attitude towards the language of neuromythology. His excellent piece, which makes many of the points covered in this Dictionary, is strongly recommended. It should be compulsory reading for anyone – neurobiologist, cognitive psychologist or philosopher – proposing to mix neurology and metaphysics.

The Dictionary

> An orator uses ink to trace out his writing; does that mean that ink is a highly eloquent liquid?
>
> Jean-Jacques Rousseau, *Essai sur l'origine des langues*

Calculations (Computations)
Complexity (Sophistication)
Fodor
Goals (Functions, Objects, Purposes, Aims, Plans)
Grammar
Information (Knowledge)
Instructions
Interpretation (Translation)

Language (Code)
Level
Logic
Memory (Stored Information)
Misplaced Explicitness
Pattern
Process (Processing)
Representation (Model)
Rule

Calculations (computations)

According to Johnson-Laird[3] the 'key concept [of cognitive science] is computation ... Cognitive science tries to elucidate the workings of the mind by treating them as computations, not necessarily of the sort carried out by the familiar digital computer, but of a sort that lies within this broader framework of the theory of computation' (p. 9). This view is reiterated at the end of his book: 'Mental processes are the computations of the brain' (p. 391).

In its original (and still very much living) sense, computation is concerned solely with calculation. The Oxford English Dictionary defines 'computation' as 'The action or process of computing, reckoning or counting; a method or system of reckoning; arithmetical or mathematical calculation.' Computation extends beyond calculation in the narrowly defined sense of 'doing sums'. Most definitions of computers include *logical as well as arithmetical operations, as do computational models of the mind.[4] Others extend the concept further to include all aspects of '*information *processing'. For example, Paul Churchland asserts that the input states 'of organisms that display natural intelligence ... *represent many more things than just numbers, and the "computations" they execute are concerned with far more things than mere arithmetical relations. They are also concerned with *logical relations, for example, and with spatial shapes, social relations, linguistic structures, color motion, and so forth'.[5] Nevertheless, calculation in the ordinary sense remains the paradigm computation and the basis of all the other computations. The computer expresses its 'concern' with logical relations, spatial shapes, etc. in sums of various sorts – vector transformations, etc. For example, a computer builds up an image by assigning digital values to the elements of the image and manipulating the digits. So, in looking critically at computational models of the mind, it is neither too literal-minded nor illegitimate to focus on calculations.

There are two relevant questions:

1. Is the mind essentially a calculator?
2. Do computers actually calculate?

Let us address these questions in turn.

1. *Is the mind essentially a calculator?* This is a rather complex question, taking in many subsidiary questions; for example: Is it possible that the mind is made up of calculations? Does a vast number of calculations add up to a mind? Do these calculations somehow throw in their lot together to make something bigger than themselves? Can computational calculations amount to a mind that is able, among other things, consciously to calculate?

Suppose we took really seriously – as opposed simply to using or glossing over – the idea that the mind is like a mass of calculations or, in some non-trivial sense, analogous to it, we would have to identify what it is about the calculations themselves (as opposed to *someone doing the calculations*) that is mind-like. What is quasi-conscious about 2 + 2 = 4? (I have taken a short calculation because there is no reason why a long calculation should be more like a mind than a short one, or a calculation with many steps spread over a period of time be closer to mind at any given moment than a one-step calculation.) What is it about 2 + 2 = 4 that makes it closer to the mind than 2 alone? In what, according to this model, does the mind reside? The individual symbols? The plus sign between them? The result, i.e. 4? If mind is composed of computation, on which side of the equation is it to be found? Does mind reside in *moving towards* a result? Or is mind the result itself – or a heap of results? (And what of my awareness of doing a sum – as when I consciously calculate the square root of 81 – is this a meta-sum, a sum of sums, or a sum that manages, mysteriously, to be about itself?)

It is enough to pose the questions in this way, to take the computational model with sufficient literalness to denude it of a nimbus of vagueness, to discredit it. It is obvious that the mind, or 'mind-ness', cannot reside in any of the things considered in the preceding paragraph; or not, at least, in any one of them more than any of the others. Nor in all of them together – the two symbols, the process of addition, the addition sign and the resultant sum – for in what (or how) would they come together? Nor is there any reason for believing that the mind resides in the operation of sentential (as opposed to numerical) calculus (as Patricia Churchland – see note 4 – suggests) or any other kinds of mathematical or logical operations, such as vector-to-vector transformation (as suggested by Paul Churchland – see note 5). The same unanswerable questions arise irrespective of whether the operations are performed on numbers, sentences or abstract entities such as vectors.

Patricia Churchland's suggestion that mind 'is a kind of *logic machine* operating on sentences' (italics mine) advances the even more implausible notion of mind as being located not in the *operations* of the computer (or the Arithmetic-Logic Unit) but being identified with the machine itself – either the material of which it is made or the electronic 'structure' that can be abstracted from it.

So it is difficult to see how one could make sense of – never mind prove or test – the idea that the mind consists of number-cruching or logic-crunching or sentence-crunching. To suggest that it is any of these things seems anyway to invert the hierarchy of levels of conscious activity. Common sense suggests that sensations are more primitive than abstract ideas and that abstract ideas are more primitive than the numerical or logical operations performed upon them. The notion that the basic material of mind is logico-numeric runs counter to this intuitive ordering. Since, moreover, logico-numeric operations must presuppose sensations if the mind is to get a purchase on the world, computational theories of the mind seem to be like an Escher staircase where the top flight (the most sophisticated function of mind) is found to underlie the bottom flight (sensation). Granted, science progresses by criticising and overthrowing our intuitions, by undermining common sense, but it has to produce powerful reasons to justify this. The evidence here, however, points in the opposite direction, suggesting that the inverted hierarchy of the computational theory of mind has little basis. Whereas for computers enormously complex calculations are 'elementary' and achieving the equivalent of ordinary perception beyond their reach, for minds exactly the opposite holds.

2. *Can computers calculate in the sense necessary to support the computational theory of mind?* The assumption that computers calculate seems so self-evident it is hardly visible. Nevertheless, it is legitimate to ask whether they really can do this – in the way that you and I calculate; whether pocket calculators calculate – in the sense that those who use them calculate; whether brains calculate – in the sense that people do. The (to some surprising) answer to all these questions is: No. Calculating machines are extensions of the mind, yes; but they are mind-like (or perform mental functions) only in conjunction with minds. They are mental prostheses or orthoses, not stand-alone minds.

In the absence of a consciousness derived from somewhere else, the electrical events occurring in computers are just that – electrical events – and not calculations.

Surely it makes sense to speak of a computer performing a calculation? Yes; but only in the limited way in which it makes sense to say that watches tell the time. Watches tell the time only if they are consulted by someone to whom the symbols on the face make sense. More generally, they require an interpreting consciousness to whom to tell the time. The *meaning* of the events in the watch – as a continuous statement of what time it is – is not intrinsic to them. And if, for example, there were a nuclear catastrophe that wiped out all conscious life on the planet, the watch face, arrested at the moment of the explosion, would not constitute a standing assertion to the effect that 'It is five past eight' or 'The explosion took place at five past eight'. Of course, one can imagine a subsequent time, thousands of years after the explosion, when the descendants of those survivors who happened to be away from the planet when it took place, visit Earth and come across the watch. To them, the watch would seem to be stating the time of the explosion. They might be tempted to think of the watch as having *stored* *information* about the time of the explosion. But this would only be as legitimate, or illegitimate, as the claim that the scorched rocks and other evidences of devastation stored *information about the catastrophe.

The calculating computer, then, is analogous to the time-telling watch. I can calculate to, and for, myself. A computer can 'calculate' only for others and those others have to be conscious. The events that take place in a computer do not count as calculations without the presence of an interpreting consciousness to transform the electrical events into meaningful symbols. Consciousness, unlike a calculator or a watch, makes sense to of for itself.

Now it might be argued that 'more *complex' computers do, indeed, calculate. Consider, for example, a robot that, on the basis of the distribution of light energy reaching certain of its photosensitive plates, is able to avoid bumping into an obstacle. It could be argued that it, or its computer, had indeed made the necessary calculations to determine its position in relation to the obstacle and that it had acted upon the result of that calculation. In other words, that it must have carried out a calculation since it could not otherwise have consumed or used the result of the calculation. The force of this argument comes from the fact that, in contrast to the case of the watch 'telling the time', the computer seems to be doing something with the events occurring within it; it seems to be using the result, just as a conscious being would use it. It seems, in short, to be acting on *information received, in this case the product of calculations.

The fault of this argument is that it anthropomorphises the output of the computer/robot. The robot is not really acting, in the sense of consciously achieving a certain end. So it is not using the result of the calculation in the way that conscious humans use calculations. Consequently, it is wrong to think of it as calculating in the true sense of the term. A calculation is an act; the events in the computer, on the other hand, are no more acts that its inputs are acts. The algorithm that relates the input to the output isn't also able to transform an input of events into an output of acts.

Even the most *sophisticated computer is no more capable of 'calculating', in the way that you or I do, than is a five pound calculator bought at a petrol station. One could labour this point by saying that calculators, irrespective of their size, calculate without feeling the qualitative size of the quantities they 'handle'. Moreover, the events that take place in the *logic circuits of the cheap calculator – which I presume few people would claim was conscious – are essentially the same as occur, on a much larger scale, in, say, a Super-Cray. In which case, the fact that computers calculate (in this sense) does nothing to carry them over the mind machine barrier. Attributing calculating power or calculating activity to evidently unconscious machines does the computational theory of consciousness no service whatsoever. For it disassociates computation from consciousness.

Curiously, that there is nothing intrinsically conscious about computing or even so-called computational events in the brain is often emphasised by the most ardent computational theorists of consciousness. What, then, are we to make of the explanatory status of the claim that 'mental processes are the computations of the brain' if all sides agree that the vast majority of 'cerebral computations' are unconscious? *The truth is, we cannot hold that the brain is a computational machine* and *that it carries out calculations, most of which are unconscious* and *that these calculations are the basis of (and the essence of) consciousness.* If the unconscious calculations of the cerebellum ('a neuronal machine') – which permit navigation through the world by automatic pilot dead-reckoning – are the paradigm of the computational activity of the brain, then such activity must have little to offer in explanation of consciousness, and its typical manifestations – such as deliberately picking one's way across the world, and knowing why one is doing it, and where and who one is.

To summarise, machines do not of themselves calculate. If the brain is a machine, it cannot really compute or perform calculations without being coupled to a consciousness external to it to transform the events that take place in it into 'computational activity'. Those events cannot themselves, therefore, constitute consciousness or mental processes. This is in fact half-acknowledged by computational theorists who recognise that the vast majority of the 'calculations' that take place even in the simultaneously anthropomorphised and physicalised cerebral machines are unconscious: they neither enter, nor contribute to the making of, consciousness.

There is some interesting equivocation by Johnson-Laird on the question of the computational model of the mind. Is the mind a computational phenomenon? he asks. No one knows, he replies. But then adds:

> *Theories* of the mind, however, should not be confused with the mind itself, any more than theories of the weather should be confused with rain or sunshine. And what is clear is that computability provides an appropriate conceptual apparatus for theories of the mind.
>
> (Johnson-Laird, p. 51)

He then asserts that 'this apparatus takes nothing for granted that is not obvious – any computation can always be reduced, if need be, to a finite set of instructions for shifting a tape and writing binary code on it'. It is, of course, not at all clear that computability provides 'an appropriate conceptual apparatus for theories of the mind'. This may be why Johnson-Laird, a few lines later, adopts the baldly prescriptive position that 'theories of mind should be expressed in a form that can be modelled on a computer program'. This prescription may make the theories testable (in a way that will satisfy cognitive psychologists) but will not ensure that they are not misconceived. We have here an example of how methodological constraints on the investigation of something start to dictate the way we see that something. Johnson-Laird's position seems to be that there is little or no evidence either way as to whether or not the mind is a computational phenomenon, but we may as well assume that it is because approaches using this assumption produce interesting and testable (i.e. computer modellable) theories. One is reminded of the drunk who having lost his key in a dark street looks for it next to the street lamp, not because he thinks the key is there but because that is where the light is.

Complexity (sophistication)

There are *materialist* theories of mind, theories which claim that what we call mental states and processes are merely sophisticated states and processes of a complex system.[6]

Talk about 'complex' or 'sophisticated' machines (or 'sophisticated' states of such machines) is so commonplace – both in everyday parlance and in the discourses of cognitive scientists and other machine theorists of the mind – that it is difficult to remember that it represents an extremely gross case of epithet transfer. The epithet transfer is from the minds of the people who dreamt up and created the machine to the machine itself; or from the description of the functions or purposes that it serves to the supposedly inherent properties of the machine. Of course, in most cases, talk about the 'sophistication' of machines is not intended literally. It is meant rather loosely, as when we speak of a 'clever design', where the (conscious) cleverness is, of course, a property of the designer rather than of the object that is designed (cf. 'smart' cards). Sometimes, however, it *is* meant literally, as when philosophers and other theorists appeal to 'the increasing sophistication' of computers as indicating that they will more closely approximate consciousness. ('As computers become increasingly sophisticated, so they will become more mind-like'.) In either case, it is as if it is expected that a bit of the sophistication of the minds of the engineers will rub off on the machines and awaken them from their mechanistic slumbers.

Even more widely used than 'sophisticated' (which should, after all, be rather too obviously anthropomorphic a term to be taken seriously) is 'complex' (and 'complexity'). 'Complex', too, is an anthropomorphism or a transferred epithet when applied to machines or unconscious matter, but it is more difficult to spot this. It is important to do so because the term carries enormous spurious explanatory force.

It is often stated that new properties can emerge in complex machines that are not evident either in simpler machines or in the components of more complex machines. Complexity is appealed to as that which will explain the emergence of 'higher' functions. At a certain '*level' of complexity, consciousness will emerge or 'supervene'. The brain, for example, is 'incredibly complex' and this fact should disarm our surprise that it uniquely carries consciousness.

By what criteria does the brain count as complex? The most obvious is that we do not understand it and, indeed, have very great difficulty in making progress towards understanding it. But that criterion is clearly not good enough for a thoroughgoing physicalism, as it is too obviously subjective and anthropomorphic. Besides, it does not generate the discriminations we need. After all, there is nothing in the world that we understand fully, and the harder we try to understand something, the harder it becomes to understand. Modern physics has revealed how infinitely complex ordinary common or garden matter is. We don't fully understand the single atom.

So more 'objective' markers of complexity are invoked. The brain, we are often reminded, is sufficiently complex to support higher functions because it is composed of some 10,000,000,000 neurons; and, as if this were not sufficient to leave one gape-mouthed with uncritical awe, it is pointed out that each of these components connects with numerous other components, so that the possible number of sub-units or combinations exceeds the number of atoms in the universe. With that kind of kit on board, *anything* must be possible.

Unfortunately, this does not amount to an objective case for the special complexity of the brain. For any object can be seen to be composed of a very large number of units. Just *how* large will depend upon how it is looked at. A pebble, for example, may be seen as one large lump or as many billions of atom-sized pieces. And the same applies to combinations of its components. We may abstract an infinite number of different sub-sets of atoms from a pebble. The argument that these sub-sets do not have any real existence because they do not work together in a co-ordinated way, unlike the sub-systems we can identify in the brain, does not wash either, because all atoms in some sense can be regarded as influencing all other atoms and one could generate an enormously (indeed, 'incredibly') complex description that would summarise the combined influence of one sub-set of atoms upon another.

If the pebble example does not convince, one could point to huge, explicitly organised interacting systems in plants and nonconscious animals in which the supposed emergent properties of consciousness have not emerged. But to do so would be to miss the point which is this: *'complexity' is not an intrinsic feature of certain states and arrangements of matter*. No one bit of matter has a right to be thought of as intrinsically more complex than any other. Complexity is in the eye of the beholder and it reflects our ability, or more precisely our inability, to comprehend the object in question. In relation to human artefacts, our measures of complexity will reflect our estimate of the ingenuity and multiplicity of the thoughts and processes that led to its manufacture. When we speak of complex systems, we are as surely transferring epithets from minds to machines as we are when we speak of sophistication. To suggest that complexity leads to mind is to put the cart before the horse; for it is mind that finds, and defines, complexity.

Compare, here, the concept of 'order'. Writers often speak of 'highly ordered systems'. Is this an objective property of certain bits of matter compared with some others? Apparently not; the harder one looks at any bit of matter, the more one will find order and disorder, according to the criteria one chooses. For there is no objective measure of order. Nor is there a 'degree of complexity or orderedness'. A system may be ordered or disordered, depending on how it is described. One could go further: a piece of matter may be a system or not, depending on how it is described. Strictly, physicalism knows no systems (or systems as opposed to non-systems).

Fodor

Not a term used by cognitive scientists but a philosopher of cognitive science whose work lies at the very heart of most of the muddles dealt with in this Dictionary – which could as well be entitled 'A Critical Dictionary of Fodorese'. A separate *ad hominem* critique would be excessively tedious. However, connoisseurs of homuncularity, anthropomorphosophistry and transferred epithets might like to savour the following sentence from an article on Vygotsky:

> It is tempting (perhaps it is mandatory) to explain such inter-actions [between the senses] by assuming that sensory channels transduce stimulus data into a central *computing *language rich enough to *represent visual, tactile, auditory, gustatory and olfactory *information as well as whatever abstract conceptual apparatus is involved in thought.[7]

Goals (functions, objects, purposes, aims, plans)

Human beings have goals. Their actions, and the things that assist them in their actions, have functions, purposes, objects, aims. They formulate plans in order to execute actions and to achieve their objects and purposes. And so on. All of this seems sufficiently obvious, though nearly forty years ago the realisation that behaviour was not controlled and shaped entirely by external events but was regulated by plans, aims and goals counted as one of the great discoveries (or rediscoveries) of psychology. Prior to that time, behaviourist dogma had forbidden acknowledgement of the obvious. Since then, the wheel has come full circle: once nobody had goals; now everything has; once it was heresy to attribute sense of purpose to human beings; now it is quite acceptable to attribute it to lower organisms and even machines. Even automata have feelings, it seems.

'When you develop a plan', Johnson-Laird says, in his excellent exposition of Newell and Simon's study of plans, 'you have in mind an *initial state* and a *goal*, and your task is to devise a sequence of *operations* [a production system] that will get you from one to the other'.[8] Well, possibly, though this description sounds as if it suffers a little from the widespread complaint of *misplaced explicitness*. This is not surprising because it conflates the normal execution of a plan with the process of getting a machine to execute one of our plans or of devising a machine that will do this. That is not too worrying. What is worrying is that the subsequent discussion of plans and productions moves seamlessly between machines, machine designers and human beings (in particular children). Humans as well as machines seemingly execute sub-routines; machines as well as humans have sub-goals. A single descriptive term – 'production systems' – encompasses both human beings engaged in purposeful, goal-oriented activity and the machines that human beings may requisition to assist such activities.

It should be unnecessary to have to point out that (unconscious) automata do not have goals; and if they execute plans, it is our plans (of which they are quite unaware) and not their own which are executed with their (unconscious) assistance. But it is all too easy to slip from a valid teleological account of a machine (or of a process within an organism, or a sub-system within the brain) to an anthropomorphised account of it; to move from saying 'the aim of this machine is to ...' to 'this machine aims to ...'. Why we tend to make these attributions is explained by Searle in his classic paper:[9]

> it has to do with the fact that in artifacts we extend our own intentionality; our tools are extensions of our purposes, and so we find it natural to make metaphorical attributions of intentionality to them.

And so we drift by stages to the absurd position, such as that adopted by John McCarthy (which Searle's scorn has made famous), in which even simple devices such as thermostats perceive things and try to change them. McCarthy's suggestions are crass, but at least they do not try to clothe their crassness in smoke-screen talk about *complexity. Moreover, they have been defended by, for example, Dennett.

Dennett has advanced a curious defence of the attribution of intentionality to machines.[10] 'The intentional stance', according to Dennett, has enormous predictive advantage and can be understood and justified solely in terms of these advantages (rather than on the basis of the objective reality of intentionality). If we were to try to predict the next move of a chess-playing machine, for example, we would not have a hope of doing so unless we appreciated its purpose. More specifically, our best strategy is to assume that it has a *goal*, that it is *trying to win the game*. Only this would make sense of its activities or, to describe this less contentiously, of the events observed to take place in it; only thus would we come anywhere near to predicting (and understanding) its output. The intentional stance – which is neither the physical stance (no one could hope to predict the output of a chess machine from considering its molecular structure) nor the design stance (for the design of chess-playing machines is so complex that designers may not predict how the machine will respond to a particular move) – justifies one in thinking of the machine as having certain *information available to it, as possessing certain goals and, on the basis of these, working out the best move. According to Dennett, it is then 'a small step to calling the information possessed by computers beliefs, its goals and subgoals its *desires*'.

The same considerations, Dennett believes, apply to animal organisms – and to human beings. I could, in theory, predict your behaviour from a consideration of your molecular structure and content and applying the laws of physics – the Laplacean approach. But this would be extremely laborious and require an almost infinite amount of knowledge. A much quicker way will be to assume the intentional stance and work out what you are going to do next on the basis that you believe certain things and desire to bring about certain ends.

Dennett's defence of the attribution of goals and other intentional states to machines is perverse. It implies that there is as much justification in crediting machines with such states as in crediting humans with them because in both cases doing so is merely an expedient to aid prediction. The intentional stance, *whether we are talking of humans or machines*, is just a 'manner of speaking' or, more precisely, a manner of describing: 'goals', 'beliefs', 'desires', etc. are not peculiar inner entities possessed by human beings but essential components of the most effective *description* of the systems (machines, animals, humans) in question. Dennett, in other words, *is able to defend the ascription of*

intentionality to machines by denying the objective reality of intentionality.
Machines have goals in the sense that humans have; and humans do not
'really' have goals, just as machines don't. The intentional stance is
as much 'as if' for humans as for machines. Goals are ascribed – to 'intentional systems', that is to say, to systems considered for the purposes of
effective description as intentional – but they are not possessed by,
inherent in, etc. the systems or entities themselves. This is a peculiar twist
to the transferred epithet story: the goals and other intentional states we
ascribe to humans have themselves been transferred from the descriptions that, only for purposes of predictive power, attribute them to many
(human and mechanical) *complex systems. Intentionality isn't in the
system but in the eye of the beholder of the system; in the tongue and
pen of the describer of the system!

Dennett's position is a curious one. According to him, *my goal in
trying to explain his ideas exists only as an attribution to me (this human
system)*. In the absence of an interpreter of my behaviour I would be
goal-less. This is in itself absurd but it is also incomprehensible. For it
does not account for the power, the usefulness, of intentional explanations (if they are just a *façon de parler*); nor, more importantly, does it
deal with the apparent intentionality of the descriptions themselves. In
adopting the intentional stance towards a machine or a human being,
I am surely in an intentional state. My descriptions are, after all, *about*
their objects. Intentionality is therefore real. The democratising move
of asserting that ascribing intentionality to machines is as justified (or
unjustified) as ascribing it to humans misfires.

One final point. What does it *mean* to attribute goals, objects,
purposes, etc. to machines? Or to programs? (McCarthy attributes
intentions to programs.) Does a chess-playing program really *hope* to
come out on top, or at least to break even? Does it *want* to win? Does it
try? Does it feel satisfied if it wins? Does it feel disappointed, frustrated,
ashamed if it doesn't? Or are satisfaction, frustration, etc. secondary
things that are not part of goal-pursuit? The answers to these questions
do not, I think, need spelling out.

Grammar

Grammar is a very handy word for mediating between minds,
brains and computers. Cognitive scientists and others will readily
talk of the grammar of the brain, of the grammars of computer
programs and of the grammar inherent in the natural languages

used by conscious speakers. Grammar here is clearly something rather larger and more exotic than that grammar we learned (and mis-spelled) in school.

During the period in which cognitive science has been establishing itself, the term grammar as used by linguists has undergone spectacular transformations. In the olden days, grammar had rather a narrow group of senses. It was first of all a branch of the study of a language that dealt with 'its inflexional forms or other means of indicating the relations of words in the sentence, and the *rules for employing these in accordance with established usage' (OED). It was concerned with seemingly superficial features of language; with visible syntax, inflexion and word-formation. Grammar tended at times to be pre-scriptive, evaluating and correcting speech and writing that did not conform to accepted usage. The relation between grammar and the consciousness of the speaker was quite an intimate one: speakers were, to a lesser or greater extent, aware of speaking grammatically. The *rules of grammar could be taught and were anyway available in books – 'grammars'.

With the advent of scientific (and sometimes scientistic) linguistics, this has changed. Grammar is now understood more widely as that part of the systematic description of language which accounts for the way in which words are combined to form sentences. Syntactic theory is an attempt to describe the general principles of sentence con-struction that speakers must know implicitly in order to use sounds to convey meanings. At its most ambitious, a grammar of a language is a theory or set of statements that tells us in an explicit way which combinations of the basic elements of the language are permitted and which are not: it may be seen as a device for generating all the well-formed formulae of the language and no ill-formed ones. It is an exploration of the *system* of language, of the *rules in accordance with which an infinite number of sentences can be generated out of com-binations of a finite number of words. Grammarians conceive of a total grammar which will encompass all the *rules necessary to gener-ate the entire corpus of well-formed sentences in a language and to exclude the inadmissible ones. Hence Chomsky's generative syntax that dreams of becoming a complete account of the *rules according to which the rule-governed creativity of the natural language speaker operates. Grammars would know themselves for the first time, as sets of rules for domains of symbols (or languages) that characterise all the properly formed constructions, and provide a description of their structure.

Since Saussure, linguists and others have become accustomed to the idea that the greater part of the system of language is actually hidden from the language user. There has been a decreasing emphasis upon the *rules the individual knows and has been taught by other individuals – so-called surface features of syntax – and more upon those *rules which can be discerned in language by experts, though they are unknown to the ordinary speakers who nevertheless conform to them.

Modern grammar, then, is concerned with the form of language rather than its accidents and with deep structures available to scientific derivation and analysis rather than surface features and *rules available directly to subjective intuitions. This changed notion of grammar connects naturally with the idea of language as a system that drives itself, rather than being driven by users; an autonomous structure that requisitions voices for its realisation; a structuralist *langue* that speaks through speakers rather than being spoken by them.

The *rules of such a grammar prove to be so complex and so numerous that it seems unlikely that they can be learned, never mind taught. Parents do not teach children their native language; they simply provide an environment in which it can be acquired. The acquisition of language is the work not of a conscious individual or of the product of interactions between conscious individuals. The speed of acquisition of the *rules, despite the poor quality of the material served up to the learner, argues for a special faculty in the brain for extracting grammars from rather unstructured presentations. This faculty, the Language Acquisition Device, is primed with a Universal Grammar which it can then apply to the particular linguistic material served up to it.

With Chomsky, then, the concept of grammar was finally separated decisively from grammar books, from the conscious application of *rules of good discourse, and from correctable lapses. It went underground, hidden in the deep structures discerned by experts and buried in a notional organ of the brain that did the work of the language learner for him. This created a favourable background for its use as one of the key metaphors in the burgeoning of cognitive science and for the invasion of brains by grammars, codes and languages.

One of the first beneficiaries of structuralist and subsequently Chomskeian approaches to language was computerese. A grammar was seen as a 'device' connecting an input to an output, operating on the raw material of individual symbols to produce the finished product of sentences. A grammar could be understood as a set of algorithms. It was but a short step to see a general relation between programs and grammars. The output of any program can be captured in a grammar. But a grammar by itself can do nothing. It is waiting to be used to produce symbols or analyse them. Programs, however, are capable of doing things. They can use a grammar to produce or process strings of symbols.

A grammar is a kind of virtual machine (and language was described in machine terms by Chomsky and everyone who followed him). And machines – in particular computers – have grammars: there is a grammar of their behaviour. Other things have grammars: there is a grammar of the behaviour, or, indeed, of all the input–output relations, of organisms.

A word that passes so readily between brains, organisms and computers has obviously considerable attractions for someone wanting to cross the machine/brain barrier. But what of the mind/brain barrier? How can it ease the passage across this impermeable wall? For some this presents no problem. Consciousness, or the mind, is cast in language – 'the language of thought' or 'mentalese'. This – despite its title – need not be a language used or participated in consciously. The massive, unconscious depths Chomsky and structuralists have uncovered in language in the form of the grammar and deep structures permits the language of thought to be something that is not necessarily accessible to the thinker nor corresponding to what we would normally recognise as a language. However, such a language lies at the root of thoughts and languages as we more usually understand them. It is from the language of thought that natural languages derive their peculiar properties.

> The basic concept is simple but striking. Assume that there are such things as mental symbols (mental representations) and that mental symbols have semantic properties ... The semantic properties of the words and sentences we utter are in turn inherited from the semantic properties of the mental states that language expresses.[11]

There is, *Fodor also tells us, 'a considerable consensus ... that there is a "semantic" level of grammatical representation – a level at which the meaning of sentences is formally specified'.[12] The language of thought is 'the medium for computations underlying cognitive *processes'.[13]

Grammar has an additional attractive ambiguity – like that of 'history' which may be used to mean either what happened in the past or the study of what happened in the past, i.e. historiography. This ambiguity – which allows grammar to be both something someone is conscious of and the *rules according to which someone acts irrespective of whether she is conscious of them – makes it a very useful passport across the brain/mind barrier.

Information (knowledge)

This is the big one, an absolutely key term in cognitive science and much contemporary thought about brain function, the mind and the relationship between them. According to popular thought, what the mind–brain does, above all else, is acquire, *process and store information.

What is information? 'Information' is a term that has a multiplicity of senses, some everyday, some highly specialised and technical. Much of the explanatory force of 'informational' explanations of consciousness and the mind–brain depends upon unobserved shuttling back and forth between these various senses.

Let us begin at the beginning. The Oxford English Dictionary lists numerous senses of the word 'information'. The most important of these is 'Knowledge communicated concerning some particular fact, subject or event; that of which one is apprised or told; intelligence, news'. This ordinary sense is very different from the specialised sense used widely in cognitive and other sciences.

At first the specialised, technical sense of information was to be kept quite separate from the ordinary sense, as was emphasised by the communication engineers who first introduced it. This specialised sense was occasioned by the need to *quantify* information, in order to evaluate the work done by, and the efficiency of, communication channels charged with transmitting it. It is worth looking at this in some detail because it has pervaded the entire universe of discourse of cognitive science.

Since to be informed is to learn something one did not know before, information can be understood as something that resolves an *uncertainty* about how things are or how they are going to be. Uncertainty itself can be quantified in relation to the number of possible states of affairs that might be the case. *In engineering terms*, the information content of a message is proportional to the amount of prior uncertainty it resolves. If there are only two possibilities, and hence only two possible messages, then the successful transmission of one of messages – the actual message – will convey a selective information content of one bit or binary digit.

The amount of information carried by any message will be determined by the number of possible alternatives that have been selected from and the relative prior probabilities of the different messages. The more unexpected, or unexpectable, a message is, the greater its information content. A totally expected message, one that has one hundred per cent prior probability, resolves no uncertainties, is redundant and, in engineering terms, has no information content: it is not worth paying for. Redundancy is both good and bad. It is good, inasmuch as it allows for a degradation of the message without loss of information transmission: the redundancy in written messages permits accurate decipherment of the most appalling handwriting, despite our inability to read certain individual letters. Redundancy is bad in so far as it may be uneconomical.

It will be clear from this that the engineer's sense of information, and in particular information content, has little to do with information in the ordinary sense. Weaver, one of the first to think of information in the way just described, underlined this:

> Information in this theory is used in a special sense that must not be confused with its ordinary usage. In particular, *information* must not be confused with meaning. In fact, two messages, one of which is heavily loaded with meaning, and the other of which is pure nonsense, can be exactly equivalent from the present viewpoint as regards information.[14]

Indeed the meaningful statement may have less information content than the meaningless one. Supposing A asks B if she loves him. B's 'Yes' is one of only two possible alternatives and, assuming he has no idea of the answer, will have an information content of one bit. Consider, by contrast, a meaningless message composed of randomly generated letters of the alphabet. At any given moment, if all letters are equally probable, then the occurrence of any one letter will have a likelihood of 1 in 26. This will give the letter/message an information content of between 4 and 5 bits – several times higher than that of the answer to the question 'Do you love me?'. It is all a matter of the range of alternatives from which the message has been selected and their prior probabilities. As Shannon, another pioneer of the mathematical theory of communication, wrote, 'the semantic aspects of communication are irrelevant to the engineering aspects' (see note 14).

In the specialised technical sense, then, information is measured by the reduction of uncertainty; the number of possibilities and their prior probabilities are measures of the quantity of transmitted information. Before long, this objective way of measuring information (which is quite separate from how *informative* – never mind how interesting, important, exciting – it seems to the recipient of the information) becomes a definition of information itself, the method of measuring the thing defines it: information *is* uncertainty reduction. And this uncertainty may not even have to be experienced as such by the individual but only inhere in the quantity of objective possibilities presented to him.

The engineering notion of information entered the sciences of the mind via the psychology of perception. From the early 1950s onwards, sensory perception was interpreted as the acquisition of information, and sensory pathways were seen as channels transmitting information from the outside world to the centre. These 'channels' had 'limited information handling capacity'; they could cope with only so much at a time. Using the notion of information in the engineering sense, it was possible to make certain predictions that proved to be true. For example, Hick[15] found that the reaction time of human subjects to a stimulus depended on its *selective* information content; it depended, that is to say, not upon its actual content but upon the number of alternatives that had to be selected from. This, in turn, determined how much information had to be *processed before the subject could react. (The stimuli in question, it is not irrelevant to point out, were extremely simple: letters, numbers and simple pictures.)

From this, it was but a short step to see *perception* as information *processing and to regard the function of the nervous system as that of transmitting information from one place to another. It is a strange and contradictory move because it both dehumanises perception and anthropomorphises the organs of perception. The perceiver is placed on all fours with a telephone receiver, while the sense organs are treated as if they were devices that had certain goals and aims and functions. Nevertheless, over the last forty years, the rhetoric of information has dominated thought about mental, cerebral and neuronal function. The apparent success of this mode of thought depends upon an almost continuous unacknowledged vacillation between the engineering and the ordinary senses of information. The information-theoretic account of perception makes intuitive sense because we think of the bearer of the nervous system being informed in the ordinary sense by what is going on in her nervous system as well as acquiring information in the narrow sense of selecting between alternative possible states. By narrowing the conception of consciousness or awareness to that of being in receipt of information and widening that of information way beyond the engineering sense that gives it scientific respectability, and not acknowledging (or noticing) either of these moves, it seems plausible to give a scientific, information-theoretic account of consciousness and of the nervous system. We can speak without embarrassment of consciousness as being identical with information or being the outcome of the information-processing activity of the nervous system.

It is worth dwelling on the inappropriateness of reducing consciousness to information – particularly when the notion of information is itself reduced to the engineering concept of uncertainty reduction or selection between alternatives. It amounts to expanding information to encompass the whole of awareness while drastically shrinking the meaning of 'information'. Under this interpretation, an ordinary conscious being is literally steeped in information; the perceptual field is a multi-modal sphere of information. It is slightly odd, to say the least, to think of me, as I sit here in this room, as sitting in a sphere of information coterminous with my sensory field; and equally odd to think of all-encompassing being-here as reducible to streams of data. Being situated does not quite amount to being informed – otherwise simply to be conscious would be to be well informed to the point of saturation.

Unfortunately, not everyone is able to see the absurdity of this consequence of extending the notion of information to include all of conscious experience. Even fewer seem to be able to see that the engineer's use of the term information cannot apply outside of its legitimate provenance – that of devices designed by human being to help them communicate with other human beings. Although information-content understood in engineering terms is distinct from meaning, its sense depends ultimately upon *the intention* to convey meaning, or to resolve uncertainty through the transmission of meaningful events. If we remove this essential element – human intention, explicit purpose – in particular its involvement in acts and instruments of conscious and deliberate communication, then 'information states' or 'information-bearing states' can be made to encompass pretty well everything that happens or exists: the scar on my leg is comparable to a statement that I have injured my leg in the past; the position of a pebble a confession of its fall from a cliff and its subsequent inertia. The information-theoretic account of *perception* tries to have its conception of information in the aseptic, semantics-free scientific sense while eating it in the ordinary sense (otherwise the events in the afferent pathways would not count as perceptions).

It stands at the top of a slippery slope at the bottom of which lies the lunacy of those who claim that the entire universe is composed of a process of transmitting and receiving information.

The first step down the slope carries information beyond the body, and devices that are designed to serve the information needs of human beings, into the energy incident upon the body. Those who believe that consciousness arises out of the interaction between the nervous system and objects outside of it, that it is the transfer of energy from external objects to sense endings that accounts for perception, would seem to be faced with a problem: how does the *energy* impinging on the nervous system become transformed into *consciousness*? For, although the nervous system seems quite good at transducing various forms of energy in the outside world into its own intra-cerebral dialect of energy (nerve impulses are mainly propagated electrochemical changes), it doesn't seem to do anything corresponding to *the transformation of energy into information*.

One 'explanation' is that, while the events in the periphery of the nervous system are indeed *energy-to-energy* transductions, those that take place centrally somehow add up to a *pattern, and this adding up to a pattern is an *energy-to-information* transformation. Why this is a non-explanation will be discussed in the entry on PATTERNS; for the present, we may content ourselves with the observation that patterns cannot be the basis of the consciousness- and information-bearing capability of the brain since patterns exist only in so far as they are discerned by consciousness. How, then, shall we account for the 'fact' that, according to Patricia Churchland, 'nervous systems are informa- tion processing machines'?[16] Clearly you can't process something you haven't got: a stomach isn't a dinner-processing machine unless it gets a dinner from somewhere. If the impulses in the nervous system convey information rather than making it themselves (as we are conventionally told), where does the information come from if all its inputs consist of energy?

According to some, information is actually present in the energy that impinges on the nervous system! The job of the nervous system is consequently simply to extract and transmit it. Johnson-Laird[17] notes approvingly that 'J.J. Gibson emphasised that light reflected from surfaces and focused on the retina contains a large amount of informa- tion' (gossipy stuff, light). Astonishingly, this has been 'demonstrated' by Longuet-Higgins' analysis of the projective geometry of images. There are, however, no entirely free gifts: 'no matter how much information is in the light falling on the retina, there must be mental mechanisms for recovering the identities of things in a scene and those of their properties that vision makes explicit to consciousness'. Still, the information built into the light itself is a flying start.

This must surely be the easiest solution to the physicalist's puzzle of how (to use his own terms) energy is transformed into information: the information is *in* the energy; it simply has to be 'extracted' from it. The older magic thinking – the animistic intuition of 'mind among things' – has been supplanted by an 'informationistic' one.

This not the end, only the begining, of the story. For some writers, information amongst things does not have to be extracted by the nervous system: it is there for the taking. Or, rather, it is there whether it is taken or not, irrespective of whether the information-bearer interacts with the nervous system. According to some authors, not only are unconscious organisms information-processing devices, but the individual parts of them are as well. Indeed, information is embodied in all organisms, most notably in the genetic material. For example, Richard Dawkins (whose views on this matter are by no means heterodox) takes it for granted that DNA is itself information, and carries instructions for transmitting and preserving information. 'If you want to understand life, don't think about vibrant throbbing gels and oozes, think about information technology.'[18] 'The information technology of the genes is digital ... since we receive our inheritance in discrete particles.' The difference between DNA and a floppy disk is merely a question of the storage medium used – chemical as opposed to electronic – but the essentials are the same. 'Each individual organism should be seen as a temporary vehicle in which DNA messages spend a tiny fraction of their geological lifetimes' (pp. 126–7). And what an enormous number of messages there are! DNA is ROM (Read Only Memory) and it is comparable to a laser disk in terms of the amount of information it packs into a small space (pp. 152–3): 'at the molecular genetic level, every one of more than a trillion cells in the body contains about a thousand times as much precisely-coded digital information as my [Dawkins'] computer' (p. xiii).

Such anthropomorphism – which makes the cells of my body infinitely better informed than I could ever hope to be – is not unusual and, indeed, has a long intellectual pedigree. It is rooted in a cluster of notions about the relations between *information, entropy* and *order*. Entropy is the degree of *dis*order in a system. Living systems, which are (according to the conceptual schema of one particular species of living system, namely man) uniquely ordered, therefore, entrain a high degree of negative entropy. They are also highly improbable because of the universal tendency, expressed in the Second Law of Thermo-dynamics, for the degree of disorder in any system to increase. They should not come into being in the first place and should decay as soon as they do.

The argument behind the supposed relationship between informa-tion, entropy and order is well summarised by Colin Cherry:

> Entropy, in statistical thermodynamics, is a function of the prob-abilities of the states of the particles comprising a gas; information rate, in statistical communication theory, is a similar function of the probabilities of the states of a source. In both cases we have an *ensemble* – in the case of the gas, an enormous collection of particles, the states of which (i.e. the energies) are distributed according to some probability function; in the communication problem, a collection of messages, or states of a source, is again described by a probability function.[19]

The idea that *information is equivalent to negative entropy* derives from Szilard's discussion of the Maxwell demon problem. The demon is conceived as 'receiving information' about the particle motions of a gas on the basis of which he is able to direct particles to one side or another of a partition. By this means, the gas may be put in a highly ordered, lower entropy state; for the demon may choose to place all the faster-moving particles on one side of the partition and all the slower-moving ones on to the other side. In other words, the information received by the demon enables him to decrease the entropy or disorder of the system and consequently to increase the energy available in it. This could be used to drive a heat engine. Since separating fast and slow particles costs only 'information', the demon seems to have discovered the secret of a perpetual motion machine. In making use of his information in this way, he is seemingly violating the Second Law of Thermodynamics in accordance with which the energy available for work in a closed system tends to decrease and entropy to increase. This is not, however, the case: he is not merely an observer of the system, he is also a participant; he is part of the system because he must receive energy in order to make his observations; he must be affected by the system in order to observe it. Szilard demonstrated that the selective action represented by the demon's observations results in an increase in entropy at least equal to the reduction in entropy he can effect by virtue of this information. There seems therefore to be a tradeoff between entropy and information; from which it is concluded that information is, in a sense, negative entropy.

This analogy has a certain amount of intuitive attraction, as Cherry, from whose account of Szilard's thought-experiment the above paragraph has been derived, explains:

> In a descriptive sense, entropy is often referred to as a 'measure of disorder' and the Second Law of Thermodynamics as stating that 'systems can only proceed to a state of increased disorder'; as time passes, 'entropy can never decrease'. The properties of a gas can change only in such a way that our knowledge of the positions and energies of the particles lessens; randomness always increases. In a similar descriptive way, information is contrasted, as bringing order out of chaos. Information is then said to be 'like' negative energy.

Cherry, however, warns against too literal an interpretation of these analogies and, even more severely, against too wide an application of them. Entropy is 'essentially a mathematical concept and the rules of its application are clearly laid down' and 'any likeness that exists [between negative entropy and information] exists between the mathematical descriptions which have been set up'. Moreover, the term entropy is usually applied to closed systems, which are utterly isolated and unable to exchange energy with their surroundings, are in a state of near-randomness and are enormous. This hardly applies to the communication systems in which humans and other organisms participate. Cherry's final comments on this matter are especially worth quoting:

> Mother Nature does not communicate to us with signs or language. A *communication channel* should be distinguished from a *channel of observation* and, without wishing to be too assertive, the writer would suggest that in true communication problems the concept of entropy need not be evoked at all. And again, physical entropy is capable of a number of interpretations, albeit related, and its similarity with (selective, syntactic) information is not as straightforward as the simplicity and apparent similarity of the formulae suggests.
>
> (p. 217)

Such warnings have gone unheeded by psychologists, for whom the notion of a sensory pathway as a channel of communication (and indeed the entire nervous system as an information transmission or information-processing device) is an apparently undislodgable received idea; by biologists for whom mind is the information-processing activity of the brain; and by not a few philosophers for whom the equation between order and information and information and mental function is beyond dispute.

The idea that order is information (and the preservation of order is the transmission of information through time – or *memory) is implicit in Dawkins' description of DNA as ROM. The equation between organic order and higher mental function is explicit in Paul Churchland's use of the entropy/information metaphors. Churchland at times seems to espouse a conventional behaviourist account of intelligence, describing it as 'the possession of a complex set of appropriate responses to the changing environment'.[20] Such a definition is interactionist, as befits an evolutionary outlook which sees intelligence as an instrument to help the organism to survive on a potentially hostile planet. Under the influence of a series of metaphors derived from ectopic thermodynamics and information theory, Churchland's conception of intelligence moves inwards until it becomes inscribed in the actual order or structure of the organism:

> If the possession of information can be understood as the possession of some internal physical order that bears some systematic relation to the environment, then the operation of intelligence, abstractly conceived, turns out to be just a high-grade version of the operating characteristics of life, save that they are even more intricately coupled to the environment ... Intelligent life is just life, with a high thermodynamic intensity and an especially close coupling between internal order and external circumstance.
>
> (p. 174)

A system has intelligence inasmuch as

> it exploits the *information* it already contains, and the energy flux through it (this includes the energy flux though its sense organs), in such a way as to *increase* the information it contains. Such a system can *learn*, and it seems to be the central element of intelligence.
>
> (p. 173)

The 'especially close coupling between internal order and external circumstance' would not seem to be a distinctive feature of life, Indeed, if one accepts the physicalist world picture within which Churchland writes, it should be the common condition of all existents: slugs, crystals, pebbles. So, far from being the great achievement of life, one would have thought that it was precisely the kind of thing that life – and intelligent versions of it in particular – has been trying to escape. So all one is left with to distinguish intelligent life is 'thermodynamic intensity' which, if this means anything, is the high level of information and negative entropy which Churchland and others think is embodied in *complex structures.

We have already discussed the anthropomorphism inherent in the use of the soubriquet *'complex' with reference to (unconscious) physical systems. All systems (or tracts of matter) are, under the democratising eye of physics, equally complex or equally simple. (And if this is the case, then the very notions of complexity and simplicity – which are comparative, contrasting and interdependent terms – vanish.) But what about the idea that there is information implicit in systems, that *order is embodied information*? There are two types of problems with this very popular and potently misleading belief. The first is a similar problem to that associated with the term *complex: from the physicalist standpoint, all pieces of matter are both random and highly ordered, depending upon how, or at what level, they are viewed. Order, ultimately, means explicit, visible or perceived order; and this, in turn, means order according to a human viewpoint. Without consciousness-born criteria of order (what shall count as ordered or as disordered), material entities are neither ordered nor disordered. (This is not to say that man *imposes* order on an intrinsically disordered world; rather that he merely finds it *once it has been defined according to his criteria*; or, rather, he imposes order only to the extent that he imposes chaos.[21]) Order may be defined mathematically; but this is only a useful stipulation and has only a tangential relationship with order in the sense meant in ordinary life.

A rather different and even more serious criticism of the idea that the structure or internal physical order amounts to information (as if one's material assets can be capitalised as information flow) is that, quite apart from the dubious thermodynamics upon which the metaphor is founded, the structure of an organism is not available to it in the way that information is. It is certainly not part of consciousness. If one's structure *were* equal to information (about that structure?), then being a crystal would be a sufficient condition of being a crystallographer – albeit one expert on only a single specimen. A pebble's 'experience' may change its structure, but that changed structure does not embody the experience. And the same applies to any organism where learning (and acquired information) is not thought to lead to conscious *memory.

(The habit of conflating structural order and functional information is connected with a more widespread tendency to fuse structural and occurrent memory. In a computer, and at a micro-anatomical level, it is not possible to make this distinction – which is why the use of *memory with respect to computers and bits of brain is invalid. But in real life the distinction is all-important: it is the difference between implicit and explicit past, implicit and explicit being there. This will be discussed further under MEMORY.)

Once information is uprooted from consciousness – and from an informant or from the experience of being informed and of wanting (or, come to that, refusing) to be informed – then any kind of nonsense is possible. According to the information theorists we have discussed so far, the unconscious structure of organisms contains information and the energy impinging on the nervous system also contains information. It is possible to go further than this: for the fully paid-up information theorist, information is simply and literally everywhere. The 'informationalisation' of the universe has been taken to its logical conclusion by theoreticians such as Fredkin, Toffoli and Wheeler[22] for whom the fundamental particles that make up the world – atoms, quarks, etc. – boil down to bits (binary digits) of information. The universe is composed of combinations of such binary digits; and atoms are 'information-processing systems'. The universe, it seems, is not only incredibly well informed about itself – a huge polymath set out in boundless space, an infinity of omniscience – it *is* information. Fredkin's 'digital physics' has a further twist: it is based on the hypothesis that the universe no longer processes information like a computer, but that it *is* a computer, still processing a program that was installed at the beginning of time, possibly by a 'Great Programmer'. Whether or not this Computiverse is carried on the back of an elephant has not yet been determined.

The rationale behind this kind of thinking is clearly set out by Davies:[23]

> Compare the activity of the computer with a natural physical system – for example, a planet going round the sun. The state of the system at any instant can be specified by giving the position and velocity of the planet. These are the input data. The relevant numbers can be given in binary arithmetic, as bit strings of ones and zeros. At some time later the planet will have a new position and velocity, which can be described by a new bit string: these are the output data. The planet has succeeded in converting one bit string into another, and is therefore in a sense a computer. The

'program' it has used in this conversion is a set of physical laws (Newton's laws of motion and gravitation).

Physical systems are thus computational systems, processing information, just as computers do, and scientific laws may be considered as algorithms. This extraordinary view is apparently supported by the observation that in post-classical (quantum) physics many physical quantities normally regarded as continuous are in fact discrete: nature is thus more readily amenable to digitisation. In other words, the universe is not merely a huge computer: it is a huge *digital* computer. Digital physicists have not yet gone so far as to specify that it has an IBM operating system.

Some of the arguments surrounding digital physics are instructive – if only because they illustrate how completely consciousness can be overlooked. According to Wolfram (quoted in Davies, ibid., p. 119):

> One expects the fact that computers are as powerful in their computational capacities as any physically realisable system can be, so that they can simulate any physical system.

If this is true, then any physical system complex enough can in principle simulate *the entire physical universe*. For those convinced so far, this raises an interesting question: if computers can mimic all physical systems, what distinguishes a simulated universe from the genuine article? The answer is even more interesting: nothing – once small problems of time-reversibility, are overcome. For Fredkin, the entire universe *is* its own simulation – by a giant cellular automaton. Frank Tipler, who also believes this, counters the objection that the map (the simulation) is distinct from the territory (the universe) by asserting that this objection is valid only from a perspective outside of the computer. If the computer is powerful enough, it will encompass everything; there will be no outside and, for beings necessarily within the computer, the simulated world will be real.

As Davies points out, Tipler has to assume that a computer can simulate consciousness. Neither of them seems to regard this as a fatal flaw, but it is. Consciousness cannot be simulated for two reasons: first, the Cartesian reason that it is enough to think that you are conscious to be conscious; and second, consciousness is logically prior to simulation – there have to be (deceived) human beings for a something (an event, an object, a state of affairs) to count *as* a simulation. Through these cracks, the light of common sense comes pouring in. In the absence of consciousness, physical events do not count as 'information' or 'information-processing. Nor do the laws of physics have *explicit* existence as 'algorithms' (which is not the same as saying that, in the absence of consciousness, the behaviour of the universe is unlawlike). Without consciousness, there are no data and no symbols. Even the classification of some event as 'input' and others as 'outputs' depends upon taking a viewpoint, a reference point. Without the latter, there are neither inputs nor outputs: every event is potentially either and therefore intrinsically neither; for every exit is an entrance to elsewhere.

Digital physics and its notion that the entire universe is composed of information or is a giant information-processing system – that, according to Wheeler, It = Bit – is what lies at the end of a long chain of unchecked metaphors. Little by little, we arrive at lunacy. As is so often the case, the first steps on the path to lunacy are often innocuous. The most important and the seemingly most innocuous is that of accepting the idea that information can be 'stored' – outside of the human body, outside of conscious organisms – 'in' books or 'on' disks. In the loose sense of 'inform', I, who have derived a lot of information from a book I have read, may regard it as 'informative'. Likewise, a book I am writing may be informative; so (again, in a very loose sense) I am filling my book with information. The books I read inform me and the books I write are informed by me. Once the books are born, surely they can inform one another: information may be passed from book to book. Once this has been accepted, then information, informing and being informed start to be liberated from a *consciousness* being informed or wanting to inform. If it sounds odd to talk of one book informing another, consider what is often said about 'information stored on disks': information may be copied from one disk to another; information may be transmitted from disk to disk. This is perfectly normal computer talk; and it encourages the idea that information can be given and received without the involvement of consciousness. This is, of course, misleading: the information in a book, or on a disk, is only *potential* information. More generally, it is not information but only *potential information* that can be inscribed outside of a conscious organism. Information remains potential until it is encountered by an individual requiring and able to receive it, able to be informed. In the absence of such a (conscious) organism, it is sloppy and inaccurate to refer to the states of objects as 'information'; but such loose talk has started the word on a very long journey and sent those who use it down a long slide into lunacy.

In conclusion, 'information' is absolutely pivotal to establishing the conceptual confusions so necessary to the seeming fruitfulness and explanatory power of much modern thought about the mind and the brain. By playing upon different meanings of the term, it is possible to argue that minds, brains, organisms, various artefacts such as computers and even non-living thermodynamic systems are all information-processing devices. Because they are seen as essentially the same in this vitally important respect, they can be used to model each other; homology and analogy can run riot. Once the concept of information is cut loose from the idea of *someone being informed* and from that of *someone doing the informing*, anything is possible.

Instructions

In computer terminology, an instruction is 'a set of bits or characters specifying an operation to be performed by the computer and identifying the data on which it is to be performed'.[24] A program is a sequence of instructions. So far so good. As long as it is appreciated that the instructions in a computer are ultimately, being issued by operators and that the computer is designed to carry out our, not its own, instructions, the anthropomorphism is harmless. For we must remember what a program is: an explicit description of an effective procedure. And the latter is a procedure which reaches *a desired goal* in a finite number of steps using only a finite amount of knowledge. *We cannot separate the idea of an instruction from that of a desired goal and the latter must connect, however indirectly or remotely, with a desire.*

Problems begin when this is forgotten and we start to think of computers as issuing their own instructions; or when, extending computer terminology beyond computers, we begin to talk (and presumably think) of naturally occurring objects as issuing instructions. For example, it is often said that DNA is a set of instructions for building an organism. Dawkins describes the process of evolution thus: 'The nonrandom survival and reproductive success of individuals within the species effectively "writes" improved instructions for survival into the collective genetic memory of the species as the generations go by.'[25] It is significant that 'writes' is in inverted commas but not 'instructions'.

So long as the metaphorical status of 'instructions' – outside of its application to human beings or to artifacts understood as acting on their behalf – is appreciated, no harm will result. If it is not appreciated, we are on the road to rampant anthropomorphism.

Interpretation (translation)

A central problem of perception is how the brain interprets the patterns of the eye in terms of external objects.[26]

In everyday terms, interpretation is making sense of something one has encountered – seen, heard, read, etc. – as a result of which one understands it, or understands it better. Interpretation is a fundamental activity of human consciousness. There is a narrower everyday use of 'interpretation'; translation from one language to another or from a code into a language one understands. This narrower sense is rooted in the primary meaning of making sense (for oneself or for others) of something, or of making better sense of it.

There is a computational sense of interpretation which is not necessarily, and certainly not necessarily directly, related to understanding and consciousness. The interpreter in a computer is 'a programme that translates each statement in a source programme into machine language, executes it, and repeats the process for each new statement until the entire programme has been executed'.[27] No consciousness is necessary and conscious understanding does not result. This difference between ordinary and computational senses of 'interpretation' is fundamental. There are, of course, points of similarity between human and computational interpreters and between everyday and computational senses of interpretation. The most important of these seems to be that some human interpretation (language translation) and, apparently, all computational interpretation involves the replacement of one group of *symbols by another. But this does not close the gap between human and machine interpretation. Replacing French symbols by English is not the same as understanding a statement in French (or in English). Searle demonstrated this with his famous 'Chinese room' argument.[28] He envisaged an individual ignorant of Chinese provided with a set of Chinese symbols and a set of rules for using them. Such an individual could respond to an input of Chinese symbols with an appropriate output without knowing the meaning of either input or output.

That the replacement of one (input) symbol by another (output) symbol in accordance with an algorithm does *not* amount to interpretation in the ordinary sense of the word is less obvious than it might be because of the anthropomorphic resonance of terms like *symbol. If we describe the substitution by a computer of one symbol by another as 'interpretation', it is very difficult not to think of the symbols meaning something to the computer. If, moreover, we think of the meaning (and reference) of the symbol as its causal relations – the effects it has or the cause that has brought it about and may be inferred from it – this attribution of meaning-acquisition to computational interpretation becomes irresistible. The analogy, of course, remains invalid: the computer lacks semantics because the symbols remain uninterpreted: the passage from one (uninterpreted) symbol to another (uninterpreted) symbol does not count as interpretation. (Actually, I am not even sure that, in the absence of semantics, the string of symbols can be considered as having syntax, except in a narrow, technical sense. It is difficult to see how one can allocate terms to parts of speech in the absence of knowing what they mean.) The input relations of its symbols do not confer semantic content upon them and the causally downstream events in the peripherals are not their meaning, either.

When we read, therefore, that 'The instructions of the universal [Turing] machine enable it to interpret the instructions encoded in the binary numeral, and to carry them out on the data' (Johnson-Laird, p. 51), or that 'RNA interprets the instructions encoded in DNA', we should be on our guard.

Language (code)

The ubiquitous misuse of these ubiquitous terms has contributed almost as much as the misuse of 'information' to the present state of happy conceptual confusion in contemporary cognitive science. We hear of 'languages' of the brain and of nervous systems and DNA 'encoding' information. We learn that computers use and somehow seem to speak 'computer languages'. In the ordinary run of things, language is something used by a conscious entity to convey information or other sorts of meanings to another conscious person. In the world of computer-speak, languages may be spoken fluently by non-conscious entities such as laptop computers, single neurons and nucleoproteins.

The frequent preference for the term 'code' over language is revealing, suggesting a certain amount of embarrassment with the suggestion that computers and neurons and large molecules are chatty. It should not relieve any embarrassment, of course, because codes are secondary developments from languages and dependent upon them. Morse code users are more, not less, sophisticated, than ordinary speakers; for in order to be able to use Morse code, one has to understand the first-order language (such as English) which it encodes as well as the second-order language (Morse) in which it is encoded. The attraction of the term 'code' is that the elements, like those of Morse, do not make immediate sense: they are remote from the terms used in ordinary languages. And a code has a highly formalised, explicit *grammar. We are therefore more inclined to believe that DNA speaks fluent Morse than that it speaks fluent English (with or without a Northern accent).

A couple of related terms that are used with particular frequency in cognitive scientology are 'signal' and 'symbol'. In everyday life, signals are events that deliver meaning to conscious organisms; and they are typically emitted by conscious organisms in order to convey meaning, though they may be read without being written. In cognitive science, signals are found at much lower levels. For example, clusters of nerve impulses – even where they occur in parts of the brain that are not thought to be conscious or related to consciousness – are described as signals (or messages). Indeed, for Patricia Churchland, 'the distinctive thing about neurons is that they are instruments of communication', receiving and emitting signals.[29] Of course, the brain does not signal in English; it talks to itself in code. The events in the nervous system encode events in the world – and hence the world itself. Gregory tells us that

> What the eye does is to feed the brain with *information coded into neural activity – chains of electrical impulses – which by their code and the *patterns of brain activity represent objects.[30]

The code is sometimes rather Byzantine; for example, the activation of a certain group of neurones at a certain intensity will constitute a point in a taste space and hence encode a particular taste. Or would, if there were someone to decode it.

According to Johnson-Laird, all mental representations are 'symbols'; it is 'a major tenet of cognitive science that the mind is a symbolic system' and 'perception leads to the construction of mental symbols *representing the world ... nerve impulses and other electrochemical events can therefore be treated as the underlying primitives – perhaps analog in form – out of which the symbols are constructed.'[31]

Level

Everyone can see that a thought is different from the passage of ions through semi-permeable membranes and that a friend is more than a collection of molecules. And yet, according to physicalists, and, in particular, identity theorists, the thought and the passage of ions, the friend and the collection of molecules, are the same thing. This apparent paradox and apparently fatal weakness of physicalism is overcome by appealing to the notion of 'levels'. The friend and the collection of molecules, the thought and the passage of ions through semi-permeable membranes are the same things – but *observed or described at different levels*. To cite an analogy often invoked in support of the 'levels' argument, a picture in a newspaper is at one level just a collection of dots of different size and at another a representation of, say, a face. So what is at one level merely a collection of molecules is, at another, a conscious human being. An entity that is a mindless collection of material particles when observed at the molecular level may be the intelligible basis of consciousness at another. The transition from one level to another is sufficient to explain the emergence of consciousness.

The levels argument is inadmissible. The reason very briefly is this. When we talk about levels, we are, at least implicitly, talking about levels of *appearance*, or of *representation*, or of *description*. Different levels of appearance, representation or description cannot explain consciousness, or its emergence from matter considered to be essentially and intrinsically unconscious, because levels, etc. *presuppose* consciousness, *presuppose* a viewpoint upon the object in question.

The levels argument is so widely invoked (either implicitly or explicitly) that it is unnecessary to give chapter and verse. I shall confine myself to a couple of exemplary instances. The neuroscientist Szenthagothai writes:

> Although distributed over large parts of the brain (not exclusively the cortex), the reflective level of the mind has the same material substrate as the brain, the only difference being that while ordinary brain functions can occur in separate, even rather small, portions of the nervous system, the reflective level (or mind) is a global function of all or most of the central nervous system. There is thus no gap to be bridged as regards the neural substrate of mind: the problem is only how anything emerging on the reflective level can act back upon the neural level.[32]

'The reflective level' is 'a global function of all or most of the nervous system' in two senses: it is dependent upon the nervous system acting as a whole; and it is something that the nervous system as a whole can do or bring about – something the parts are not capable of.

Levels not only have an existence independent of any observing consciousness – so they are out there in material unconscious things – but they have, apparently, causal efficacy. Or at least according to John Searle they do.[33] Searle tries to reconcile his biological naturalism (the view that 'mental states are as real as any other biological phenomena' and are caused by and cause biological phenomena) with the fact that mental states are totally different from physical ones. He does this by stating that 'mental states are both *caused by* and *realised in* the structure of the brain (and the rest of the central nervous system)' (p. 265). This is precisely comparable, he claims, to the way in which 'the liquid properties of water are both *caused by* the molecular behaviour and *realised in* the collection of molecules'. The analogy leads Searle into some very muddy waters indeed:

> So if one asked, 'How can there be a causal relation between the molecular behaviour and the liquidity if the same stuff is both liquid and a collection of molecules?', the answer is that there can be causal relations between phenomena at different levels in the very same underlying stuff.

An entity or stuff can causally interact with itself in virtue of being seen at two levels!

It is worth spelling out what is wrong with Searle's argument because, although fallacious, it is not particularly unorthodox. It is the logical outcome of the unthinking use of levels in discussions about the relationships between mind and brain, between thoughts and ionic movements, and between persons and molecules.

First of all, there is something profoundly suspicious about the analogy (never mind the homology):

Brain states: Mental states :: Molecular behaviour: Liquidity

It implies that the relation between the physical and the mental is similar to the relationship between one type of experience of the physical and another, between one way of being conscious of, or describing, a physical entity and another. This seems odd because both the molecules and the liquidity of the water are on the same side of the mind–matter divide: either on the matter side if they are thought of as intrinsic properties of material water; or on the mind side if they are thought of as different ways of experiencing or observing water.

Second, it suggests that there can be causal relations between these types of experiences or levels of description. 'It is tempting', Searle says, 'to think that whenever A causes B there must be two discrete events, one identified as cause, the other as effect.' But this temptation must be resisted: events at a macro level are caused by events at a micro level; so one can get out of two levels all that one has hitherto wanted to get out of two separate events. In the case of the mind/brain, the levels are apportioned as follows: 'The intrinsically *mental* features of the universe are just higher level *physical* features of brains.'[34]

The notion of the causal interaction between mind and body as being essentially the same as a causal interaction between descriptions is rather obscure. Searle believes, it seems, that when matter acts upon mind (to alter mental states) and mind acts on matter (to bring about intentions), it is a question of one description of a system acting upon another – as if the level of description of the system were not only part of the system (which of course it is not) but also enabled that system to interact with itself. Without such levels of description, or observation, one must presume, matter could not give rise to mind nor mind act upon matter. This confusion of descriptions with objects described is even more spectacular than Hacker's witty analogy with 'buildings talking to one another in the language of classical architecture'.[35]

Searle's talk of levels takes the 'transferred epithet' approach to the mind/brain problem one step further: we have transferred descriptions!

Logic

Since time immemorial, logic has been associated with consciousness and logical operations regarded as distinct achievements of consciousness at its most developed and sophisticated. Man may not be the only rational animal, but he is unique in the degree to which he engages in explicitly logical thought. This uniqueness is denied by some and we are frequently asked to believe that nonconscious machines, or even parts of machines, carry out logical operations and that logical operations may be carried out in the lower reaches of the brain without surfacing in consciousness. Logical operations may be executed without consciousness. This, it is believed, has momentous consequences for the philosophy of mind. According to Dennett,[36] the development of modern computers has taken away the force of Descartes' argument that reasoning betokens a non-physical substance.

There are several strands in this conception of logic disassociated from consciousness. Each deserves separate critical inspection.

1. Logic is in machines

Electronic engineers and computer experts talk about 'logic circuits' and 'logic gates'. Such talk is clearly anthropomorphic. A NAND gate does not, of itself, execute logical operations. It requires a conscious individual to turn this input/output relation

$$1 \overline{} \\ 1 \underline{} \Big] 0$$

into a logical operation corresponding to 'not (A and B)'. And the same applies to more complex logical operations, even those conducted by 'expert systems' in natural language. The electronic events within the machine count as logical operations only if they are understood as relations between inputs and outputs that are themselves understood, i.e. interpreted by a conscious human operator.

2. There are logic circuits in the brain

Parts of the brain are spoken of as if they were organic computers ('wetware') executing logical operations. We are told that there are 'logic gates' in the spinal cord and the cerebellum; if–then circuits in the cortex; and so on. This is a particularly complex mess to unravel. It seems to involve three steps:

a) 'machinomorphic' attitudes to the brain: the brain thought of as a kind of *device*, as if it were an artefact that had been made with some purpose in view;
b) the anthropomorphising of machines in line with *1* above;
c) the application of the anthropomorphised conception of machines to the de-anthropomorphised brain, so that its operations can be termed 'logical' and its neuronal elements logic circuits.

3. The mind is a kind of logic machine

According to Patricia Churchland, 'the mind is a kind of logic machine that operates on sentences'.[37] The concept of machine is brought right into the heart of mind: logic and mind are reunited but no consciousness results or is necessary. Mind-logic remains machine-logic. This position is the end-point of a bio-logic which derives ultimately from Helmholtz, who first suggested that perception was based upon 'unconscious inference'. For many cognitive psychologists, perceptions are inferences from sensory and stored data or the result of inference mechanisms operating on sensory '*information'.[38] According to Richard Gregory (quoted in ref. 38, p. 228): 'To understand perception, the signal codes and the stored knowledge or assumptions used for deriving perceptual hypotheses must be discovered ... . perceptions are inferences based on signalled data from the senses and stored in memory.'

The fundamental error behind the machine-bio-logic claim is that it fails to distinguish between conscious reasoning, which may be quite effortful, and events that may have the same apparent input–output relations as conscious reasoning but are not even effortless. The logic of the logic circuit is not strictly logic because the events have been totally uprooted from – and in fact never bore any relation to – the process of reasoning, the business of being reasonable. We may use machines to assist us to draw logical inferences but it is we, not the machines, who draw the inferences. The output of a machine is no more an inference than natural processes are inferences: without explicitness, without consciousness, there are events but no true logical operations.

Of course, we can attribute our own intentionality to the machines we devise for our own purposes, in the same way as we can regard a cloud as a standing assertion to the effect that it is probably going to rain. Likewise, when one stone falls on another and the second stone is broken in two, we could regard this as a valid calculation to the effect that $1 + 1 = 1 + 1/2 + 1/2$ or even an invalid calculation to the effect that $1 + 1 = 3$. In either case, we are committing the error – common in cognitive science – of *misplaced explicitness.

Memory (stored information)

Computers, we are told, have memories as well as logic; and so it doesn't seen unreasonable that we can use computers to model minds which, importantly, have memories. Now there are many senses in which it is roughly true to say that computers have memories – *but there are many others in which it is not at all true.*

In its original and true sense, memory is inseparable from consciousness; in an extended sense, it is separable from but closely serves consciousness; and, in a greatly extended, metaphorical sense, memory has nothing to do with consciousness. The neuroscience ploy is to apply the term in its metaphoric, unconscious sense to machines, brains-considered-as-machines, organisms and even to non-living non-artifactual matter, and then to gloss over the differences between this sense and the primary, stricter, sense of memory – the sense which gathers up the really interesting and mysterious aspects of the phenomenon.

The primary sense of memory corresponds to occurrent or episodic memory: conscious memory for particular facts or events which may be recalled involuntarily or at will – in either case explicitly. Amongst these are personal or autobiographical memories which relate to things that one has oneself experienced. In the case of such memories one often recalls not only the event but the fact that one was there to witness it. The recollection is imbued with a sense of a past self. The memories are explicitly past *experiences*; they are related consciously to one's self and to a past which is one's own and for which one feels in part responsible.

Other senses of memory are less directly related to conscious-ness, less rooted in recalled past experience. Procedural memories (remembering how to do something), acquired skills which one may deploy more or less consciously, habit memories (behaving differently as a result of past experience), may be retained independently of any accessible episodic memory. There are many forms of amnesia in which it is possible to learn new skills without acquiring new occurrent memories. In such cases, the individual is unable to recall anything about the circumstances in which the new skill was acquired. Such pathological cases dramatise the difference between procedural and occurrent memory. The past may be active in the present even though one may not explicitly recall it.

This distinction is, perversely, used to license the complete separation of memory from consciousness and the further extension of the term 'memory' to encompass the enduring effect of any event upon any object – as if procedural or habit memory were the real thing and occurrent, episodic or declarative memory an unimportant sub-type. If I fall over and cut myself badly, a scar will form which may remain with me for the rest of my life. This scar is a record of the event that caused it and, by preserving it intact, my body has, in a sense, 'remembered' the event, long after *I* have forgotten it. The general notion is that, if an event causes a permanent change in an object, that change is a memory of the event, 'stored *information' about it: the permanent change has stored the past. In this extended sense, all sorts of naturally occurring stuff has – or is – memory. For example, DNA. Or a rock bearing the marks of an antediluvian geological catastrophe.

It is worth teasing out the logic here. If order is information and memory is the transmission of information over time, any ordered system that endures will seem to have, or to be, memory. Of course, once the concept of memory is extended to include any permanent change that has taken place as the result of the impact of an event, or the interaction between objects, then memory is everywhere: the present state of the universe could be seen to be a continually changing memory of the entire past of the universe. And the more inert the universe, the more it would appear to be saturated with, or identical with, memory.[39] The most impressive feats of memory will be exhibited by rocks that do not alter over many millions of years.

It will be obvious that something has gone wrong. If the sense of the term 'memory' has been so extended that it now includes the entire state of the universe – irrespective, moreover, of whether it has any conscious inhabitants – then it has no meaning distinct from stability or, as I have said, from inertia. This result lies at the bottom of a slope at the top of which is the decision to separate our idea of the nature of memory from that of a conscious rememberer. This is a perfectly acceptable move, so long as it is not then forgotten that memory now has several distinct meanings and that memory without consciousness is a rather specialised meaning, the metaphorical extension of a term whose primary meaning is connected with consciousness.

The primacy of conscious memory – and in particular of autobiographical occurrent memory – is demonstrated by the fact that those in whom this is defective though all other aspects of memory are intact are regarded as profoundly amnesic and severely impaired. Germane to this primary sense are deliberate and conscious recall, the savouring of memories, reminiscence and nostalgia. These aspects of human memory are not minor or optional characteristics. For they are connected with the central fact of personal memory: its being rooted in the sense that 'this happened to me', 'this memory is about me', 'this is *my* memory'. Moreover, true memory is implicated in our sense of the present: the familiarity of objects and of the world and its feeling of being related to me and me to it. And our sense of the past inasmuch as it is our own past; and so our sense of ourselves as more than a succession of unconnected moments.

Until such time as computers, or DNA, or elastic show convincing signs of nostalgia, we should be on our guard whenever we hear that they have, or encode, or embody[40] memories. They may help us to recall things but they do not themselves remember their 'memories'. In this regard, there is no metaphysical difference between an interactive laser disk and a knotted handkerchief. They are not so much memories as reminders; and they are able to remind only those who actually have memories in the real, primary sense.

(We should be equally guarded when we encounter the term 'memory store' or '*stored information'. Of the making and occurrence of data-bases there is, it appears, no end. But the concept of stored *information is only a useful shorthand and it should not be taken literally. While it is in store it is only potential *information: *information that is not informing anyone is not information. See INFORMATION.)

As an example of just how muddled neuro-computational cognitive psychology can be on the topic of memory, the following is worth pondering:

> Despite their limitations, simple auto-associative memories show many of the valuable properties of neural computation. What they remember is the pattern of activity created across their units by the external input. All learning rules store some aspect of the pairwise co-occurrence statistics in the units in the weightings on their connections.[41]

From my sudden recall of a happy or unhappy moment in my past to 'pairwise co-occurrence statistics' is a long journey during the course of which memory – at least as those of us who are not wedded to computational theories of the mind understand it – entirely evaporates.

Misplaced explicitness

There are things that we do (deliberately, explicitly) and things that happen. The abiding mystery of conscious human beings is that they are able to create doing out of happening, to fashion agency out of agent-less event, to carve choice out of the unchosen, deliberation out of mechanism. Thus, my deliberately going for a walk is predicated upon a complex hierarchy of reflexes necessary for directed ambula-tion. *I* walk, yes, but *it* provides the walking mechanisms; *I* do walking, but I do not 'do' the modulation of tone regulated by vestibulo-spinal and other pathways necessary to permit walking to take place.

One result of the inversion of the hierarchy of mental phenomena (so that calculations are at the bottom and sensations at the top), noted in the discussion of *calculations, is that deliberate operations, displaced from the higher reaches of the mind as the latter are computerised, reappear surprisingly at lower levels. Consider Johnson-Laird on vision (op. cit., p. 114):

> Your visual system constructs a description of the perceived object and compares it with some sort of mental catalogue of the three-dimensional shape of objects. It can recognise them from particular viewpoints and then make automatic extrapolations about the rest of their shapes.

This sounds a jolly sight more difficult than simply seeing the object and recognising it! Here we have 'the visual system' doing all sorts of clever things: constructing descriptions, comparing them with mental catalogues, recognising them from particular viewpoints, making automatic extrapolations about the rest of the shapes of objects. Johnson-Laird's account illustrates how, when explicitness and deliberation have been displaced from the places where it is usually considered to be – ordinary behaviour – they reappear elsewhere in the *mechanisms* postulated to underlie ordinary behaviour. The terminology appropriate to conscious, indeed higher-order conscious, activity also reappears – precisely where, *ex hypothesi*, consciousness should be absent. That it *should* be absent is evident from Johnson-Laird's own assertion (on the same page of his book) that 'the machinery of [visual] identification is unconscious in the Helmholtzian sense'.

Whenever you try to drive out consciousness from the places where it is ordinarily thought to be, from its rightful place, it will return in places where it obviously has no right to be – the only genuine example, perhaps, of Freud's 'return of the repressed'!

Pattern

The appeal to 'patterns' is rather like the appeal to '*levels': both are invoked to help explain how an entity such as the nervous system whose elements are very simple and unquestionably made of matter can give rise to something – the mind – that is apparently neither. All nerve impulses are roughly the same; they differ only in the *patterns* they form which can encode the extraordinary variety of the perceived world. These patterns emerge at a higher *level.

The criticisms directed at the use of the notion of *levels apply *a fortiori* here: patterns are viewpoint-dependent. To illustrate this, consider the following diagram, intended to represent an array of neurones in a state of excitation:

```
*   *   *   *
*   *   *   *
*   *   *   *
```

What is the pattern of activity here? It could be read as

```
*   *   *   *
*   *   *   *
*   *   *   *
```

or as

```
*   *   *   *   +   *   *   *   *   +   *   *   *   *
```

or as

```
*   *       *   *
*   *   +   *   *
*   *       *   *
```

or as a collection of six pairs. The truth is that, from an array of activated neurones, any number of potential patterns could be extracted. *Which* of these is *the* pattern of activity is an unanswerable question. Intrinsically, from the physicalist point of view that neuroscientists espouse, it is none of these: a consciousness, a viewpoint, is required in order to decide between possible patterns; in order that one pattern rather than another should emerge victorious; in order that there should be a particular, and hence *any*, pattern. If the nervous system is to be viewed as a physico-chemical system, as something that has no viewpoint, then the events in it have no more intrinsic pattern than do the events in a stone or an avalanche. In short, the emergence of patterns is dependent upon consciousness; they cannot, therefore, explain the origin or emergence of consciousness.

Process (processing)

For the thinker bluffing his way across the brain/mind barrier, travelling is always easier to handle than arrival. Despite the alternating machinisation and anthropomorphisation of terms, it still sometimes remains difficult to deal with them when they approximate old-fashioned unreconstructed consciousness. Even *information can embarrass; so instead, arrival is replaced by further journeying and writers sometimes prefer to talk about 'information-processing' rather than 'information'.

Consciousness is thus sufficiently distanced from self-presence to be convincingly machinised. Consequently, seeing becomes 'optical information-processing';[42] and neurons are 'information-processing devices'.[43] Indeed, we are often told that the brain is 'an information processor of almost incredible complexity'.[44] This conventional view is endorsed fulsomely by Johnson-Laird, who seems very keen to ensure that journeying entirely displaces arrival:

> What do mental processes *process*? The answer, of course, is a vast number of perceptions, ideas, images, beliefs, hypotheses, thoughts and memories. One of the tenets of cognitive science is that all these entities are mental representations or symbols of one sort or another.[45]

The very things that we would regard as the contents of (conscious) mind – ideas, thoughts, memories, etc. – are relegated to the material that is processed – by mental processes. There is raw material and processing (starting point and journeying) but no product (arrival). The mind is more convincingly machine-like if, like machines, it does jobs rather than being composed of mental states. For example, the following is seemingly more convincing for being about 'information-processing' than about mental states:

> Information processing is achieved in neural systems by a large number of highly interconnected units that affect each other's levels of activation through broadcast signals that are modified at the receiving end by local connection strengths ... The dynamic change of activation under the influence of external input, current state, and internal connections constitutes information processing, and modifications of the connections constitutes learning.[46]

This emphasis upon processing rather than upon products also makes it easier to identify mental phenomena with nerve impulses which also exist in travel rather than arrival.

Finally, there are useful ambiguities in the idea of 'information-processing': is it a question of turning something that is not information into information; or is it a matter of turning one sort of information into another sort? These uncertainties stop one looking too closely and asking what form information – or information-processing – takes in neural terms.

Examples of information-processing often revolve around the events that take place at a synapse – the junction between two neurones – where two sub-threshold pre-synaptic excitatory impulses add up to one that actually breaks threshold to cross the synaptic cleft, or where two impulses, one excitatory and the other inhibitory, partly cancel one another out. But is one entitled to think of this as the processing (production/transformation/enhancement) of information? After all, convergence of 'signals' at a synapse may be equally regarded as loss, rather than use, or gain, of information. If the central pathways receive only the result of the convergence of incoming activity at synapses they have lost access to the components that made it up. If we are given the answer '4', we do not know what elements went into that result: $2 + 2$ or $3 + 1$ or $1 + 1 + 1/2 + 1/2 + 1/2 + 1/2$.

In short, we have no idea how energy is turned into information, and fudging the issue by talking about 'information-*processing*' does not help, either – except in so far as it unfocuses the question and makes it easier to enjoy the illusion that one is answering it.

Representation (model)

Careers have been built upon 'representation' and upon 'model'. 'Representation' is a key term in *Fodorese and, indeed, throughout cognitive psychology. The roots of its current usage are philosophical, though within cognitive psychology it has taken on a life of its own. According to Johnson-Laird, 'One of the tenets of cognitive science is that all the entities are mental representations.'[47]

Representationalist theories of the mind begin with the claim that we do not have direct access to external reality, only to mental representations of reality. What we have contact with is not, say, the surface of objects, but a mental event or content caused by the external object. Representationalist theories of the mind follow naturally from the causal, interactionist, theory of perception, according to which perception (and hence consciousness) is, or is the result of, the *effect* the external world has on a specialised part of the body, namely the nervous system. The question then arises as to what form the representations of the world in the mind (or the nervous system) take. The naive assumption is that the mind mirrors the world; or, at the very least, the mental phenomenon has some feature in common with the object or property it is about, for example, a common form, so that the mental phenomenon is *isomorphic* with the physical object it relates to. This view quickly runs into difficulties, though, as we shall see, thinkers are drawn back to it again and again. Since the representation of the object is the result of an *interaction* between the object and the nervous system, it cannot simply look like the object. This was pointed out by Helmholtz, who, unfortunately, went on to suggest that the events in the nervous system were *symbols* of external reality.

Contemporary representationalism in psychology may be traced to the immediate postwar writings of Kenneth Craik, who took the idea of symbols further and suggested that the mind or the nervous system constructed a *model* of reality out of these symbols: external reality is known to us because it is reconstructed or symbolically represented within our nervous systems/minds. We have direct access not to the world but to transformations, models, representations of it. This view, now ubiquitous throughout cognitive psychology (whose commitment to mental representation is what distinguishes it form the old, despised behaviourism), philosophical psychology and artificial intelligence, achieved one of its its most highly elaborated expressions – indeed its apotheosis – in Johnson-Laird's *Mental Models*.[48]

The main and the most obvious criticism of the representational or model theory of mind is that it raises the homunculus problem. To what or to whom are the representations representing (re-presenting) the world? This is particularly obvious if mental models are thought to be pictures in the mind: who or what is going to look at them? For pictures imply spectators and, indeed, spectators able to interpret their elements, translating them into the elements of the depicted object or state of affairs. This difficulty is equally obvious (despite a considerable amount of fast footwork) if the representations are propositions cast in some postulated 'language of thought' – in, for example, Fodor's Mentalese; for the language of thought seems to require someone to whom it is addressed and who will also interpret its symbols. If representations are neither of these homunculus-generating things, then it is difficult to know what they are.

For Johnson-Laird,[49] who distances himself from both the image and the proposition versions of representationalism, they are 'internal tableaux'. These, however, seem to require homunculi to use them at least as much as images and propositions do. Despite strenuous denials, the homunculus problem cannot be driven away from representational theories of mind. Indeed, it becomes more apparent the more representationalists try to wriggle away from it. Johnson-Laird asserts that, 'unlike a propositional representation, a mental model does not have an arbitrarily chosen syntactic structure, but one that plays a direct representational role since it is analogous to the corresponding state of affairs – as we perceive, so we conceive' (ref. 49, p. 156). The structure of mental models 'is identical to the structure of states of affairs'. This claimed isomorphism seems to solve, or dissolve, the homunculus problem by the following logic: if the mental model is structurally identical to the state of affairs it models, it will self-evidently be about that state of affairs and will require no further interpretation; if the model requires no further interpretation, it will not require the consciousness of a homunculus for whom it is a model in order to be a model. The second claim does not, of course, follow from the first: a transparent model requires a homunculus just as urgently as does one requiring more active interpretation. The homunculus doesn't have to be so clever – a thick homunculus will do – but he/she is still needed.

It is clear that, as mentioned already, naive mirror representationalism remains a perpetual temptation, often taking the form of a proposed isomorphism between the physical and the mental, between the external objects and the internal ones.[50] This raises two new problems: how, for example, yellow could be represented isomorphically in the nervous system by non-yellow phenomena; and how that representation is itself consciousness or is presented in consciousness. The first question is often answered by claiming that the different properties of the outside world are represented by sites in 'vector space'. According to Paul Churchland, 'activity vectors form the most important kind of representation within the brain' (ref. 5, p.165): there is a 'unique coding vector' for each kind of sensation, which is described by the firing frequencies of different kinds of neurones. But this 'coding' dodge reintroduces the problem of decoding and the question of how the representation is 'understood'. The second question leads to a retreat from representationalism altogether in the hope of abolishing the homunculus problem. Johnson-Laird's transparent (because isomorphic) representations may represent a half-way retreat from representationalism. It has been characterised by Russell as follows: 'mental models aren't just representations. Why, they're the real thing ... though still mental, of course.'[51]

Despite these insuperable difficulties (and the fact that representationalism solves no problems itself or even provides a framework for solving problems), its intuitive attractiveness makes it irresistible. For it provides a framework within which the real problems can be bypassed and the illusion of progress maintained. Yates' review[52] begins by suggesting that the central claim of cognitive psychology 'is that information about the world is coded in the form of mental representations that are distinct from external information and sensory information' (p. 249). He argues that 'the content of awareness consists of constructs that account for sensations by representing patterns of the environment relevant to the set of possible actions that might be taken'. The data upon which these constructs are based do not correspond solely to sensations: perceptions are representations of the world that are incompletely accounted for by what reaches the sensorium from the world. The models that constitute our awareness are based upon centrally directed inference from sensation.

Such a direct identification of models or representations with awareness is particularly embarrassing to those who would avoid the homunculus problem. There are several ways out. Johnson-Laird, writing several years after *Mental Models* (ref. 3, p. 389), talks of 'implicit representations': 'The brain itself may represent much of its knowledge in an implicit representation based on parallel distributed *processing.' An implicit representation is, presumably, one that no one in particular is explicitly conscious of: it doesn't represent anything to anyone. Once we admit the possibility of implicit representations, then representations may be found anywhere. The universal *grammar of human language may be represented in the brain of a newborn child. Truth-tables may be represented in the logic circuits of a pocket computer. The *instructions for making an organism – genetic information – may be represented in its DNA. *Rules may be represented in unconscious computational systems. Newton's laws of motion may be represented in planetary orbits. And so on.

The fundamental flaw in representationalist thought is that it overlooks the primary sense of representation – that of *re*-presentation. A picture is a representation of something that may in its own right be present. Representation is secondary to presentation – to presence – and thus requires consciousness. It is an indirect presentation – via signs – of *something to someone*. Things are represented to – just as they are presented to – consciousnesses. *A representation cannot therefore be the basis of, but presupposes, consciousness*. And for this reason, the description of something as a 'representation' in the absence of a consciousness to or for which it represents – unless it is explicitly acknowledged that a consciousness is potentially there – should arouse suspicion. 'Unconscious representation' is a deviant form and should prompt vigilance. At the risk of labouring the point: there can be no re-presentation without presentation.

Since presentation itself presupposes presence, consciousness cannot be founded upon representation, cannot be understood as emerging effortlessly from modelling of the world, understood as the generation of internal transforms of the world within, say, a nervous system. Presentations presuppose someone – a consciousness – to whom the presentation is presented, to whom, at least, it is present. Without that someone, or that consciousness, it is difficult to know by what right the object or entity counts as a presentation, or a re-presentation.

In the topsy-turvy world of cognitive psychology, we are allowed to speak of representations in the absence of consciousness – though representations require consciousness – and to speak of consciousness as a set of representations – though consciousness is the terminus at which representation gives way to presentation, to presence. Some explanation of this craziness is necessary. It lies, perhaps, in the ambiguities of 'representation'. Let us look at a couple of these:

1. It is acceptable to say that pictures represent things – but only because it is assumed that they are being, or have been, or will be, looked at by someone. By itself, a picture is simply an object and lacks intentional reference to any other object. At best it is a *potential* representation of something. We tend to forget this seemingly pedantic requirement and, as a result, think of the picture itself as a 'representation'. This paves the way for thinking of other things – nerve impulses, etc. – as being able to represent things and so becoming the basis of consciousness or of a model of consciousness.

2. Cognitive scientists often frame their fundamental question as follows: 'How is the world represented in the brain?' This is open to two interpretations: what representation (image, etc.) does the world have in the brain (or what transforms of its image are in the brain)?; and in what form is it present in the brain? To underline the ambiguity of the question, compare the two ways in which the Pope may be represented: through a picture; or through a representative, a legate. Representation in the first sense allows a meaningful incorporation of the world into the brain. This, however, raises the homunculus problem – since meaning has to mean to someone, pictures have to depict for someone. Representation in the second sense closes off the homunculus series; for the representative is a kind of terminus. A legate is not a picture and is in himself a terminus.[53] Such ambiguity keeps representationalism alive.

Rule

An entire family of anthropomorphic terms gathers round this word. It is particularly useful for assisting the passage across the mind/brain, mind/matter barrier, since following a rule, which is something that conscious creatures do, also seems to be something – like conforming to (physical) laws – that unconscious entities are capable of. Rule-following, that is to say, has one foot in mechanism and one in deliberation.

Cognitive psychologists and others would have us believe that:

1. Computers act in accordance with rules.
2. Automata obey rules.
3. There are rules *represented/embodied in the brain.

The use of 'rule' would be considerably less carefree if it were appreciated that acting in accordance with a rule – as opposed to showing patterns of occurrence in accordance with certain natural laws – requires consciousness. Or if it were understood that the concept of 'implicit' rules (and unconscious rule-obedience) requires an extension of the usual sense of rule. The primary sense of a rule is of something that is inculcated and is explicitly obeyed.

We distinguish a rule from a law of nature. Although the laws of nature describe in the most general terms what happens as a rule, they are not prescriptive. As a rule, objects tend to fall downwards. This does not mean that they consciously obey the rule 'fall downwards'; or that they consult the rules in order to discover that they should fall downwards. The objects governed by the laws of nature do not try to follow that law, nor can they fail to act in accordance with it, least of all as a result of misunderstanding or misapplying it. The notion of following a rule is closely connected with that of the possibility of accidentally making a mistake or of deliberate transgression. This is quite different from being subject to a (natural) law where one can hardly be mistaken and even less be in a position to flout the law.

Now it might be argued that a computer, or some other automaton, may follow the rules according to which it has been designed or programmed without 'knowing' those rules; it may exhibit rule-governed behaviour.[54] Is it not, therefore, possible to obey rules without being conscious of them, or indeed, of anything? Well, yes, in this specially extended sense of rule-obedience, it is possible. But even here *someone* – a user, an observer – has to be conscious for the events in the automaton to be rule-obeying, for them to *count* as rule-obeying. Unless the rules are housed in a consciousness *somewhere*, the events are not rule-following.

One might go even further and adopt the Wittgensteinian position that rule-following is an essentially social practice, that it requires not merely one consciousness but a community of consciousnesses: 'a computer has neither inwardness nor society ... so *it* is not following rule...'[55] For some, this may be going too far; but it emphasises how following a rule is quite different from conforming to a natural law are rarely respected in computer-talk and other areas of cognitive psychology where rule-obedience seems to take place as well without as with consciousness.

Notes and references

1. Ludwig Wittgenstein, *Philosophical Investigations*. Trans. G.E.M. Anscombe (Oxford: Blackwell, 1963), p. 115.
2. Peter Hacker, Languages, Minds and Brains. In: Colin Blakemore and Susan Greenfield (eds.) *Mindwaves* (Oxford: Blackwell, 1987).
3. P.N. Johnson-Laird, *The Computer and the Mind* (London: Fontana Press, 1988).
4. Patricia Churchland, *Neurophilosophy* (Cambridge, Mass.: MIT Press, 1986) p. 252: 'Oversimplifying, one could think of the mind as essentially a kind of logic machine that operates on sentences.'
5. Paul Churchland, *Matter and Consciousness* (Cambridge, Mass: MIT Press, 2nd edn 1988), p. 92.
6. Paul Churchland, ibid. p. 2.
7. J.A. Fodor, Some reflections on Vygotsky's 'Thought and Language', *Cognition* (1972), 83–95.
8. Johnson-Laird, pp. 159 et seq.
9. John Searle, Minds, Brains, Programs. In: *The Behavioral and Brain Sciences*, vol. 3 (1980). See also, Minds and Brains without Programs. In: *Mindwaves*, op. cit., pp. 209–34.
10. See D.C. Dennett, Intentional Systems, *Journal of Philosophy* 8 (1971), 87–106. This is reprinted in Dennett's *Brainstorms: Philosophical Essays on Mind and Psychology* (Montgomery VT: Bradford Books, 1978), and its consequences further examined in his collection *The Intentional Stance* (Cambridge: Bradford Books, 1987).
11. J.A. Fodor, The Mind–Body Problem, *Scientific American* (1981), 114–23.
12. J.A. Fodor, *The Language of Thought* (Hassocks: Harvester Press, 1976) p. 125.
13. Fodor, ibid., p. 65.
14. This passage and the quotation from Shannon below are also cited by Hacker, op. cit. They come from C.E. Shannon and W. Weaver's classic text, *The Mathematical Theory of Communication* (Urbana: University of Illinois Press, 1949).

15. W.E. Hick, On the Rate of Gain of Information, *Quarterly Journal of Experimental Psychology*, 4 (1952), 11–26.
16. Patricia Churchland, op. cit., p. 36.
17. Johnson-Laird, op. cit., p. 14.
18. Richard Dawkins, *The Blind Watchmaker* (London: Penguin, 1988).
19. Colin Cherry, *On Human Communication* (Cambridge: MIT Press, 2nd edition, 1966) p. 215.
20. Paul Churchland, op. cit., p. 174.
21. Even the most amorphous event or object can be analysed as if it were highly ordered. Fourier analysis presupposes that any time-series can be analysed as the sum of (rhythmic) sinusoids of different frequencies. And the more amorphous it is, the more complex its analysis and, consequently, its apparent order.
22. The classic paper is Tommaso Toffoli, Physics and Computation, *International Journal of Theoretical Physics* 21 (1983), 160–7.
23. The best account of the 'computationalisation' of the universe is in Paul Davies, *The Mind of God: Science and the Search for Ultimate Meaning* (London: Penguin, 1993). The present discussion is particularly indebted to Chapter 5, 'Real Worlds and Virtual Worlds' (pp. 117–39).
24. L. Darcy and L. Boston, *A Dictionary of Computer Terms* (London: Fontana Paperbacks, 1984).
25. Dawkins, op. cit., p. 119.
26. R.L. Gregory, *The Intelligent Eye* (London: Weidenfeld and Nicolson, 1970) p.15.
27. Darcy and Boston, op. cit.
28. Set out in John Searle, 'Minds, Brains and Programs', op. cit.
29. Patricia Churchland, op. cit., p. 48.
30. R.L. Gregory, *Eye and Brain: the Psychology of Seeing* (London: Weidenfeld and Nicolson, 3rd edition 1974), p. 9.
31. Johnson-Laird, op. cit., p. 35.
32. See J. Szenthagothai, The Brain–Mind Relation: A Pseudo-Problem?, In: *Mindwaves*, op. cit., pp. 323–35.
33. See Chapter 10 of J.R. Searle, *Intentionality* (Cambridge: Cambridge University Press, 1983).
34. Searle, *Mindwaves*, op. cit., p. 225.
35. Hacker, op. cit., p. 487.
36. D.C. Dennett, Can Machines Think?, In: *How We Know*, ed. M. Shafto, (San Francisco: Harper and Row 1985) pp. 1–26.
37. Patricia Churchland, op. cit., p. 252.
38. For a comprehensive critical review of this notion, see S.G. Shanker, Computer Vision or Mechanist Myopia, In: S.G. Shanker (ed.) *Philosophy in Britain Today* (London: Croom Helm, 1986).
39. The analogy with what follows when the concept of *information is uprooted from consciousness, from individuals giving and receiving *information, will be obvious.
40. The equivocation here is instructive. We are told that DNA is 'stored information', is genetic memory. It does not, however, have this memory. It does not remember; it *is* 'memory'. When I remember, I do not become

my memories; I have them. This distance is an essential part of memory in its true, that is to say human, sense.

41. W.A. Phillips, Brainy Minds. *Quarterly Journal of Experimental Psychology*, 40A(2) (1988), 389–405. The passage quoted appears on p. 392.
42. Paul Churchland, op. cit., p. 114.
43. Ibid., p. 133.
44. C. Longuet-Higgins, Mental Processes, *London Review of Books* (4 August 1988), 13–14.
45. Johnson-Laird, op. cit., p. 28.
46. Phillips, op. cit., p. 392.
47. Johnson-Laird, op. cit.
48. P.N. Johnson-Laird, *Mental Models: Towards a Cognitive Science of Language, Inference and Consciousness* (Cambridge: Cambridge University Press 1983).
49. *See Mental Models*, Chapter 3 – What Mental Models Are Not.
50. For a discussion of isomorphism, see the section Exhibiting Consciousness in Chapter 8 of Raymond Tallis, *The Explicit Animal* (London: Macmillan, 1991).
51. James Russell, *Mental Representation and the Psychology of Knowledge* (London: Macmillan, 1986). This is by far the best account I have come across of the problems of contemporary representationalism in psychology and the various ploys that have been used in an endeavour to kill off the homunculus.
52. J. Yates, The Content of Awareness is a Model of the World, *Psychological Review*, 92(2) (1985), 249–84.
53. Szenthagothai's definition of mind – 'the *level of representation of wholeness, self and purpose' (*Mindwaves*, p. 324) – is a classic.
54. For a discussion of tacit rule-following (and, rather less illuminatingly, of *representation), see D.C. Dennett, Styles of Mental Representation. In: *The Intentional Stance* (Cambridge, Mass.: Bradford, MIT Press, 1987).
55. A.C. Grayling, *Wittgenstein* (Oxford: Oxford University Press, 1988), p. 72.

3
The Poverty of Neurophilosophy

Neurophilosophy

In the last decade or so, there has been a stream of books, both popular and semi-professional and in both philosophy and cognitive neuro-science, purporting to demonstrate that contemporary neuroscience is advancing our understanding of the mind.[1] While none of these books suggests that the mind has yet been fully explained by the neuro-scientists, the implicit assumption is that they are, at last, on the right track: it is just a matter of time. It is also suggested that the earlier approaches, typified by the philosopher in the armchair dreaming up hypotheses that are either untested or, more likely untestable, are now simply out of date. A philosophy of mind that is not rooted in, driven by and checked against the findings of the neuroscientists is archaic and empty.

The title of Patricia Churchland's nearly 600-page volume, *Neuro-philosophy*, captures the fundamental notion underpinning such books: that at least one particular philosophical problem – the philosophy of mind – may be solved by neurological investigation. Of course, the solution to this problem would have wider implications. It would be a signal advance in our understanding of our own nature and might help us to make progress in other areas of philosophical investigation – for example, understanding the basis of human agency and our apparent free will; determining our place in the natural world and the overall scheme of things; and even solving ethical problems and getting a better understanding of the right way forward for human society. The implicit claims of neurophilosophy are thus even more wide-reaching than their explicit ones.

Some, but not all, neurophilosophers make bold assertions about the extent to which contemporary neuroscience has solved, or shortly will solve, the mysteries that have baffled philosophers for so many centuries. These claims are broadcast in the titles of the books: Daniel Dennett's

Consciousness Explained (1993) and Stephen Pinker's *How the Mind Works* (1997) are just two extreme examples. While, in the preface to his book, Pinker disavows any claim to understanding how the mind works, this, in the light of his title, is disingenouous to say the least, particularly since he argues that cognitive neuroscience has transformed certain issues in the philosophy of mind from mysteries into problems.[2] I wish to argue here that not only has neuroscience cast no light on how there is such a thing as the mind, how it comes about and how in a fundamental sense it 'works', but also that it is unlikely to do so.

The relationship, or non-relationship, between mind and brain is, of course, a huge subject which has generated a massive bibliography. I myself have contributed to it; in particular, *The Explicit Animal*[3] attacks the notion that biological science has helps us to understand the extraordinary nature of human consciousness. I will not attempt a survey of current neurophilosophy. Suffice it to note that there are two theses which may be regarded as central: the belief that consciousness can be explained in biological terms and the parallel belief that it is both appropriate and fruitful to think of the mind as a complex computer or a set of computational functions. The biological dimension of neurophilosophy itself has two elements: the notion that human consciousness can be explained within the framework of evolutionary theory (so that the emergence of consciousness, even specifically human aspects of consciousness, is explicable as a product of natural selection); and the claim that consciousness is somehow accounted for by the neural activity of the brain. Several of these strands are brought together in Pinker's assertion that 'the mind is a system of organs of computation designed by natural selection to solve the problems faced by our evolutionary ancestors' (op. cit., p. 21).

In the present chapter, I shall address the poverty of neurophilosophy. Because I have already discussed the unsupportable claim that human consciousness can be explained in evolutionary terms, I will not revisit this here: the reader is referred to the relevant chapters (2 and 6) of *The Explicit Animal*. Nor shall I attempt a comprehensive discussion of the computational theory of mind. The language of neuromythology, to which the computational theory owes most if not all of its plausibility, is subjected to an extended critique in Chapter 2 of the present volume; and other arguments against the computational theory are set out in 'Computerising Consciousness', Chapter 4 of *The Explicit Animal*, so I shall glance at the theory only in passing here. Nor, finally, will I address the problematic relationship between neural activity and sensations in great depth, though I shall briefly examine the fundamental problems besetting attempts to reduce sensations and other mental phenomena to patterns of nerve impulses.

My primary purpose in this chapter – as will be evident from its title – is to focus on the extent to which neural theories of mind put forward or assumed in cognitive neuroscience, despite their role in raising our awareness of the enormous complexities that are embedded in even the simplest act or the simplest decision, actually impoverish our idea of human consciousness and our mental life. I am, however, not unaware of the major contributions that neuroscientists have made to advancing our understanding of the brain. An additional purpose of this chapter will, therefore, be to try to indicate ways in which neuroscience may contribute to a true neurophilosophy. At any rate I will endeavour to determine the relationship between findings of neuroscience and a true understanding of the nature of the mind. This last question, which is to me the most pressing, will also be dealt with only briefly, not because I have addressed it satisfactorily elsewhere but because I am still unsure how it should be addressed. I will, however, attempt to indicate what is needed if I am to reconcile within myself the believing clinician – whose central interest in medicine is in neuroscience and who in daily practice talks like the most hard-line materialist neuroscientist – and the sceptical philosopher who on a Sunday morning criticises neuromythology.

The case for neurophilosophy

The founding assumption of neurophilosophy is that we can explain mental phenomena in terms of certain processes in the brain; that we have empirical evidence in support of such kinds of explanation; and that this evidence is derived at least in part from the discoveries of modern neuroscience. This assumption is connected with several other theses:

a) that mental phenomena are identical with neural activity (or *patterns* of neural activity – and thereby hangs a tale) taking place in certain parts of the brain;

b) that in the case of perception, this activity is caused by energy (originating from the perceived world) impinging on the brain ('the causal theory of perception');

c) that the brain, in this regard, is like a computer ('mind is the information-processing activity of the brain');

d) that mind/consciousness can be understood in terms of the evolutionary processes that gave rise to the brain.

Irrespective of whether or not the mind really is a computer (or it is correct to think of the mind as the sum of the computational activities of the brain) and whether its emergence can be explained in Darwinian terms, everyday observations seem to give overwhelming support to the notion that there is an intimate relationship between brain and conscious experience. For example, the *content* of my experience is determined by the location of my brain: I am experiencing this room in Bramhall, rather than a room in London, because Bramhall is where my brain presently is. More specifically, I can change my experience by altering the energy that impinges upon my brain via my sense organs; for example, I can alter my visual experience by turning my head in one way or another. I can alter my auditory experience by putting my fingers in my ears. The easiest way of interpreting this is that it prevents a certain kind of energy reaching my brain in the transduced form of nerve impulses. In other words, my mind is where my brain is, my consciousness is more less *of* where my brain is *at*: in at least one important sense, in waking life, the world of which I am conscious is the world which objectively seems to surround my brain. In contrast, my mind is not necessarily where my leg is: I could leave my leg in London and, so long as I had not bled to death, my mind could still be in Bramhall.

In addition to this compelling evidence of the connection between the brain and consciousness, there are all the many everyday observations that indicate that brain nick and mind nick are closely correlated: a head injury may remove vision, impair memory, alter personality, all of which suggest that vision, memory, personality – everything from the most primitive buzz of sensation to the most exquisitely constructed sense of self – depend crucially on the functioning of the brain.

If these homely observations are thought to cut metaphysical ice, then the more sophisticated ones of science are not required to take us any further. However, on top of this folk database, there is the huge mass of observations made by neuroscientists over the last few hundred years showing close correlations between holes in the brain and holes in the mind, between cerebral dysfunction and abnormalities of consciousness. These observations – which seem somehow more authoritative than what Mrs Smith of Wigan knows from daily life in Wigan or what I observe of myself – range from crude lesion experiments through to the kind of exquisite studies using functional neuro-imaging that currently dominate the literature in cognitive neuroscience.

Importantly, the scientific data include not only negative but also positive observations: certain parts of the brain are seen to be active, to light up, in anticipation of, or during the course of, the discharge of certain mental activities. Magnetic resonance imaging, functional magnetic resonance imaging, position emission tomography, electro-encephalography, magneto-encephalography and other techniques have shown exquisite correlations between activity in certain areas of the brain and mental functions. Under the heading of positive observations, I would also include the effects of brain stimulation, beginning with the famous experiments of Penfield in waking human subjects undergoing epilepsy surgery, in which he observed quite complex memories being switched on by electrical stimulation of the appropriate parts of the cerebral cortex. And then, finally, there are the strong correlations between the pattern and distribution of cerebral activity as recorded by electro-encephalography and global states of consciousness: sleep/waking, coma/alertness, attention/inattention.

The problems with neurophilosophy

Everyday life and neuroscientific observations – neurology, neurosurgery, neurophysiology, neuro-anatomy, neuropathology, neurochemistry, neuropsychology, neuroradiology, etc. – would all seem, therefore, to point inescapably to the conclusion that consciousness is due to certain activity in the brain; or that mental activity is neural activity. The confident claim that (for example) 'our sensations are simply identical with, say, a set of stimulation levels (spiking frequencies) in the appropriate sensory pathways'[4] seems close to being unassailable. But actually, there are many insuperable objections to the jump from observing the dependency of mind nick on brain nick to concluding that brain activity somehow explains mind or consciousness boils down to brain activity.

The first objection is that the way in which the objectively observed neural activity brings about or is in some sense implicated in the subjectively experienced contents of consciousness is far from clear. Indeed, it is profoundly puzzling. There are three front-running accounts of the relationship between nerve impulses and conscious experiences: the dual aspect theory; the causal interaction theory; and the identity theory.

Dual aspect theory

Some have suggested that neural activity and conscious experience – or at least certain 'central' events in the brain and qualia – are two aspects of the same events. However, this so-called 'dual aspect' theory has been largely rejected because most people do not feel happy with the notion of a single event that has two ontologically different aspects – a physical front-side and a mental back-side. It would be a very odd hybrid indeed.

Causal interaction theory

Others have suggested that the neural activity *causes* the mental activity – just as banging on a table causes a loud sound. Under this interpretation, there are therefore two types of events in the brain: on the one hand, nerve impulses which are the material causes; and on the other, the contents of consciousness (sensations, memories, thoughts, etc.), which are the immaterial effects of these impulses. This essentially dualist account runs dangerously close to making mental events mere epiphenoma, digressions from the causal net, ontological diverticula from the material world, which have no role in bringing about other events:

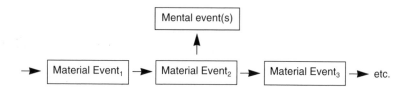

This is obviously unattractive, since it contradicts our firm belief that our conscious experience to some extent drives our behaviour.

If, however, it is claimed, to counter this objection, that the mental phenomena themselves have causal efficacy and are able to bring about material events, in particular the nerve impulses essential for voluntary action, then we have the unexplained situation of a continuous causal chain or net, a material nexus of which we are part, that inexplicably passes into and then out of a mental phase. This is particularly awkward if we believe that material events do, and immaterial events do not, have a location in space. We have, furthermore, to accept the existence of a section of one strand of the causal net – which itself extends indefinitely into the material world of which it is a small inlet – where consciousness inexplicably emerges and initiation, volition is possible; an utterly mysterious area in which the soluble fish of agency and doing somehow crystallise out of the sea of causation and mere happening:

Identity theory

So most philosophers and neuroscientists (when they have a view) prefer to espouse the idea that neural activity is *identical* with conscious experience. This may seem to incur the difficulties of both the dual aspect theory (one entity, two natures) and the causal theory (an immaterial/material entity embedded in a material causal chain). But it also, of course, raises the objection that neural activity is not at all *like* contents of consciousness. Nerve impulses – waves of electrochemical activity – don't look like sensations. In the wake of this objection comes the further objection that there is nothing in a nerve impulse to explain the specific qualitative features of the sensation it is supposed to be identical with – nothing in, say, impulses in the auditory system to make them specifically the basis of hearing rather than sight. In other words, neither the phenomenal content of consciousness nor the difference between different phenomenal contents of different bits of consciousness has any plausible neural basis. Nerve impulses don't look like sensations and the differences between nerve impulses don't look like the differences between types of experiences.

Let me deal with the issue of differences between experiences or mental contents first. Most neuroscientists agree that one lot of nerve impulses looks pretty much like another lot of nerve impulses. The contrast between the monotonous similarity of the nervous system and the infinite variety of the perceived world seems therefore rather puzzling. The argument that *location* of the activity in the brain explains all – that hearings are experienced when the hearing neurones are excited and sights are experienced when the visual neurones are excited – is self-evidently circular. So, too, is the argument that impulses in the visual cortex give sights because

Identity Theory

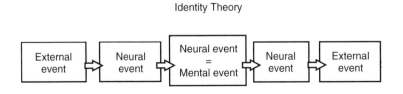

they are triggered off by light and those in the auditory cortex give rise to the experience of sounds because they are triggered off by sound. In fact, it is even less helpful than might seem at first sight; for, according to orthodox physical theory, qualities such as brightness and loudness do not exist in nature. There is, for example, nothing in the intrinsic properties of the electromagnetic energy called light that corresponds to brightness or colour. These qualities – secondary qualities – have therefore to be generated in the nervous system – by some unspecified means.

Even if there *were* some way of generating these qualities, how would we account for the discrepancy between their *variety* and the monotonous activity of the nervous system? All nerve impulses are pretty much the same. According to most writers who believe in the identity theory, the basis for the necessary variety is to be found not in the individual impulses but in their *patterns*, the patterns of large numbers of impulses considered together.

This is discussed in the entry on Patterns in Chapter 2, but is worth reiterating here. The patterns argument says, yes, all nerve impulses are indeed pretty much alike but there are millions of profoundly different possible *patterns of impulses* and it is the variety of these that underwrites the infinite variety of the experienced world. The trouble with this argument, however, is that patterns do not exist in, even less for, the elements that make up the pattern, only for an external observer, a consciousness that extracts the pattern.

An Array of Dots

Consider, for example, the array in the figure. It could be seen as a single array of nine dots; as an array of six dots on the left and three on the right; or as an array of three dots on the left and six on the right; or as any of a vast number of other possibilities. What this tells us is not that the array contains all these patterns – that it is 'infinitely rich' in patterns – but that it has no inherent pattern; that its patterns exist only in so far as they can be and, indeed, are *extracted*. Unfortunately for the identity theory, they can be extracted only in so far as they are perceived. Likewise there are no intrinsic patterns in the large numbers of nerve impulses that make up brain activity. They do not pick themselves out. The patterns are in the eye of the beholder. If, however, they exist only in relation to a perceiver, and we have to 'send out' for such a perceiver then the patterns in themselves cannot be the basis either of perception or of its variety.

What about the more fundamental objection to the identity theory that nerve impulses don't seem anything like sensations, qualia, experiences, etc.? This objection has been countered by an argument from 'levels' of description or observation. (Also addressed in Chapter 2.) This argument goes as follows. Granted that nerve impulses aren't at all like sensations or other more complex experiences, but neither are molecules of H_2O at all like water. So we can explain the huge difference between nerve impulses and experiences by thinking of the relationship between nerve impulses and conscious experiences as being like that between water molecules and water. Water molecules are totally unlike water: they do not possess the properties of wetness, shininess, liquidity, etc. But no one regards this difference between water molecules and splashes and dribbles and puddles of water as an argument against the well-accepted belief that water is identical with the water molecules that make it up. Molecules of H_2O are unquestionably identical with drops of water which have phenomenal properties of liquidity and wetness, etc.: H_2O molecules and drops of water are the same thing observed at different levels. Surely, then, it may be argued, by analogy, that neural activity and conscious experience are also the same thing perceived at different levels.

There are, however, many seemingly insuperable difficulties with this solution to the problem of the dissimilarity between neural activity and conscious experiences.[5] The most obvious is that the concept of levels – like that of patterns – implies levels of observation: H_2O molecules and water as it is experienced pouring out of the tap correspond to different ways of observing water – water as disclosed to a particular kind of scientific investigation and water with its secondary qualities as disclosed to ordinary perception. *Levels of observation* surely presuppose observation and observations – viewpoints, perspectives, etc. – presuppose consciousness and so cannot be legitimately invoked to explain the relationship between the seemingly unconscious third person neural activity of the brain and first person conscious experience. In addition, the 'levels' argument shares some of the weaknesses of the dual aspect theory, except that, instead of having the same phenomenon seen from the front and the back, as it were, we have the case of a phenomenon seen respectively from the air and from the ground; or a front end which is an aerial viewpoint and a back end which is a view from the ground.

The levels argument, in common with the dual aspect theory, has the additional failing that it does not explain why some neural activity has the characteristic of being identical with consciousness while most neural activity – for example, that which takes place in the cerebellum, the spinal cord, the peripheral nerves, as well as much of the activity recordable in the cerebral cortex – does not. This is rather as if some molecules of H_2O counted as water and others didn't. Or as if some had the propensity to add up to phenomenal or secondary qualities such a liquidity and wetness and others did not.

Nor, most crucially, does the 'levels' explanation go any way towards accounting for the fundamental and unique characteristic of conscious experience, namely, its intentionality, its character of being *about* something. For example, my consciousness of the cat refers to something outside of myself, in particular outside of my brain. How do these neural discharges in my brain refer back to the object that triggered them off? This puzzle is set out below:

Identity theory: the mystery of
intentionality

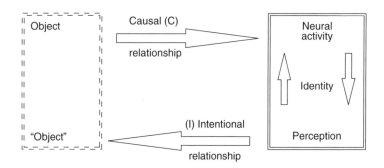

The inward causal chain (C) leading from seen object to impulses in the visual cortex fits with our conventional materialistic scientific framework; but the outward intentional (I) link – whereby the visuo-cortical impulses 'reach out to', refer to, are about, the seen object – most certainly does not. There is nothing else in nature corresponding to this. Moreover, the object they refer to does not itself have the attributes, those secondary qualities of brightness, loudness etc. that any perceiving consciousness finds in them. Physical objects are odour-less atoms that reflect colourless light waves and soundless vibrations in the air. And, moreover, in view of the endless causal chain or causal network of which the brain's activity – according the identity theory – is a small part there is no reason why this reaching back should stop at a particular point – at a so-called object of perception:

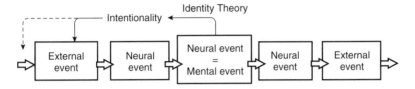

This final point has led some philosophers to abandon the notion of intentionality altogether and suggest that nerve impulses reveal only themselves: that all we know is some of the contents of our brain. This raises the question of how we manage to infer a world from these contents – or rather how the impulses manage to infer a world from themselves; and, moreover, how different brains manage to infer and inhabit a shared, or agreed world – the very world, the public material world, that neurophilosophers believe our brains to be part of. To this there is no answer.

And actually the endeavour to dispose of the problem of intentionality by claiming that impulses disclose only themselves and that all we know is our own brain contents, runs into even bigger problems – as becomes apparent as soon as we ask the question what is the self that the self-disclosing neural impulses would disclose. It is not possible to say what inherent properties they would have. Being physical events, they would have no secondary qualities.[7]

The complexity of ordinary consciousness

These are the particular, as it were technical, arguments against a neural explanation of mental phenomena and, more specifically, conscious experience. Less technical, but equally potent in my view, is the argument advanced by Colin McGinn in a classic paper published in *Mind* in 1989:[6] that it does not seem intuitively satisfying to explain human consciousness in terms of the passage of sodium and other ions across semi-permeable membranes. Neural activity seems the wrong kind of thing to explain consciousness. Of course, neuroscientists – and indeed philosophers – are right to be suspicious of the intuitively satisfying and to remind their critics of the point made so well by Lewis Wolpert[8] that science progresses towards truth by going beyond the intuitively satisfying to the counter-intuitive. More pointedly, philosophers like Stephen Stich have urged us to set aside what he calls 'folk psychology'.[9] However, even if we were to accept this rather special defence of the failure to remain within the intuitively plausible, this would not get the neurophilosophers off the hook. For the failure of neurophilosophy to give an account of consciousness that in any way matches our sense of ourselves and of our conscious lives is profound indeed.

This mismatch is not merely at the 'atomic' level discussed so far – the level at which the neural basis of consciousness fails to explain particular sensations in terms of particular clusters of impulses in particular circuits. The identity theory fails most signally at the higher level, in accounting for the organisation of ordinary human conscious-ness, the infinitely complex lacework of the aims, goals, intentions, notions ambitions, etc. that comprise our daily lives. I want to argue that, even if the identity theory did somehow explain consciousness, on a one-to-one basis for sensations, such a theory would not take us much further because it would not explain the complex unity of the conscious moment (which presumably involves huge quantities of activity in different areas of the nervous system), nor the coherence of conscious activity over time necessary for the moment of under-standing that corresponds to the present self or, even more so, for the coherence of the understanding self. There are impulses here and impulses there but no place where it all comes together in my sense of being someone here now discharging complex plans of the kind that fill most of our ordinary days.

It is worth dwelling on this and reminding ourselves about the long-range, explicit internal connectedness necessary to be the kind of responsible agent who is able to operate effectively in our complicated world. The notion of agency – of the individual as a cause, rather than as an effect – is inseparable from that of explicit purpose, of responsi-bility, of the expression of the rational will. This requires relating to things across time, to larger situation-frameworks than are available to the instant of consciousness. The temporal framework of an ordinary human agent – you, me – is huge and complex.

Consider the situation, routine for an academic, of giving an invited lecture. (The trigger for this present chapter.) Typically the commit-ment to speak is undertaken many months, perhaps a year or more, before the appointed date. Fulfilling the commitment – one of many thousands of small- and large-scale commitments in the period between agreement to speak and the actual lecture – connects the moment of that commitment with many other moments: those in which the title of the talk is discussed with the host, those in which ideas are jotted down, the hours in which the text is written and rewritten, the moments in which all sorts of implicit knowledge are deployed in order to find one's way via car and railway and tube and foot to the venue at the right time and in the right place – and all of this, while one is in the grip of a thousand other preoccupations and is floating in a sea of relevant and irrelevant sense data. However much the audience may come to regret the speaker's success in pulling off the feat of getting to speak at the right moment several months after the idea was first floated, it is a remarkable tribute to the complex inner organisation of his life and its extendedness across time. This example illustrates why bursts of electricity in the wetware of the brain don't somehow seem adequate to the exquisitely structured mind that we humans have.

The troubles go deeper than this. There has to be convergence in the unity of the conscious moment, but this must not take the form of a merging of the actions, knowledge and experiences relevant to the dozen macro- and micro-projects in progress at any given time, otherwise these projects would lose their distinct identity. If you think of all the things that would have to be going on in my brain in order to sustain the different levelled activity necessary to underpin my giving a lecture in the right place at the right time you would have the image of a vast number of overlapping circuits supporting a huge ensemble of different functions, and it is difficult to see how they could be kept apart so as not to interfere with one another – while at the same time they somehow relate to one another in or through something like a self. Even if we do not have to find space in separate parts of the brain for each of the many different functions or modules of the mind that we may distinguish – for, after all, as Stephen Pinker says, 'the beauty of information processing is the flexibility of the demand for real estate' – we still have problems of keeping them and the separate projects they are engaged in apart. (And we have to remember that one of the major effects of cognitive psychology has been vastly to increase the number of component tasks identified in the seemingly simplest activities, such as reading: trying to design robots to simulate ordinary cognitive functions is, as Stephen Pinker says, 'a kind of consciousness-raising'.)

I used the phrase 'different levelled' just now and it may be worth while spelling this out, to highlight the complexity of ordinary consciousness and the corresponding complexity of the task that would be faced by a cognitive neuroscience that had a clear idea of its object of study. There is the level at which all the elements of the lecture come together. At this level, there is a convergence between the conversations that set up the speaking engagement and the many different moments of thought that contributed to the final form of the lecture. These moments of thought are just as likely to occur while one is thinking of, or busy with, or engaged in, some other pressing task as they are in the setpiece hours of composition in the study. An idea for the lecture may come while one is hurrying to catch a train or worrying about the cost of the mortgage, or coming across a word in a book that triggers off a just-connected thought about a better phrasing of a key step in a component argument. The haystack in which needless have to come together is huge. At a lower level, which must always keep the higher-level goals in view, there are the practicalities of writing the lecture – making sure the laptop is working, ensuring a supply of disks, clearing sufficient free time to be able to work on it undisturbed. These practicalities will keep things like deadlines, other commitments, etc. in mind. At a lower level still, there will be the various components of the actions that are necessary to meet the commitment. For example, if the lecture is in another city – London, say – there will be all the elements that comprise the journey and preparation for it. Think of locking up the house in a hurry because one has calculated that one is at risk of being late for the train that will enable one to get to London in good time. 'Locking up the house in a hurry' itself has a vast number of component behaviours whose style will have been radically altered by the knowledge that one is in a hurry. Each of these components in turn will have numerous other components; for example, closing the door and turning the key will involve many elements of ballistic control of the limbs regulated by an overarching sense of their shared goal. Something as seemingly simple as 'getting to the station' will be made up of a myriad element, all of them custom-built to the occasion. When, for example, I walk from the car to the ticket office, I will have to take account of the day's particulars: the cars I have to avoid, the person who is coming in the opposite direction, the dog-dirt to be navigated round. And I must take account of these without losing sight of the general purpose towards which the components are directed – that of catching the train – or the singular purpose to which this instance of a general purpose, this train journey, is subordinated: that of giving a particular lecture in a particular place at a particular time. In the meantime, despite the overriding priority of giving the lecture, I cannot afford to be sealed off from either the rest of my life or the rest of the world: the phone will ring, I will remember something I haven't done, I will catch up on my other work on the train, I will remember to get a present I had wanted to purchase opportunistically in London, I will answer the query posed by the person opposite me in the train. Nevertheless – in the sea of relevant and irrelevant events, actions and sensations – I will still keep my overarching purpose alive. Moreover, the lecture engagement itself may relate to a higher level of purpose and goal in my life: my sense of who I am, of what my job is, what I think is important, of where I am going to in my life.

And so we have an immensely complex situation: many elements, at many different levels (ranging from the ballistic control of my arm as I reach for the door handle in my train-catching hurry to the aims and goals of my career), all converging in my continuing sense of what I ought to be doing at any given moment.

This should seem to present overwhelming difficulties to anyone who wished to explain ordinary consciousness in terms of the neural activity of the brain. If it seems to be less of a problem than it in fact is, this is in part because neuroscientists, when they think about neural activity, tend to forget that the abstract logic circuits (which can be multiplied indefinitely) have to be embodied in the wetware of the brain. Information-processing may (to refer back to Pinker) make 'flexible' demands for real estate; but it still does require real estate. After all, the neural theory of mind – even when it has been computerised – requires that all the different mental activities should be embedded in some way in the brain. This inescapable fact licenses us to think of this activity in an ordinary brain as a thousand sets of ripples in a pond created by the impact of a dense shower of hail and to imagine adding all sorts of internal sources of ripples. Neuroscientists are then required to explain how each ripple or a very complex set of ripples – such as those supposedly corresponding to a plan to give a particular lecture on a particular theme on a particular day – retains its separate identity. There seems no way of conceiving how this could be possible. The multidimensional lacework of a vast number of projects with their overarching structures and purposes and their subordinate elements, all of which draw upon a holistic world of interpenetrating meanings, presents a much greater threat to the neural theory of mind even than the 'combinatorial explosion' problem poses to the notion of the brain as acquiring its world through information-processing.

Someone might object that the analogy of ripples interfering with one another is unfounded because the neural circuits are insulated by myelin. But we can't appeal to electrical insulation when we talk – in the way, as we have noted, cognitive scientists do talk – of *patterns* of activity. It seems even more impossible if we remember that, ultimately, the nervous system will have to allow everything to come together in the moment of present consciousness, steeped in present meaning, but retaining its relation to a highly structured near and distant past and protending into an equally structured future of expectation, responsibility, timetable, ambition and life plan: so that the ballistic control of my arm in trying to lock the door in a hurry ultimately relates to my ambition to get my ideas accepted as true by a wider community of people.

The bluffing by people like Daniel Dennett who are wedded to computer analogies (of which more presently), which license them to talk of the functioning brain as sustaining a multiplicity of simultaneous virtual machines and nascent modules, clearly cannot answer this problem of the ultimate unity of the intelligent conscious moment: unity and distinctiveness. In this moment everything has to be brought together – so that I know where and who I am – but in it vast numbers of projects, programmes, duties, unscheduled reactions to unforeseen events, etc. must be kept distinct. To make things even more difficult, those distinct projects must be intelligently connected with many others as each contributes to the others' framework of possibility or acts as a constraint. My giving a lecture that I perceive as important explains my not getting drunk the previous night to celebrate – as I would most naturally do – Manchester United's failure to win the Premier Division.

The challenge to the neurophilosophers, then, is to explain how the distinct identity of a vast number of patterns of ripples could be retained while *at the same time* those patterns have to interact with and be open to one another. And this is the killer: my ordinary consciousness has to retain its global openness in order that I can enact my planned activities in a setting which will be effectively a sea of unplanned contingencies: for example, avoiding the bicyclist who might have killed me as I crossed the road in Manchester on my way to accomplishing the timetabled complex task of giving my lecture in London. A multitude of overarching and subordinate intentions, large- and small-scale, ranging from the micro-level of co-ordinated movement to the macro-level of life plans have to coexist and interact without merging into mush and at the same time be able to take account of the huge kaleidoscope of the unforeseen particulars of every actual moment during which real plans are enacted.

I have already indicated how complex and subtle these interactions are. But let me illustrate with a real-life example just how much more complex they may become. When, the other week, I had some difficulty getting the key to turn in the front door and I was indeed anxious about missing a train taking me to London to give a lecture on consciousness, I thought of this as an example I might use of the interaction between the micro and the macro and here I am using it. I wanted to note this example down as soon as I though of it and the only quiet place was the station buffet. I didn't want to buy a coffee as my train was due in a couple of minutes. However, I was conscious that the buffet was quite full and I would have to legitimise my use of a table in the eyes of the rather large assistant who had some months before expressed concern about my occupancy of a seat when I had not purchased anything to be consumed on the premises. I therefore bought a packet of biscuits which I did not want but which I could carry away. I then thought of presenting this packet of biscuits during the lecture as (to quote the jotting on the Post-It I wrote on in the buffet) 'a startling tribute to the exquisitely organised, but open to the winds, structure of my consciousness and to the fact that my ordinary intelligence is quite unlike, and unimitatable by, the co-operation of automata portrayed in contemporary neuropsychology'.

There is a problem, therefore, of modelling, in electrical ripples, the fact that we bring together, and yet keep separate and apart, so many things. Compared with the extraordinary openness of my consciousness necessary for me to enact even a relatively simple task in the real, unpredictable outside world of our multitudinously engaged minds, even the most powerful all-purpose SuperCray seems almost laughably narrow in its dedication. Everything has to be brought together in this moment – so that I know where (in the widest sense) and who (in the deepest sense) I am – but it must *at the very same time* keep myriads of projects, actions, micro-projects, micro-actions, distinct.

We tend to overlook the complexity of our own lives when we think about the neurophysiological basis of consciousness. I would go further: neurophilosophy seems half-way plausible only if it is predicated on a desperately impoverished account of our many-layered, multi-agenda-ed, infinitely complex but wonderfully structured and organised selves. Dementia is salutary in this regard by being an indirect reminder of the fact that to be human is to be explicitly extended in and across time; and this connectedness over time has to be *sustained across an extraordinary interdigitation of preoccupations, themes, locations, situations.*[10] We do not require continuous summative recall to secure psychological connectedness and preservation of identity but we do require sufficient recall to give a context to the present, to give it temporal depth – the implicit depth of recognition and the explicit depth of specific reference back. It is impossible to imagine how this could be embodied in the ripple-tossed pond of the brain, and how, in addition, this brain could sustain the act of deliberate recall of an episodic memory – housing the recaller, the act of recall and that which is recalled.

The mystery of the first person

This question of the open but ring-fenced unity of consciousness itself opens on to an even deeper problem: that of accounting for the fact that there is such a thing as the first person – the me, here, now – to which the boundless variety of experience is ultimately referred. Without such a unifying element – based upon what Kant called the unity of apperception, and rather unfortunately described as 'the I think that accompanies all my perceptions' and which linked the moments through some kind of transcendental ego – the brain would simply be a colloidal suspension of not-quite-haunted modules – which is how the cognitive scientist seems to present it. The third-person neural activity of the brain as seen by neuroscience can provide no explanation for the unified Tallis who is putting together this critique of the neuroscientific explanation of the consciousness of Tallis and his conspecifics.

I have raised the question of the first person in the context of the mystery of the coherence of my consciousness – of my world and of myself as an agent in it. But this in its turn connects with a deeper mystery: the origin of the sense of me, here, now; of the suffering agent, the responsible creature who is a viewpoint on the world. It is no use saying that *my* brain gives me the sense of me here now because it is *my* brain and it is here and now: looked at through the third person materialistic eyes of conventional neuroscience, the brain is just an object in the world, like a brick or a pebble, and it has no intrinsic ownership and therefore offers no basis for the fundamental sense that I am this thing here and now. The difference between the ionic activity in the brain and the atomic jigging in the pebble does not yield this ownership out of which arises the sense of being this thing here and now. And yet this sense is required if I am to have the feeling that I am here now, that I am, to use Heidegger's phrase, a being whose being is an issue for itself. The fact that things matter to this brain cannot be accommodated within the neurophysiologist's account of the brain. More generally, mattering has no place in the materialist world picture of the identity theorist.

These are very deep waters and the thoughts they give rise to are elusive. Suffice it to say, there is no basis in the brain for the unified consciousness and the connected fundamental intuition of self: the sense that *I am this thing* and that *I am here*. There is nothing in the brain to make it my brain; it cannot underpin the first person, the viewpoint, the deixis, that make the ordinary moments of life a matter of me, here, now. Such indexicality has no place in the materialist world-picture of the identity theorist. And this connects back with something that I alluded to at the beginning of this chapter: the folk observation that I (my consciousness, my mind) am where my brain is. This 'where I am' cannot be taken for granted as a given. There is nothing in the brain, as neuroscientifically construed, to provide a foundation for this 'where I am', for the viewpoint that results in my brain (or at least my body) assuming the position of the 0, 0, 0 point in the Cartesian grid or the 0, 0, 0 of personal or hodological space. The third-person world of science offers no basis for the first-person viewpoint; in short for viewpoint *per se*. The folk observation I alluded to at the outset – that my mind is where my brain is – could just as well be turned on its head: my brain is where my mind is. For without consciousness, there is no 'where', no 'here' for my brain to be 'at'. And my brain is ownerless.

The fugitive thoughts that arise from here seem to me to be thinkable about once a fortnight. To return to slightly shallower waters, it is interesting to gauge just how far we are from comprehending the ordinary fact of the coherence of the self in neural terms – a coherence back-lit by its disintegration in dementia. This is betrayed by the eccentricity of some recent theories advanced by some extremely respectable people. One of the frontrunners is the idea that the global nature of consciousness is made possible by the micro tubules in neurones which, because of their peculiar biophysical properties, are able to host quantum coherence (Bose-Einstein condensates) which, it is conjectured, can extend across an appreciable part of the entire brain.[11] Unfortunately, this model – in which an entire system containing a large number of particles behaves like a quantum state of a single particle and thus provides the basis for the unitary sense of the self – would, even if it were coherent itself, fall foul of two facts: that microtubules are present in many human and non-human biological tissues that are not conscious; and that quantum coherence occurs outside of living tissue.

The language of neuromythology to the rescue (see chapter 2)

All of this would seem to force us to the conclusion that ordinary, intelligent consciousness cannot be due to activity in the brain; or, to put it at its most charitable, neural activity is an inadequate explanation of mental activity. And yet this is a message that has certainly not got through to many neuroscientists and their neurophilosophical fellow travellers. Why is this? Because they speak to themselves in a language that conceals from them the barrenness of their explanations. The language of neuromythology is what permits the neurophilosopher to cross the mind/brain barrier without solving the problems that I have alluded to. I shall refer to this language only briefly because it is dealt with at length in Chapter 2.

The key step is to redescribe the mind in mechanical terms – and so remain within the materialist and even biological framework of neuroscience – but to think of the mechanisms as operating like a machine (which has purposes and functions) and, moreover, a very special sort of machine – a computer – which can be readily spoken of in highly anthropomorphic, or mindly, terms. Brainy minds and mindly brains meet in the idea of the computer; the mind is the computational activity of the brain; or brain is to mind as hardware is to software.

Computers are very obliging models because, for a long time, it has been traditional to use anthropomorphic terms in describing their functions, however, humble they are. For example, we talk about a pocket calculator having a memory, or executing a series of instructions or mobilising its logic. This is fine, because it is not likely to lead us to believe that it also experiences nostalgia, is subserviently obedient or wonderfully rational. In short, the transferred epithets – transferred from the human users to the small plastic object they use – are harmless. They are less harmless when they are used in neuroscience, because then we start taking the terms in both literal and metaphorical senses.

In order to get across the mind–brain barrier, all you have to do is take two easy steps:

a) describe the activity of the brain in terms of the functions of a computer;
b) describe the computer in 'mindly' terms.

The oscillation of terms between the mental and the physical realms lies at the root of the myth that modern neurological science has somehow explained, or will explain, or has advanced our understanding of, what consciousness truly is. Of all the terms that straddle the mind/brain barrier, the most important is 'information'. When Stephen Pinker preaches the Official Doctrine that mind is the 'information function' of the brain, he has solved the mind–brain problem without making one discovery or conceptual advance. Janus-faced words like 'memory' and 'information' – which look in the direction of both man and machine – dissolve the very problems that philosophically are most interesting. In truth, neurologically-based, biological and computational explanations of consciousness begin beyond the point where the real questions are to be found.

I believe that the progress neuroscientists imagine that they have made across the mind/brain barrier – so that the brainy mind and the mindly brain merge into one another – has nothing to do with any empirical observations and everything to do with the presuppositions, half-hidden because embedded in the terminology they use, that inform their discourse about those observations. A truly illuminating account of the relationship between mind and brain would not be one that had 'information' on both sides of the mind brain barrier: it would explain how physical energy (which is all that there is in the material world of which the brain is a part) was transformed into information, knowledge, consciousness: how light energy became the object of sight; how light (which does not know itself) became the seen, the visible world.

Provisional conclusion: cognitive science does not and cannot explain mind

In the absence of such an explanation, one has to stand firm and say that there is as yet no satisfactory account of the relationship between brain and mind and that current research and the current neurocomputational framework for research is not taking us anywhere. Indeed, the complexities thrown up by cognitive psychologists' own analysis of relatively simple mental functions compound the challenge by revealing the massive complexities that stand in the way of materialist or computational accounts of mind – complexities that, even at a surface level, are evident to anyone who reflects for more than a minute or two on the way we have to function in ordinary life. For my money, no multiplication of automata forming co-operatives will be able to replace the conscious human being knowing what he or she is doing: there is something called 'conscious understanding' that goes beyond a mass of modules, notwithstanding that being able to do what one intends – and even formulating intentions – requires, is built upon, the smooth working of various automatic systems which lies beyond the reach of consciousness. That conscious understanding is necessary not merely to meet our need for an intuitively satisfactory account of the processes underlying ordinary behaviour but also to get the outputs that are needed. Some neurophilosophers – Pinker, for example – aware that we cannot explain qualia, would like to separate 'cognitive functions' such as intelligence from sentience because they recognise that sentience is not yet explicable in neural terms:

> At least for now, we have no scientific purchase on the special extra ingredient that gives rise to sentience. As far as scientific explanation goes, it might as well not exist. It's not just that claims about sentience are perversely untestable; it's that testing them would make no difference to anything anyway. Our incomprehension of sentience does not impede our understanding of how the mind works at least.
>
> (p. 147)

While this is better than Dennett's attempts to deny the reality of subjective experiences, or at least of qualia, dismissing them as cognitive illusions, it is still somewhat unsatisfactory. Though Pinker's position is consistent with, indeed necessary to support, the extraordinary claim that 'Thought and thinking ... are mechanical processes that can be studied' (p. 131), its inadequacy will be apparent from what has already been said. Not only is to leave out qualia, effectively, to omit the contents of consciousness – and so reduce the mind to a set of mechanical functions – but it also makes it impossible to see how the typical activities of conscious human beings are achieved. We cannot make sense of intelligent behaviour without assuming that intelligent behavers are conscious of what they are doing. From which it follows that we cannot 'park up' trying to understand sentience for the present (because it is too difficult) and proceed to investigate intelligence without it.

The observations made earlier strongly suggest that on the contrary we cannot begin to get a handle on intelligence without assuming, and hence explaining, sentience: in short, intelligent behaviour requires *knowing what one is doing*. (Only to a neurophilosopher could that seem disputable and reasserting it a revelation.) All the computing power in the world, any number of mysteriously co-operative automata, would be insufficient to stand in for the necessary sense of 'knowing what I am doing' – which, at the very least, would require that intelligence was informed by sentience. Sentience is the first and not the last requirement of intelligence and to try to understand the latter while not taking into account, never mind understanding, the former, is like trying to build a house by starting at the second floor. It may be desirable, methodologically, to set aside the problem of sentience because it seems more difficult in principle to investigate neuroscientifically; but this does not reduce the problems that arise out of having done so.

Sentience, is the first, not the last, problem (or mystery) of psychology. It is not merely the most difficult of the problems of consciousness or mind; it is also the pivotal one and addressing it cannot be postponed until one has solved the 'easier' problems such as those pertaining to 'cognitive functions' like intelligence, memory, thinking, etc. When we humans deploy our intelligence, we do so in a wider context, in a complex framework which may be captured by the phrase, 'knowing what we are doing' (or trying to do). It is impossible to explain how the automata that are mobilised in the service of those ends are requisitioned without reference to that context.

It would seem, therefore, that nothing of what we know about the brain, or, indeed, of what we are likely to discover about it using present research paradigms, would account for the status that it enjoys among neuroscientists as that in virtue of which we are conscious; its unique status as a piece of matter in virtue of which matter discloses itself and becomes the contents of the consciousness of the individual identified with the brain. Nor is there anything in neural activity that would explain how all this disclosing is organised into the unified moment of consciousness. Nor is there anything that can account for the extremely elaborate, unified, many-layered multiplicity that is the necessary substrate of and background to the ordinary acts of the ordinary human agent, acts which relate to numerous hierarchies of overarching and subordinate frameworks of intention. Nor is there likely to be.

Neurophilosophy: separating the neuroscience from the neuromythology

And that would seem to be that. And yet, and yet, I, too, am a neuroscientist of sorts and a humble toiler in the field where many individuals much more talented than myself are working, thinking, speculating and experimenting. And the truth is, I don't *really* – or fully – believe either that the mind has nothing to do with the brain or that scientists have made no progress in understanding the physical conditions of the mind.

How, then, am I to reconcile the warring views within me? Or am I condemned for ever to have a split mind over the nature of the relationship between brain and mind, with my left hemisphere believing that the brain is the basis of the mind and that our advancing brain science is helping us to explain mind, and my right hemisphere saying that mind cannot possibly be explained by the neural activity of certain parts of the brain and that we are no nearer to understanding the nature of mind or consciousness than we were when Descartes suggested that mind and matter were connected through the pineal gland.

Is there a way out of this neuro-antinomy? One escape route would be to propose that, while neural activity cannot explain why there is consciousness, it can explain the shaping of consciousness, or even the fact that consciousness has specific contents and what those contents are. While my brain being in London does not explain why I am conscious of anything at all, perhaps it does explain why, given that I *am* conscious, my consciousness is of a bit of London rather than, say, of a bit of Manchester.

This escape route leads straight into yet more difficult problems. For example, it requires us to accept the notion of contentless consciousness which is, as it were, coloured in by the activity of the nervous system. This is somewhat difficult to grasp. Moreover, it does not explain how the nervous system interacts with this blank, general, consciousness-of-nothing in particular, this uncommitted awareness, to commit it to particular sentient experience. Nor, most damagingly from the viewpoint of those who are serious about trying to understand consciousness, does it suggest how this interaction might be investigated.

Another, seemingly slightly less vulnerable escape route is to invoke the distinction between a necessary and a sufficient condition. A necessary condition of something happening is the set of circumstances that has to be present in order for it to take place. In the absence of those circumstances, it will not take place. The presence of those conditions, however, will not guarantee that it will take place. It is necessary for me to be in a particular street in order to be knocked down by a bus in that street. But being in that street is not a sufficient condition of being knocked down by a bus, even by a bus in that street. A sufficient condition, self-evidently, is the sum of those circumstances which, if present, will guarantee that the event will take place. One could use this distinction to argue that a normal functioning brain, producing certain ('normal') neural activity in response external stimuli or as a result of normal quasi-endogenous activity is a necessary condition for mental phenomena, for normal consciousness, but it does not of itself produce that consciousness in the sense either of causing it or of being identical with it. To connect this with our earlier discussion about the relationship between where the brain is at and where the mind or self is at: my brain has to be in London for me genuinely or directly or truly to experience being in London; but this is not a sufficient condition of my experiencing London. The closest analogy would be with a radio: a normally functioning radio is not enough to ensure the reception of programmes; there has to be a radio station within range transmitting programmes. (The same escape would seem, incidentally, to apply to some aspects of the evolutionary theory of mind: of course, mental activity has somehow to be adapted to support the activities necessary to ensure survival in a hostile natural world. Evolutionary forces and the demands of the natural world do not, however, explain how consciousness could have emerged in the physical world. Evolutionary advantage, therefore, is a necessary but not a sufficient condition to explain the structure and functions of mind.)

But this escape route is actually fraught with difficulties, even dangers. First of all, while it might account for lesion (negative) experiments, it does not seem to account for stimulation (positive), Penfield-type experiments, in which the active nervous system seems able to work nicely on its own in producing consciousness. In other words, neural activity seems to be both a necessary and a sufficient condition of consciousness. It might be argued that such false experiences are – like hallucinations – parasitic upon, and depend upon, a track record of normally produced experiences arising out of encounters with real external things. In other words, that they have as it were parasitic or borrowed mentality or intentionality. Stimulation experiments, for example, can re-evoke memories of experiences had by a normally functioning brain, but they could not implant properly formed experiences – with all their holistic links – in a brain that had been totally deprived of experiences through the normal routes. I am not clear how strong this argument is.

A more worrying concern is prompted by the very analogy that I used to illustrate the difference between a necessary and a sufficient condition – that of the radio receiver. This would seem to suggest that the nervous system is merely a tuned device to receive consciousness from elsewhere – from some kind of 'within' in the case of volitions and from without in the case of perceptual experience. The former would be a return to a homuncular kind of thinking that we all shrink from, the latter to a kind of mystical thinking that would bear a rather unnerving resemblance to the lunatic new age ideas of certain thinkers (I shall withhold their names for the sake of their families) who have argued that, for example, memories are picked up by 'morphic resonance' between the brain and a kind of ether in which the impressions of the past are held. One of the reasons why such mystical notions are unattractive is that they do not suggest any kinds of research programmes, even less specific experiments. They can only be dogmatically asserted or equally dogmatically rejected. Perhaps making sense of the relationship between the brain and consciousness will require an epistemological and ontological rethink.

The requirement for an epistemological rethink – for a new theory of knowledge that goes beyond the idea that knowledge itself is based upon experiences arising out of energy impinging upon the excitable tissue in our bodies – is, surely, not surprising. All the things that neuroscientists have discovered about consciousness, or think they have discovered, have been based upon observations that amount to a very small sample of our consciousness. It would be extremely surprising if this small part of consciousness were able to dig beneath (all) consciousness to discover the basis of the latter; or if, on the strength of a relatively few perceptions (even high-quality expensive, specialised ones such as are enjoyed in neuroscience laboratories), we were able to find and understand the basis of all perception. The belief, underpinning the neurophilosophical expectation that the basis of mind is a matter for empirical investigation with our minds, is intuitively implausible for all its tenacity. And it is connected with the assumption – which I hope by now will be recognised as ill-founded – that our world, ourselves as viewpoints sustaining personal worlds, could be housed in, and explained by, the functioning of a small something in that world.

As for an ontological rethink, in *The Explicit Animal* I expressed the view that we would need a new ontology to make sense of the relation between matter and mind, or between brain matter and consciousness; that we should abandon not only dualism (which leads to all the problems of Cartesian epistemology) but also materialism (which is the implicit framework of much contemporary neuroscience and in particular the neural theory of consciousness). As others have done before me, I floated a third possibility: a neutral monism that took as ontologically foundational the category of *presence* (which spans both subject and object, perceiver and object of perception). I also, regrettably, made the routine, facile appeal to the new physics (in which the ghost of mind haunts even the microphysical world, being the necessary condition of the wave-packet collapse of otherwise indeterminate quanta).

None of this is very satisfactory. Nevertheless, I do feel sure that the founding myth of neuromythology – that conscious experience is created out of the impingement of various sorts of physical energy upon the excitable transducers of the sensory system and that the evoked neural activity is identical with that experience – must be set aside. That, in other words, our whole approach to the consciousness of embodied creatures such as human beings must be radically revised. And this is all to the good; for neurophilosophy seems to require a drastically impoverished account of our own nature as wholly mysterious animals, at once a part of nature and at the same time uniquely distanced from it – as reflected in our ability to articulate it.

But all is not doom and gloom. While thinkers are trying to formulate the new framework for thinking about perception, etc., neuroscientists may be reassured that what they are doing is far from worthless or unilluminating. Even if they are not discovering how the mind works, or how it is constructed in the brain, they are defining with ever-increasing precision the conditions under which normal experience and volition are possible: the necessary but not the sufficient conditions. And, for my money, as a clinician concerned to re-create or encourage those necessary conditions in patients from whom they have been withdrawn, that is good enough. Metaphysics it is not; supremely worthwhile it certainly is. It just needs to recognise its limits, so that good science is not discredited by bad philosophy and scientism causes scientists to be accused of 'single vision and Newton's sleep'.

Notes

1. The best of these are: Patricia Churchland, *Neurophilosophy* (Cambridge, Mass., MIT Press, 1986); Paul M. Churchland, *Matter and Consciousness: a Contemporary Introduction to the Philosophy of Mind* (Cambridge, Mass.: MIT Press, rev. edition, 1988); Daniel C. Dennett, *Consciousness Explained* (Harmondsworth: Penguin, 1991); Steven Pinker, *How the Mind Works* (Harmondsworth: Allen Lane, Penguin, 1997).

2. The curious mixture of claims and disclaimers in Pinker's Preface is worth noting:

   > When we face a problem, we may not know its solution, but we have insight, increasing knowledge and an inkling of what we are looking for. When we face a mystery, however, we can only stare in wonder and bewilderment ... I wrote this book because dozens of mysteries of the mind, from mental images to romantic love, have recently been upgraded to problems (though there are still some mysteries, too!)

3. Raymond Tallis, *The Explicit Animal: A Defence of Human Consciousness* (London: Macmillan, 1991).

4. Paul Churchland, op. cit., p. 149.

5. See also the entry LEVELS in Chapter 2.
6. Colin McGinn, 'Can We Solve the Mind/Body Problem?', *Mind* (1989), 350–66.
7. Discussed in Raymond Tallis, 'The Impossibility of Neurally-mediated Disclosure: Why Neural Theories of Consiousness Will Always Fail'. Submitted for publication.
8. Lewis Wolpert, *The Unnatural Nature of Science* (London: Faber, 1992).
9. Stephen P. Stich, *From Folk Psychology to Cognitive Science: the Case against Belief* (Cambridge, Mass.: MIT Press, 1983).
10. Discussed in Raymond Tallis, 'A Dark Mirror: Reflections on Dementia', *News from the Republic of Letters* (1997), 12–16.
11. See Roger Penrose, *Shadows of the Mind: A Search for the Missing Science of Consciousness* (Oxford University Press, 1994), pp. 367–9.

4

(That) I Am This (Thing): Reflections on Deixis, Explicitness and the Tautology of the Self

The thing I am trying to grasp is the me that is trying to grasp it.

Traditional

Yet, in every possible case, being, you will agree, is still strange. To be in some particular way is stranger still. It's even embarrassing.

Dialogue: A New Fragment Concerning M. Teste,
In: M. Teste, translated by Jackson Matthews
(Routledge and Kegan Paul, 1973, p. 64)

Introduction

Philosophy begins, as the ancient philosophers reminded those who had become too caught up in technicalities and the secondary joys of polemic, with astonishment; and it should remain bathed in a nimbus of astonishment, if it is to continue to be philosophy. And yet astonishment is not enough. It is often vulnerably expressed: it seems either to state the obvious rather badly; or worse, to move at the double from the valid but obvious to the non-obvious and invalid. In this essay, I want to reflect on some of the intuitions most commonly served up by my own, perhaps rather peculiar, astonishment and try to unpack from those intuitions some non-obvious but valid conclusions that may be of relevance to some present-day disputes about the place of subjectivity in the objective world and the relations of priority between language and extra-linguistic reality, though I shall scarcely touch explicitly upon either of these huge issues here. My aim will be a modest one: to put into italics some large facts – too large, really, to be called facts but I know of no better word – about us. What follows will not be an argument in the usual manner of a philosophical essay but a meditation; or, to put it less charitably, a circling round a large truth or large realisation that defies expression.

Some exemplary astonishments

A glimpse of a girl's neck

The other day, on a hot bus, I sat behind a girl with her hair drawn up into a pony tail. This left her neck, emphatically denuded by the sunshine, exposed to my gaze. As I looked at the shadow cast by her sternomastoid muscle over the anterior triangle of her neck and observed the soft pulsing of the carotid artery, I had an overwhelming sense, beyond that of the girl's bodily presence to me, of her presence to herself, mediated by this, her body. She *was*, in some sense I found difficult to characterise, this body. And I was reminded of the extent to which *I* was, more or less, *my* body. I was reminded, that is to say, of the material tautology of my own existence.

Glimpse of my hand

I would have been tempted to state that I *was* my own body *tout court*, were it not for a variety of experiences I have had, some of which seem to cut much ice in my discussions with myself, even if they might not carry much weight in a more public metaphysical dispute.

Like Sartre's Antoine Roquentin[1] and Rilke's Malte Laurid Brigg,[2] I have been prone, from time to time, to catch sight of my own right hand. This is a strange experience; for the hand seems at once to be deeply familiar and quite unfamiliar. My hand is so close to me that it does not seem eccentric to count it as part of me; to be regarded as belonging with my very own self. And yet there are times when it seems distant from me, and my relationship to it external and accidental. I see my hand as an object (which happens to be attached to the rest of my body) or even (when, as I contemplate it, I set it in motion), as a small animal. Naturally, like most other people, I do not *see* my hand most of the time, because it is usually dissolved in my purposes, assimilated into myself through the actions which fulfil my intentions, or simply out of sight – and hence out of mind. But even under such circumstances, it may present as an entity in its own right and somewhat separate from me. If it is numbed, injured or deformed, then, of course, it may be caused quite abruptly to precipitate out of the solvent of my preoccupation and busy-ness.

Catching sight of my face

There is, of course, a huge literature on the relation between the self and the body. The most interesting and subtle (because it does not waste any time on a Cartesian dualism) is that of the existential phenomenologists such as Maurice Merleau-Ponty.[3] One has to be a least some kind of fool, as J.L. Austin said, to rush in where so many angels have trodden already. I do not therefore intend to dwell on the relationships between the subjective, the instrumental and the objective body, or to try to tease out the complex relationships between how we are related to our foot when we are using it to play football, trying to steer it into a sock or begging for it to be chopped off because of an agonising, chronic ulcer. But let me try to deepen the discussion a bit by considering the face – my face.

I look at my face in the mirror. It seems more intimately me, it goes more deeply into myself, is less of a mere possession than, say, my foot. I might fail to recognise my foot from a photograph but, unless I was seriously brain-damaged, I would always recognise my face.[4] Moreover, if I were to point to my face in a photograph, I would most likely to say 'That's me' whereas if I pointed to my photographed foot, I might well say 'That's mine'. This special relationship to the face may be in part due to the privileged status of the gaze. A kind of closed circuit is established when I look at myself in the mirror: the living eyes see a reflection that looks back – and into – the living eyes; the gaze gazes upon a gaze that gazes upon the gaze; the gaze and the gazed-upon gaze are intersleeving, looking in and looking out, and yet are identical. And there are other reasons why glimpsing my face seems to be glimpsing me: the face is that by which I am most often and most readily identified by others; it is what they think of when they think of me; and it is that by which I most immediately express myself. For these, and other reasons, we think of the face as being nearer than any other part of the body to the seat of the self. (This intuition of the privileged relationship of the face to the self antedates the discovery of the putative special relationship between the brain immediately behind the face and consciousness. Indeed, it has nothing to do with the greater proximity of the face to the brain; after all, the brain is closer than the face is to the brain and we find it difficult to identify ourselves with our brains.)

The identification of the self with the face is, however, incomplete: I still refer to 'my' face; I can, as it were, step back from it and judge it. It is an object, or surface, that may please or (more likely) displease me, when I think of the effect of its appearance on others, when I find it ugly or beautiful, stupid or intelligent, etc. As Eliot's Prufrock observed, 'we prepare a face to meet the faces that we meet'.

Our bodies, ourselves

In short, we are and we are not our bodies. There is no doubt that it is the destiny of that girl on the bus in some sense to be that body on the bus and it is the destiny of this man, me, in some sense to be this body. This is at least true in a comparative sense: I am much more this body (the body named Raymond Tallis) than anyone else is and I am much more this body than I am any other body. These are understatements: that girl is not in the slightest bit Raymond Tallis's body and Raymond Tallis is not in the slightest bit that girl's body. Our lives, our destinies, our meanings, are caught up in the destiny, the composition, the vicissitudes of one particular body:

a) At a biological level, I live out the requirements that must be met if this body is to survive and prosper, and I experience these requirements as my hungers and my appetites and my sufferings and my delights.

b) My status as an agent is mediated through this body: it is through my body that I bring about these actions that are directly or indirectly attributed to me.

c) Furthermore, my body is not only the seat of my agency; it is also the location of my viewpoint, the centre of my field of perception.[5] (Which should not be confused with a kind of 0, 0, 0 point of objective or geometric, Cartesian space: it is more like the centre of what Kurt Lewin called 'hodological space' – the space of need and history and journeying that surrounds the engaged agent.)

d) I am where my body is. My presence is, most literally and fundamentally, the presence of my body; all other modes of my presence are parasitic upon or derivative from this.

e) In summary, my being 'here' is my body's being here. My body lives my days and sleeps my nights. My body's decay is my decay, its demise my demise.

The possessive ('my' body), however, captures the ineradicable ambiguity of my relationship to my body. The adjective 'my' both connects me with my body and disconnects me from it: it suggests a distance between what I might call my 'self' (try to ignore this further possessive) and the body that carries my name. But this distance is quite different from, is considerably less than, that between myself and what are more conventionally understood as my possessions. I cannot don and doff my body. When I 'sell' my body for physical labour, I do not then continue a discarnate existence; no more does a man or woman who sells his or her body for sexual purposes. It remains mine – unless I am killed – and more, and closer, than 'mine'. It is not as unbrokenly close to me as my thoughts are but it is closer than the closeness of any other object or any other person. I could not fail to know which body was mine:[6] that this body is mine is a presupposition so deeply engrained that I cannot seriously question it. This is reflected, though not entirely clearly, in the fact that I could not fail, as a result of being uncertain whose hand it was, to know whether a pain felt in this hand (my hand) was my pain or somebody else's. (I could not, it goes without saying, feel a pain without knowing whose pain it was.) It is reflected more directly in the fact that I could not fail to know to which body I should ascribe a pain I felt.

Why am I dwelling on these obvious things? Because I wish to underline a tension in our relation to our own bodies – one which some philosophers, notably Marcel, have seen reflecting the wider tensions of the relations between having and being.[7] Our identification of ourselves with our own bodies is not as complete as our identification of others' selves with their bodies. Your body seems more inescapably you than my body seems to be me. (I cannot as clearly see the distances between you and your body as I can experience the distances between me and my body or between me and a particular part of my body.) Yes, I may intuit you, or your consciousness, or your thoughts, as being inside, as being hidden within, your body. But this intuition is intermittent. Correspondingly, I do not as readily separate you from the physical appearance of your body as I separate myself from the physical appearance of my body.

Nevertheless, despite all these 'inner' distances between ourselves and our bodies, there is something inescapable in our relationship to our own body – as inescapable as the relationship we perceive between others and their bodies – that somehow makes it right, valid, to feel a certain astonishment: a surprise that, in some residual, ineluctable sense, I *am* this body.

It is this astonishment I wish to explore at some length.

That I am this thing

Astonishment at being this thing

Looking at the girl on the bus made me aware of her being destined to be a particular thing, her being obliged to live out her life, herself, through a particular material entity. More profoundly, it made me astonished that this was true of myself. Even if I distance myself from my body and claim that it is not quite accurate to say that 'I am this body' it remains true to say 'I am this (thing)', that I am a certain particular.

Why should this be a cause of astonishment? Surely it is less astonishing that I should be a particular thing in a particular place than that I should be everywhere or nowhere, everything or nothing in particular. Maybe. But the reflection that one is a particular thing awakens two counter-factual possibilities:

a)   that I might not have existed at all;
b)   that I might have been some other thing: someone, or even something, else.

These two possibilities correspond to two not entirely idle questions:

a)   Why do I exist at all?
b)   Why am I this thing rather than something else?

The sense in which these questions are idle, the deeper sense in which they are not idle, and the deepest sense of all, in which they *are*, after all, idle but not empty, are the true themes of this paper.

What it is to be a certain particular in the way that I am it

Let us stick, for the present, with the following, unsatisfactory formulation: 'I am this body' (where the phrase 'this body' refers to the body that is named by the unique name, functioning as a rigid designator, 'Raymond Tallis'). The manner of my being this body is quite different from the manner in which a particular pebble is a pebble and in important respects similar to the way in which the girl on the bus was (and is) her body. (Or at least I am inclined to think so: this is one of the most pervasive and fundamental givens of my picture of the world.) Let me try to capture something of this manner of being my body and how this differs from a pebble's way of being a pebble.

Of myself, I am inclined to say that I am conscious of my body, that I am conscious of being that (or this) body, that I am conscious of it, at times, as *my* body, conscious above all, most importantly and most mysteriously, that there is (to use T.L.S. Sprigge's formulation[8]) something corresponding to what it is like to be the body that I am. There is, in short, something corresponding to 'what it is like to be this body' and to the contingent fact that this body is what I *have* to be, in the sense of being compelled or obliged to be it.[9] It is, as it were, as if my body had an aspect that went beyond the outer aspect: an aspect for itself that is distinct from its aspect for others. This is also true of the girl and her body. It is not, however, true of a pebble: the pebble has certain objective and visible features; but there is nothing corresponding to 'what it is like to be' the pebble – its hardness, its heaviness, its opacity, its size – but the pebble itself does not experience those features.

It is not merely a question of my being ignorant of what it is like to be a pebble – as if this were due to a failure of my knowledge, my imagination or my empathy. No: there is simply *nothing* corresponding to what it is like to be a pebble. The pebble does not, for example, experience its own hardness – any more than it experiences itself as being (actually) quite soft or as being neither hard nor soft but as 'just right' or 'medium' or 'ordinary'. So there is nothing to know, to imagine or to empathise with. The girl and I are different from the pebble in this crucial regard: there *is* something that corresponds to what it is like to be me and to what it is like to be her; and because this is not directly visible (unlike my body or her body) we are inclined to think of this something as an 'inner' aspect, hidden inside the outward and visible features of the body. It is, however, perhaps more helpful to think of this 'something' in this way: the pebble exists and that is the end of it; but my existence and the existence of the girl are explicit. We suffer or enjoy our respective beings explicitly. The post-Hegelian existentialist philosophers would put it this way:[10] the pebble has only an in-itself; whereas the girl and myself have bodies that not only exist in-themselves but also exist for-themselves or (not quite the same thing) for us. In so far as we are our bodies, so our bodies are the for-itself we are. I repeat: *in so far as* we are our bodies.

One existentialist philosopher, Heidegger, has an especially illuminating formula which captures the distinction between the pebble on the one hand, and the girl and myself on the other. He speaks of Dasein or 'being-there': Dasein is 'that being whose being is an issue for itself'. And so my being – the being of this living body and its world – is a matter of concern for itself, a subject for anxiety, joy, fear; a burden and a privilege. It is important to be careful here: although most of these anxieties, concerns, joys, etc. are mediated through the body – they are connected, directly or indirectly, with what may be described as the 'biological needs' of the body and reflect those needs directly or indirectly – it is wrong to interpret Dasein in this narrow sense; or to think that what is made explicit in the explicit being enjoyed or suffered by the girl and myself, but not by the pebble, is simply the body. For, as already noted, our relationship with our body is only patchily one of absolute identification: there is a sense in which my appendix (whose being I do not enjoy explicitly) is not part of my being (or not unless it is inflamed, anyway); and there is a sense, which we have already explored, in which my hand, and even my face, are not always or entirely dissolved into the being that I enjoy or suffer or just am.

Mindful of the distances between ourselves and our bodies, we may be tempted to be a bit (but only a bit) more neutral and say, simply, that 'I am one thing; the girl is another; and the pebble is a third'. And we can add that the way in which the girl and I are our respective things is different from the way in which the pebble simply *is*. (We shall return to that difference in a minute.) Of myself, I would say, 'I am *this* thing' and of the girl that 'She is *that* thing'.

Expressing matters thus is still not entirely satisfactory; for it is too easy to translate 'thing' into 'body'. The very word 'thing' tends to suggest, if not a material object, at least something in the third person. And the important thing about myself and the girl (and it is not true of the pebble) is that we exist in the first as well as the third person – or that we exist in differentiated (first and third) persons. (It is probably wrong to say of the pebble that it exists in the third person. The third person exists only by contrast – it presupposes a world of differentiated persons. In a universe composed solely of pebbles and material objects like them, no such differentiation would be possible. If the pebble seems to exist in the third person, it does so only courtesy of beings such as myself and the girl who sustain the distinction between first and third persons. The 'third personalisation' of the pebble is an external attribution.)

I would like, therefore, to shed 'thing' for a moment (and, consequently, the body), though I shall return to it in due course. I want to formulate more uncommitedly the astonishment I felt on the bus, as follows: 'I am this; and she is that.' Most of my astonishment focused on the first part: 'I am this.' Formulating the astonishment in this way, which does not make any assumption about the kind of particular I am, makes it possible to unpack from the astonishment the intuitions that it seems to awaken, without the distraction of arguments about the extent to which she and I are material beings. It makes more clearly visible the counter-factual possibilities:

a) that I might not have existed at all;
b) that I might have been some other particular (or collection or series of particulars) than the one currently designated by 'Raymond Tallis'.

Meditating on counter-factuals

That I might never have existed

All particular objects seem contingent. As Roquentin says, 'To exist is simply *to be there*; what exists appears, lets itself be *encountered*, but you can never *deduce* it' (*Nausea*, op. cit., p. 188). That book over there on my desk might not have been written, published and issued in that particular copy. And so, likewise, I might not have been. I can be more precise about the circumstances in which I might not have been: my parents might never have met; or, just to push the point home, one or the other might have died before reaching the age at which they could reproduce.

I might not have been this [thing, body, person ...]

The accident that I am at all seems to be compounded by the further accident that I am *this*. I am one particular rather than another. Of all the particulars that I know of, I happen to be this one. It falls to me to carry the burden of being this particular. Reflecting on this brings us back to the body; for among the consequences that follow from my being a particular – indeed, the largest class of such consequences – is that I am obliged and privileged to live the vicissitudes and delights of a particular body. Its objective fate and my (subjective) being are inextricably intertwined. If I look in a large mirror and catch sight of my body – one object among many others – I say: 'this is me' or 'that's me'. There is no doubt or hesitation.

The sense that it is an extraordinary accident that I am *this* is rooted in the asymmetry between what I know and what I am, between my knowledge and my being. What I know *of* far outweighs what I am. This is vividly illustrated when one is given back part of one's own visual field (and a part that includes one's own body) in a mirror: then one sees oneself as simply one object among a crowd of objects. The very basis of one's perceptions is seen itself to be a small perceptible object. (There is, of course, no *a priori* reason why the ground of one's perceptions should itself be a potential object of perception – why the eye should be visible, etc. It is another mystery that it is.)

But the asymmetry between my being and my knowledge – between what I am and what I know of – goes far beyond this revelation of oneself as simply one object in a crowd of objects. The universe of propositional knowledge – the one (to use Russell's terms) I know of by 'description' rather than by direct, immediate, present 'acquaintance' (as in the mirror image) – enormously outsizes me. I am one of a huge crowd of human beings – several billions over millions of years. Human beings are only a part of the biosphere, which itself is only thinly buttered over a large planet that has been in existence for many millions of years. And that planet is but a small part of the solar system, itself part of a vast galaxy and the latter just a particle of dust in a colloid of similar particles of dust. To a fully awakened knowledge, Voltaire's characterisation of an individual man as an insect on an atom of mud is a flattering overestimate of the figure we each cut in the order of things. Is it not astonishing, then, that I should be this particular thing, out of so many things? Or that my knowledge should be housed in one out of so many of the million, billion, etc. things that I know? Surely, I could well have been something else.

But I am not something else. I am this. Could it have been otherwise? Is it not inevitable that I should be *this* being; that the assertion is a kind of analytical truth, even a tautology, which, like Descartes' famous formula, is necessarily true only in so far as it is empty of specific content?[11]

The tautology of explicit being

Let me change the formula from 'I am this thing' to ' I am this being'. Replacing 'thing' by 'being' liberates the complement to some extent from the idea of a material object such as the body. Unfortunately, this still does not capture what it is about me that makes my way of being what I am different from the way a pebble is what it is. The difference between me and a pebble is that there is, to reiterate Sprigge's formulation, a 'what it is like to be' me, whereas we do not conventionally accept that there is a 'what it is like to be' a pebble. There is a fundamental difference between what it is to be a pebble and what it is to be a human being; namely, that I am explicitly what I am, whereas the pebble has an explicit existence only courtesy of other beings for whom it exists explicitly. Explicit existence does not inhere in or exist for the pebble. So I want to change the formula and say that "I am the being of this being'.

This formulation encompasses both the 'what it is like to be' a certain being and the being itself. It suggests two themes for reflection:

a) Is it a necessary truth that I am the being of *this* being (or '*this* being of being');
b) What does it mean to say that I am the being of a certain being? Of *what* am I the being? *What* is it that I have, or enjoy, or suffer, the condition of being?

I am this...

I have already considered how focusing on the fact that I am a particular wakens two sorts of surprise: surprise at the fact that I am this particular rather than another one; and surprise that I exist at all. From the left there dawns the astonishment that I am but one of many of the things that I know of; and from the right there dawns the astonishment that I might not have existed at all. And yet both astonishments seem somehow not only merely 'worked up' but actually invalid, as if they were based upon a misunderstanding. Counteracting the astonishment that, out of all the beings that exist, I happen to be this one, and that, although many beings that might have existed didn't and of the many beings that did exist the vast majority do not exist at this moment, I actually do exist, there is a feeling that these are only tautologies and nothing to get excited about. I want to address this feeling, to show the sense or senses in which 'I am this' *is* a tautology and then to try to show how it *is* something to get excited about – indeed to feel a full-blown philosophical astonishment over. (To count as truly philosophical, an astonishment should be about the most general and obvious – but the obvious more intensely lit than our typically otherwise-engaged attention usually allows.)

Two ways of dampening the excitement come to mind.

The first tries to neutralise the astonishment at the fact that I exist at all (when I might well have not) by pointing out that my existing is a necessary condition of my being astonished. If I had not existed, or indeed if I do not currently exist, I could not be astonished. There is an infinity of possible beings – and possible human beings – my childless sister's grandchildren, for example – that do not exist and, are, consequently, not astonished. No being, in short, can be astonished at its non-existence; it cannot look back, with amazement, upon the narrow escape it had from the burden of existence, the office of particularity.[12] If I cannot be astonished without existing, perhaps therefore I should not be astonished that I exist. (This is analogous to the Weak Anthropic Principle, which reminds us that there is a kind of necessity in the fact that the universe should be found to have the – seemingly highly improbable – conditions required for the existence of intelligent life on earth: if the conditions were not right for the existence of intelligent life on earth, and in particular for the emergence of the minds of physicists, then we should not have found ourselves existing here and now but somewhere else at some other time where the conditions were right. The laws of the universe could only be discovered, in other words, under conditions necessary for the emergence of physicists; those laws are, therefore, going inescapably to be compatible with the conditions necessary for the laws of physics to be discovered.)

A second way of damping down the excitement would be to reflect on the fact that, as already noted, the intuition that I might not have been *this* being is based upon the fact that I know of more things than I myself am; I know beings other than myself; I recognise a not-self, a not-me. In other words, my surprise that I am this being rather than another depends upon my being the kind of being that is aware of beings other than itself. My astonishment at being a particular being is contingent upon something that is fundamental about me – that I am capable of being aware of a boundless reality external to me. I have, that is to say, created the grounds for my own astonishment.[13]

It seems to me that neither of these observations, however, entirely invalidates the astonishment or reduces it to an empty tautology. Let me, therefore, examine the statements more directly.

We adduced two grounds for astonishment: that I might not have been (at all); and that I might not have been *this*. They merge in a single astonishment: that 'I am this'. Is it legitimate to separate the existential astonishment that I am (at all) from the astonishment that I am a particular *x*? Does it not follow from the fact that I am that I am this? Could it really be an additional accident that I am this: could I have been something other than 'this' (or a nothing other than this)? If I were not this, would it not follow that I was not at all?

Consider the grammar of the sentence: 'I am this'. The subject, 'I', is what linguists call a 'deictic shifter'. It has, as Barthes, after Jakobson, pointed out, a double structure:

[it is] an indicial symbol which unites the conventional and the existential bonds: for it is only by virtue of a conventional rule that *I* represents its object (so that *I* becomes *ego* in Latin, *ich* in German etc.), but on the other hand, since it designates the person who utters it, it can only refer existentially to the utterance.[14]

The referent of the 'I' needs a little further clarification: it might be argued that 'I' refers not to the utterance but to the person who utters. Under normal circumstances (that is when the word is being genuinely used rather than, as here, merely mentioned), 'I' means, refers to, the person who says 'I'. That is the convention that governs the referential function of the word.[15] But what, precisely, is the referent of 'I'? Is it all of the speaker? Her body, all her life, her entire CV, the sum of her effects on the world, etc.? That is not entirely a grammatical question. Its answer could be seen, arguably, to depend upon what view is taken of the unity – empirical or transcendental – of the self, of the 'I'. We could say that 'I' refers to a putative transcendental ego of the speaker; but it would be less controversial to think of its referent as the speaker's moment-of-speaking, along with all the explicit and implicit support framework that defines the speaker's individuality at that moment.

Our discussion will be more focused if we assume the less controversial referent of the 'I' and think of it as corresponding approximately to a 'speaker-moment'. 'I' when I use the word (use, rather than, as now, mention it) refers to 'Raymond Tallis at the time at which he uses it'. As John Lyons has put it:

the analysis of 'I' in terms of some underlying definite description meaning 'the one who is (now) speaking', if it is pressed to the point at which it will do the job it is intended to do, must be relativized to the very utterance that contains the first-person pronoun whose meaning it, allegedly, explicates.[16]

This is not to reduce the referent of 'I' to the utterance – as Barthes and many others who believe that language refers only to itself would claim – but to the speaker-moment defined by the utterance.[17]

So much for 'I'. What about 'this'? Lyons is again both useful and illuminating:

Demonstrative pronouns and demonstrative adjectives, like the English 'this' and 'that', as well as demonstrative adverbs, such as 'here' and 'there', are primarily deictic; and, when they have this function, they are to be interpreted with respect to the location of the participants in the deictic context. Roughly speaking, the distinction between 'this' and 'that', and between 'here' and 'there', depends upon the proximity to the zero-point of the deictic context: 'this book' means 'the book (which is) here' or 'the book (which is near to the speaker'; 'that book' means 'the book (which is) there' or 'the book (which is) not near the speaker' or, in explicit contrast with 'this book', 'the book (which is) further from the speaker (than the book which is nearer the speaker)'.

(ibid., p. 646)

Lyons comments that, though it is difficult to be precise about the difference between the demonstratives (pronouns, adjectives and adverbs), it is 'sufficient to show the connexions between the demonstratives and the participant-role of the speaker' (ibid., p. 646). It is sufficient at any rate for our purposes.

If, by definition, 'this' is 'near to the speaker', or 'nearer to the speaker', the speaker – who will be nearer than anything else to the speaker – will always be 'this', in contrast with that. 'I' will always be 'this' because 'this' is defined by relative closeness to 'I' and 'I' will always be closer to 'I' than any other candidate being will be. 'I am this', therefore, looks like a tautology, a necessary consequence of the meanings of 'I' and 'this', rather than an empirical fact. Or, to put it in terms that relate to the question that prompted this linguistic excursus: it is not legitimate to separate the fact that I am (at all) from the fact that I am this.

That is not, however, the end of the story. First, the astonishment is not directed at the 'fact' that 'I am this' – that is scarcely a fact, at all, we agree. (Or, if it is a fact, it is a fact of grammar.) It is directed at a something that corresponds to that assertion – to the fact that 'I am this X', where X may be a body, a person, a stretch of space-time, a current set of thoughts, or whatever. The astonishment, therefore, is not at the link between a naked personal pronoun and a naked demonstrative – this is, after all, merely an analytical truth, a tautology; rather it is between a clothed, realised specific 'I' and a clothed, realised, specific referent of a demonstrative noun or noun-adjective phrase – and this is neither an analytical truth nor a tautology. The question then arises (as it does with the Cartesian *cogito*) what clothes to give them; how thick and complex they should be and of what fabric they should be made.

It is not the end of the story for another reason. When I say 'I am this', and yet, at the same time, point out that this assertion is a mere tautology because 'I' and 'this' are, by definition, in this context, the same thing, it seems as if there is after all a distance inserted between 'I' and 'this' despite their being, at the same time, identical. This merged identity and difference seems to be freighted with more content than is the obvious grammatically-based tautology of 'I am me' (or, to maintain the grammatical proprieties, 'I am I') and seems closer to the less obviously grammatically-based tautology 'I am here' (rather than elsewhere). What they all have in common is an underlining of the fact that I *am*: it is an explicit affirmation of my existence.

That affirmation requires specificity in order to carry any weight, to have the effect of drawing attention to the fact of my existence. Once it has specificity, it loses its status (or lack of status) as a tautology. I am 'here' of necessity; but that the 'here' is a certain place at a certain time is not a matter of necessity. It is necessary that I should be somewhere at sometime and that that somewhere should be here and that time should be now; but it is not a matter of necessary that, as I speak, 'here' is a particular room in Bramhall and 'now' is a particular time on a particular Saturday morning. The empty necessity of the tautology is the toti-potential receptacle for holding specific realisations of my existence. The 'I am this' is the empty form of explicitness; a notional distance from which I can catch sight of myself and the unoccasioned, or insufficiently occasioned, fact of my particular, actual existence.

(We could put this another way: 'I am this' expresses astonishment at the fact that the I of the speaker-moment defined by the utterance has a privileged, indeed inescapable, connection with the series of 'I's' that are connected with other moments, other events, other actions.)

I am the being of this being

Let us now look at the tautology when, endowed with some content, it ceases to be a mere tautology. We can add content on at either end. 'I am this' can be loaded at the left-hand end and expanded to 'Raymond Tallis is this X'. However, the most useful and illuminating loadings take place at the right-hand end. What happens at the left-hand end is only the replacement of the grammatical subject by a proper name; it is on the right-hand end that we get the predicates, the real stuff of the world (After all, proper names, it has been argued, have reference largely without sense – achieve reference without the mediation of predicates.[18]) What can we add to the right-hand end without importing extraneous material?

The safest thing is to use a neutral term – such as 'being' or 'existent'. By this means, we do not commit ourselves to specifying what 'I', essentially, am: what I am in myself, what I am all the time, what I am at any given time, my enduring substance, etc. By such caution, alas, we also prevent ourselves from escaping from the circle or dot of the tautology: 'I am this being', or 'I am this existent' doesn't take one much beyond 'I am this'. Moreover, astonishment at the fact that 'I am this' usually picks on some thing and reverts back to it – such as: 'I am this body' (as when I sat behind the girl on the bus who seemed intensely bodily present to me and so made me aware of my own specific embodiment); 'I am this person' (whatever that means); 'I am the holder of this office' (bearer of these duties, carrier of these responsibilities, occupant of this post, spouse of this person); 'I am such-and-such a kind of person' (male, twentieth-century, of a kindly or unkindly disposition, middle-class, or whatever); 'I am the subject or referent of this *curriculum vitae*' (and so legitimately laying claim to this deposit account of achievement); 'I am the one who is having these thoughts' (at the present moment, over the course of my life, etc.).

It is difficult to adjudicate between these different clothings of 'I am this'. And connected with this difficulty is the fact that the 'I' can vanish in two ways: it can shrink to nothing; or it can expand to every-thing and become coterminous with 'my' world which, in turn, becomes 'the world'. We can find, like Hume in pursuit of the self, that 'I can never catch *myself* at any time without a perception, and never can observe anything but the perception'.[19] Or hold, with solipsist philosophers like Stirner, that the self is the only true reality in the world and is hence everywhere. Or even, like certain absolute idealists, that the universe is one great thought and we (or some of the more metaphysically privileged citizens among us) are thinking it: in other words, that the universe is the present moment of the consciousness that is aware of it in the form of a proposition. We can, in short, neither pin down the 'this' that we are, not can we contain it within reasonable, plausible bounds. This presents as a problem when we try to translate the sentence 'I am this' into terms that answer to the intu-itions such as those that flooded over me when I sat behind the girl on the bus: 'She is that being while I am this being.' Or, more precisely, 'She is that being plus, or incorporating, what it is like to be that being and I am this being plus, or incorporating, what it is like to be this being.' We could express these intuitions in shorthand: 'She is the being of that being and I am the being of this being.'

What is it to be the being of that being or the being of this being? This, too, is extremely difficult to specify. It is no easier to do so when we think of ourselves than when we think of others.[20] As already discussed, it is not a matter of being a particular (biological) body. Our occupancy or possession of our body is incomplete and variable. I am not entirely the being of my body – or not, at any rate, the being of my entire body. To express this rather clumsily: there is a good deal of my body that is not really animated by my consciousness, much that does not report to me. We could put this another way by saying that our relationship to parts of our body varies from the first to the third person – adding that, so long as we are alive, we have to have a first-person relationship to *some* of our body.[21] When we are dead and our body is a corpse, we have no relationship to our body: it exists only in the third person, for others. But even when we are alive, much of our body exists, if it exists at all for us, in the third person. In addition to those part of our body that are never directly present to us in the first person – our bone marrow, for example, or our brain – there are many more parts (perhaps most, perhaps all) that are only intermittently present in that sense. If I am busy working on a problem, I am not present in my toes, or even my mouth, just as I do not feel, or am not aware of, the presence of my clothes. The body may, on the other hand, be subsumed in the first person – as when we are lost in its pains and pleasures. And then there are, as we discussed earlier, intermediate states – as when, for example, I look at 'my' hand or 'my' face and enjoy a quasi-possessive relation with respect to 'my' body.[22]

What, then, is it to be the being of this being? Is it to be the being of these sensations and feelings I or my body enjoy? But these sensations and feelings are rather dispersed – spread over the space of my body, spread over time. To be the being of this being must, at the least, surely be to be the being of these sensations and feelings in relation to the *series* of sensations and feelings that I am. But how are they thus related to, made to count as part of, a *series?* Do I – that is, the being that is the being of this being (or the 'what it is like to be the being of this being') – exist, or subsist, in these relations? Or do I exist more in thoughts than sensations – thoughts which are, by definition, relational and span series? Again, yes and no: sometimes the being of my being seems to inhere in my thoughts; and sometimes my thoughts – at least in so far as they are internally vocalised or cast in images – simply accompany my essential being like fluff on a thread or static over a broadcasting or like a commentary on events. Sometimes I am my thoughts, sometimes I have them, sometimes I (actively) think them, and sometimes they simply happen and I happen to be their site – rather as, when I find myself humming a tune I have neither heard nor thought of for years, it seems simply as if the tune has taken up lodgement within me.

What is it, then, to be the being of this being? What is the being of which I am the being? And in what special sense am I being it? So long as we treat this question as one of demarcating the me from the not me, then we shall not answer it. We shall at best end up with a disputed inventory of heterogeneous items which will sometimes seem to be me and sometimes not to be me.[23] What is peculiar about my being – and that of other human beings – is that, whatever it is that I am, it exists *explicitly* and, through this explicitness, makes other things explicit – as objects of knowledge, or of need, or simply as environing me. The fundamental relation that I want to draw attention to is one which is illustrated when I have a thought, or when I, in some other way, *live* my body. It is my destiny to be at once identified with this thought and yet capable of owning it, expressing, challenging it. It is likewise my unchallengable destiny in some sense to be this body – to be the being of this body – but scope of this will differ from one moment to the next: I am the being of my teeth and mouth differently when I have toothache compared with when I do not. The central intuition, the invariant, is explicitness: to be the being of this being (whether the being can be viewed as an object, like my body, or whether it cannot, like my thought) is, so to speak, to place that being in *italics*.

This intuition, compelling though it is, may be misleading and warrants further reflection. To be me cannot be simply to be the being of this body understood as 'what it is like to be this (material) body' because this (material) body does not, *of itself*, have a 'what it is like to be' this body. There is, that is to say, no experience that is the essential experience of being a particular material object – whether the object in question is a human body or something else. For example, there is no essential experience of being a pebble. It would be odd to expect that, if a pebble enjoyed a sense of 'what it is like to be' a pebble, it would experience itself as 'hard', 'dark' or 'inert' (or even 'stupid'). One error behind the expectation that it *would* experience itself in this way is rooted in the unexamined assumption that the intrinsic properties of objects – and consequently the ones that would dawn upon them as they came to self-consciousness and enjoyed or suffered their own being – are identical with the way the objects appear to *us*, the place they have in *our* world. To believe that the 'what it is like to be a pebble' would be, or at least include, an experience of, say, hardness, is as daft as believing that it would be, or include, an experience of being 'harder than human flesh' or 'useful in primitive warfare'. Likewise, although what it is like to be Raymond Tallis includes experiences of his body, those experiences are not best described as the body's experience of itself. Even that part of 'what it is to be Raymond Tallis' is composed of experiences of Raymond Tallis's body, being Raymond Tallis is, even in part, composed of Raymond Tallis's body experiencing itself. (or, *a fortiori*, Raymond Tallis's brain experiencing itself, or the events in itself.)

Behind this discussion of what, if physical objects disclosed themselves to themselves and enjoyed a 'what it is like to be' themselves, would be disclosed, there lurks the question of the extent to which the *appearance* or the *presence* of material objects is intrinsic to them. Let us dwell on this question for a moment or two. The conventional view (shared by philosophical idealists and realists alike) that minds or consciousnesses are required to bring about appearings is, in the case of philosophical realists, associated with – and moderated by – the assumption that, whereas appearing *per se* is not intrinsic to objects (it occurs only in interaction with conscious beings), the contents of the appearings *are* dictated by the objects. This latter conclusion, though it contradicts the first, makes a kind of sense: if the object did not dictate the features of its appearings, our consciousness of it would be untrue (or unconstrained by anything outside of consciousness and so only accidentally and intermittently 'true') and, incidentally, consciousness would be of no value from the point of view of survival. However, behind this common sense (and, in addition, received-evolutionist[24]) assumption is a hidden circularity that would make it true irrespective of the truth or otherwise of Darwinian theory: we can assume without fear of challenge that the appearances of objects express (or generally express) their intrinsic nature because our only access to anything which could be described as their 'intrinsic nature' is through their appearance. If we are tempted to suppose that the appearance a pebble has to us of being 'hard' reflects an intrinsic hardness in the pebble, this is only because our sole access to its 'essential nature' is through its appearances to us, mediated via its interactions with our bodies.

The lack of a guaranteed relation between the 'objective' properties of an object and the 'what it is like to be' that object is spelt out by Sprigge in the case of the human body (p. 168).

When one imagines another's conscious state, there is no conclusive way of checking up whether one has done so correctly or not. This by no means implies that one's guess may not in fact be more or less correct. Presuming the object (that is, at least normally, the organism) with which one is concerned, is indeed conscious, then *being that organism* will have a certain definite complex quality at every waking moment, and what one imagines will (if one is right) be, in fact, a more or less correct reproduction, or (alternatively) symbolic representation, of that quality. Physical science makes no reference to qualities of this kind.

Thus consciousness is that which one characterises when one tries to answer the question what it is or might be like to *be* a certain object in a certain situation. This use of 'be' (which I have no time to discuss further) though suggestive, is most peculiar, for it is not the same thing to characterise the consciousness of an organism and to characterise that organism. An inanimate (or rather, a non-conscious) object has a definite character at every moment and *is* plenty of things, but there is nothing which is *being* that object in the relevant sense.

In summary, then, to say that to be 'Raymond Tallis' is to be 'What it is like to be' Raymond Tallis's body is to say nothing because there is no fixed or canonical form of 'what it is like to be' Raymond Tallis's body – or, indeed, of any object. It is tempting, as we have noted, to imagine that there *is* such a canonical form of 'what it is like to be object X' – and that this consists of the object experiencing its own properties[25] – or being that object experiencing its own properties. But this folds us back into the absurdity of assuming that, if a pebble had a 'what it is like to be a pebble', it would experience itself as 'hard', 'dark' or, even, 'useful in primitive war', etc. That, in other words, the pebble would experience itself as I – or as humans in general – experience it; or very generally, its enjoying a 'what it is like to be' itself would have as its content its appearing to something, or, more precisely *someone*, else. That, in acquiring a 'what it is like to be', the pebble would simply take possession of the appearances it has to an external viewpoint – its being experienced by something or someone else. The dawning 'what it is like to be' would be assimilated into 'what it is like' to be (for example) for a human being; or, even, what other things it is like *unto*. To develop this last point: it is evidently absurd to imagine that, if a pebble had a 'what it is like to be' this would amount to a consciousness of being hard, cold, dark, dense, firm, etc., as these are only comparative properties and arising in the experience of an external consciousness such as mine. It is to me (and to creatures like me), and not to the pebble, that the pebble is hard (and the sponge soft). And this is partly (though not only) because my own experienced needs and physical properties set the scale by which things are judged as hard (or soft) and light (or dark).

To be 'Raymond Tallis' cannot be simply explained as being 'what it is like to be Raymond Tallis's body' – i. e. to be the self-disclosure of the properties of the object thus designated – not only for the reasons given in the case of objects such as pebbles but also because what it is like to be 'Raymond Tallis' is not merely the self-disclosure of a particular body (a difficult enough notion, as we have seen). There is an additional complication arising out of the fact that Raymond Tallis's body is also in some very obscure sense the means by which a world is revealed – 'to' or 'in' or 'for' Raymond Tallis. As Heidegger has emphasised, Dasein is in the world 'in the mode of having a world as other kinds of entities that are in the world in the mode of spatial inclusion do not'.[26] This world, moreover, casts light upon the original self-revelation of the body; indeed, is the light through which the body is revealed to itself. Not only, therefore, is my self-disclosure, my 'what it is like to be Raymond Tallis', not just a transcript or dumb copy of my bodily properties (for example, having an appendix two inches long or having a serum potassium of 4.2 mmol/l) but such bodily self-revelation as I do experience is related to many things in the world which is also revealed to 'Raymond Tallis' as his situation. And this is to open up further layers of complexity: my world-as-situation in turn reveals – or (to use a favourite verb of Sartre's) posits – my body as being of a certain character and in a certain situation: small, near to home, in danger, etc.

The elusiveness of intrinsic properties

Let us reflects a little more upon this difficulty – arising out of the fact that human beings disclose, are open to, experience, worlds posited as being outside of, and other than, themselves – presented to the endeavour to say 'what it is like to be' a particular human. It clearly vetos the simplistic notion of humans as having a 'what it is like to be' that amounts simply to enjoying the gift of one's own intrinsic (presumably material) nature or composition transformed into self-awareness.

If I meditate now upon my 'what it is like to be', upon my own consciousness, I see it merges in one direction with consciousness of the world and in the other with self-consciousness. If I knowingly have a sensation of a pebble, this consciousness points in two directions:

AWARENESS	←	RT's SENSATION	→	AWARENESS
OF SELF		OF PEBBLE		OF WORLD
(to which the				(to which the
sensation of the				pebble belongs)
pebble belongs)				

The situation is, of course, more complicated than this diagram, which neatly separates self and world, suggests.

In short, when we are trying to determine 'what it is like to be that being', and the being in question is a human, then it is even more obvious that the 'what it is like' is not simply a *toute rendu* of what is intrinsic in or to a particular (material) body – not only because the entirety of that body is not available, even over time, never mind at at a given moment, to its (my?) consciousness, but also because what is available is interactively so: I come to my body mainly through its interactions with other human and non-human bodies and what is revealed to me, and constitutes my 'what it is like to be', is not so much the body itself as the things it encounters. Of course, it in part encounters them on its own terms, or in part translates the encounters into its own terms. But the contents of consciousness – when they are not remote from the body (as memories, preoccupations, abstract thoughts) – are revelatory of the world, of the body's outside. In other words, exteroception dominates over proprioception: the body is a more or less transparent lens on the world. Only the sick or the sexually engaged or the physically stressed body asserts itself as the main content of consciousness. Even then, the contents of consciousness – pain, nausea, difficulty moving, etc. – are not plausible as 'pure' revelations of the intrinsic properties of the human body *qua* material being. (Of course, there is a constant under-presence of our body, a sense of warmth and weight and cold and pressures and positions and volumes, even where the body is not foregrounded in pain, physical pleasure, etc.)

I have not perhaps sufficiently emphasised the interactive nature of our 'objective' knowledge of objects, including our own bodies. One of the reasons why we should not expect a pebble, if it acquired a 'what it is like to be' (itself), to, as it were 'come to' the properties we experience in it – hardness, opacity, etc. – is that these properties with which we are familiar are the product to some extent of the interaction between ourselves and the pebble. They are not intrinsic to the pebble; they are not 'pure'.

To explore this a bit further, try, for a moment, identifying the 'what it is like to be' with self-consciousness, with being rendered to oneself as contents of consciousness; more precisely, with intrinsic or objective properties being rendered to the object as self-awareness. This is difficult, if only because it is not possible to identify 'intrinsic' properties with 'objective' properties. Objective properties are those that are revealed to an external collective of consciousnesses. (The more 'scientific' the determination of those objective properties, the wider the collective. Science reports not only what you see, or what you and I see, but also what they saw in Ancient Times and what they will see in the future.) But what is revealed to the collective of consciousnesses (e.g. that the stone is hard) is derived from the *interaction* between the object and its environment – including other organisms. This interactive nature of the 'intrinsic' character of objects is reflected in the fact that standing properties, such as they are, are rendered through occurrent events. (An obvious example would be the *sound* of the pebble, but it is equally true of its hardness; of 'primary' qualities as well as secondary ones.)

In fact, there are at least two senses in which the properties of the pebble are less intrinsic than interactive:

a)   the properties are revealed in, and are relative to, interactions with other objects – the hardness of the pebble is revealed in a collision with a comparatively soft human body;

b)   and they are revealed in, and are relative to, a series of experiences of a particular evolving or developing consciousness.

With respect to a), we might ask, does the pebble in the interactions that reveal it, actually reveal itself or the other partners to the revelatory interactions: if a pebble gives out a splash when it falls into the water, what is the more revealed – the water or the pebble? Which speaks itself? The answer is that neither does intrinsically; which one does in practice depends upon the needs, interests, history, etc. of the consciousness witnessing the engagement. If I throw a pebble into the dark to see whether there is water nearby, then the resultant sound reveals the water, rather than the pebble; if I am looking at the water and hear a splash, then it is the thrown pebble that is revealed.

The obsessed lover

Sexual desire may or may not be the most metaphysical of the human appetites[27] but it is certainly true that sexual love is one of the most powerful stimuli to asking questions of a metaphysical nature, even if they are not cast in the form that the professionals would accept as fruitful. The question of 'what it is like' to be an entity other oneself is one that preoccupies, indeed obsesses, lovers. The lover wants to know what it is like to be the loved one. She is so beautiful, she is so different from me in virtue of her beauty, that I imagine that there must be something wonderful that corresponds to 'what it is like' to be her (or her body). However, it is undisclosable. The loved one could not tell me. This is in part because she has always been that body: the experience of being it is no more summarisable than 'being in the world' is summarisable. It is common to all her life and is therefore more than, and less than, a 'factor' in or 'tone' of experience that could be specified for a set of experiences that could be recounted. There will, moreover, be much in common between the 'what it is like to be' this (beautiful) body and 'what it is like to be' this other (ordinary) body. The experience of running for a bus, of being busy at work, or of having colic will not be specifically inflected in a manner reflecting the beauty, or non-beauty, of the bodies through which they are experienced. Our experience as bodies is not entirely translated – we suspect – into an idiolect peculiar to our particular body.

The lover may imagine, or hope, or fantasise that he could get to know what it is like to be the loved one through seeing her exposed in nakedness or the extremes of sexual intimacy. This, too, is an illusion – certainly if the knowledge that is sought is of the average or typical experience of what it is like to be the loved one. If he is lucky enough to gain what he imagines is his heart's desire, he will discover that his wanting to know 'what it is like to be' the loved one goes beyond the desire for carnal knowledge and is not satisfied by it (although it may be extinguished by a satiety that removes the aura of mystery from the loved one). The 'what it is like to be' this body will not have privileged exposure or disclosure in the sexual frenzies and the other special situations that preoccupy its lover. Carnal knowledge is socially and personally, but not metaphysically, privileged – under certain circumstance, it may be a supreme acceptance by, and acknowledgement of, the other person; but it is not a supreme disclosure.

It might be argued that sexual arousal is metaphysically privileged because it is an unusually complete rendering of the person as body and of the body to the person and because it is the deepest, most secret, most intense aspect of the individual that is revealed in embodiment. But this is true only if we see the most secret aspect uncovered as the most revelatory. (As a long skirt makes a glimpse of an ankle a disclosure.) Sartre addressed this thought in *Being and Nothingness* and suggested that the lover aims through sexual congress to achieve privileged access to the consciousness of the other by inducing identification of the other with his or her own body: the sensual delight experienced in the caress brings the loved one to his or her own surface – a surface which can be, and indeed is, touched by, exposed to, the lover. By this means the lover aims to possess the loved one's freedom. Even for Sartre, however, this privileged access to the other is not metaphysically privileged: the loved one's freedom eludes the lover's grasp and he or she continues as incarnated consciousness elsewhere: the lover can only, at best, seize a *moment* of the loved one's biography – perhaps a supreme moment – but a moment, none the less and not the biography itself. He or she lives on – elsewhere – to be caught up in other equally powerful preoccupations and even to forget the supreme moments in other supreme or even ordinary moments. If it is a privileged moment, it is privileged not so much, or not only, in its knowledge of the loved one, but in its making present – in making her be present .

Moreover, for the person whose body is beautiful, the wonderful, the distinctive, 'what it is like to be' probably lies more in the reactions evoked by the body – in the surplus of attention, in the power to choose it confers, in all the other social things that follow from the reactions of others to a beautiful body – than in its intrinsic properties. In short, the distinctive experiences associated with having a beautiful body come from without and belong at least as much to the outside, as much to a putative inside, world. The corollary of this is that carnal knowledge reveals the body only in a certain mode – and one of many possible interactive modes, at that. (Moreover, in sexual encounters, there are at issue many other things than knowledge of 'what it is like to be' the loved one: tenderness, conquest, moral transgression, privileged access, companionship, assertion of intimacy and love, trust and distrust, etc.)

We may relate this discussion to the point made much earlier that we are (different parts of) our bodies to differing degrees at different times. In pain we may become a foot, in physical exertion or sexual delight we might become our bodies more widely, darkened with discomfort or lit up in pleasure. Sexually, we do not uncover the essence of a person when we bring about, or attempt to bring about, a sexual frenzy in them any more than they are uncovered to us in illness. For to be the being of a human being (or a human body) is not only to feel its physical sensations – to endure its cold or its hollowness when it is hungry, or to enjoy its pleasures in sexual arousal; it is also to be concerned about an insult it received ten years ago, to worry about superannuation, to think of the future of the universe. Abstract thoughts are part of the 'what it is like to be', and this is therefore yet another reason why 'what it is like to be the being that is Raymond Tallis' cannot be reduced to being the rendition – however indirect – of the material properties of this body or even of its concern for itself, its seeking its pleasure rather than its pain, its working towards its own continuation and avoiding its extinction – complex, rich and mysterious though these are. (The full complexity of what it is like to be the being of a human being is only hinted at in my book *The Explicit Animal*.)

None of this is meant to imply that there is *no* specific 'what it is like' to be your body or even 'what it is like to be' your body rather than my body, only that the astonishment awoken by the encounter with the girl on the bus is more complex than it, perhaps, at first understood.

Postscript

> Phenomenology issues, I'm afraid, in tautologies. But tautology is, perhaps, the only metaphysical affirmation which men can reach. The most we can say about being is that it is.[28]

The train of thought set down in this essay was prompted by a particular experience that I referred to in the opening section. And yet this actual experience seems irrelevant. The thoughts would still be true – or false – if they had not occurred to me on a bus; and the girl's sunlit neck adds nothing to their validity. Even so, specifying the occasion is not entirely frivolous. It feeds back into the very mystery I have been trying to illuminate, using its own light. For the experience of seeing the girl's neck and having the thoughts prompted by it is part of my being this being, my being obliged to be the moments of this particular being called 'Raymond Tallis'. It emphasises how even my metaphysical thoughts about the extraordinary fact that I am this particular thing are themselves particular thoughts – particular realisations of a thought-type perhaps – attached to, or part of the sequence that is this particular being. The generality of our thoughts does not lift us up above the particularity of our condition – for they have to be realised in us as particulars. They are still particular moments of our particular being and not especially privileged moments, either: they will be replaced by other moments in which we shall be equally, if not more, absorbed in quite different matters – for example, trying to interpret the odd expression on someone's face, eating our dinner, running to an appointment, brooding over our troubles, getting on with our work. The metaphysical thoughts that promise to raise the thinker above the particularity of his or her condition are part of that particularity. Our thoughts are part of the unraised self. The I who struggles to have this thought, even the I who is pleased to have this thought, fall below it. I belong to a series that flows beneath the thought.

This inability to escape one's existential particularity, howsoever elevated, abstract or *sub specie aeternis* one's thoughts and pre-occupations, was one of Kierkegaard's abiding concerns.[29] It is reflected in the style of his philosophical works which provoke questions about the relationship between narrative (and the specific occasion) and abstract, or general, argument in philosophy and is connected with the tension between the specific occasion and the general thought. The occasions of philosophy are never adequate to its thoughts because the latter encompass whole classes of occasions including ones that did not prompt the thought.[30] This is explored by Marcel and is implicit in both his philosophical style and his public image. For Marcel,

> the knowing subject who apprehends the public object of know-
> ledge is in practice a specialised function of the whole man, and in
> theory an abstraction from the human situation, and must not be
> mistaken for the existing individual (infinitely interested in existing,
> as Kierkegaard put it, and therefore intermittently interested in
> thinking).[31]

Marcel's method

> is to note in his journal his trains of thought, which expose the
> intimate process of his thinking, with all its hesitations and
> audacities, its tentatives and discontinuities, its polished fragments,
> suggestive beginnings, sudden triumphs, and abandoned pursuits.
> This is at the furthest remove from system building, and far even
> from systematic exposition.
>
> (ibid., p. 66)

Corresponding to this 'doctrine of scattered occasions' is the image of the philosopher, sitting in the open air, on a park bench, writing in a notebook as the world promenades by. This is an attractive picture; but must be seen as complementing, rather than correcting, or displacing, other images: the philosopher on the podium delivering a highly technical presentation to an international audience of peers; or the discarnate consciousness, a cognitive angel, given over, without remainder, to the highest level of understanding – to 'the view from nowhere'.

Notes and references

1. Jean-Paul Sartre, *Nausea* (English translation Robert Baldick, London: Penguin, 1965):

   > I see my hand spread out on the table. It is alive – it is me. It opens, the fingers unfold and point. It is lying on its back. It shows me its fat underbelly. It looks like an animal upside down. The fingers are the paws ... it is me, those two animals moving about at the end of my arms. My hand scratches one of its paws with the nail of another paw; I can feel its weight on the table which isn't me...

   > (pp. 143–4)

   The phenomenological/Heideggerian/existentialist provenance of much of the present essay will be evident to anyone familiar with the relevant literature: it is more pervasive than the acknowledged references. However, it is equally rooted in the analytical and linguistic tradition. I hope it will, in a sense, move between both, in the way suggested by 'The Philosophies of Consciousness and the the Philosophies of the Concept, Or: Is There Any Point in Studying the Headache I have Now?' in Raymond Tallis, *Enemies of Hope: a critique of Contemporary Pessimism* (London: Macmillan, 1997).

2. R.M. Rilke, *The Notebooks of Malte Laurid Brigge* (English translation by John Linton, London: Hogarth, 1930).

3. See, for example, *The Phenomenology of Perception* (English translation by Colin Smith, London: Routledge & Kegan Paul, 1962). Of course, it is easy to exaggerate the naivety of Descartes' dualism. Descartes emphasised that he was *not* lodged in his body 'like a pilot in a vessel'.

4. Assuming it was presented to me in adequate light and I had not recently 'changed out of all recognition'.

5. This relationship between body and viewpoint is lucidly expressed in P.F. Strawson's *Individuals: An Essay in Descriptive Metaphysics* (London: Methuen, 1959):

   > We may summarise such facts by saying that for each person, there is one body which occupies a certain *causal* position in relation to that person's perceptual experience, a causal position which in various ways is unique in relation to each of the various kinds of perceptual

experience he has; and – as a further consequence – that this body is also unique for him as an *object* of the various kinds of perceptual experience which he has.

(p. 92)

The entire chapter ('Persons'), from which this passage is abstracted, is a wonderfully suggestive exploration of a variety of mysteries that touch upon our present concerns. For example, why should the different dependencies of perception – in the case of vision, eyes open and closed, orientation of head, and location – refer to the same body? And why are one's states of consciousness, including perceptions, ascribed to anything (any body) at all? Why are they ascribed to the very same thing as certain corporeal characteristics located in a certain physical situation?

6. Of course, there are conditions in which I fail to recognise parts of my body. For example, certain stroke patients with lesions of the parietal lobe may not regard an affected limb as their own and may even develop a hatred towards it ('misoplegia') and attempt to throw it out of bed. (I had once such patient who christened his right arm 'Thatcher'.) And auto-prosopagnosia – the failure to recognise one's own face – has also been described with certain lesions.

7. Gabriel Marcel, *Being and Having* (English translation unattribute, London and Glasgow: Fontana Library, 1965). See especially 'A Metaphysical Diary' pp. 91 *et seq* and 'Outlines of a Phenomenology of Having'.

8. T.L.S. Sprigge, 'Final Causes', *Proceedings of the Aristotelian Society*, Supplementary Volume (1971), pp. 149–70. One of the relevant passages in this seminal paper is worth quoting verbatim:

> One is wondering about the consciousness which an object possesses whenever one wonders what it must be like being that object. Concerning an object deemed non-conscious one cannot thus wonder. To wonder what it is like being an object is to concern oneself with a question different from any scientific or practical question about the observable properties or behaviour of that object or about the mechanisms which underlie such properties or behaviour.
>
> (p. 167)

This intuition – that the essential condition of consciousness is that there must be 'something it is like to be' the object in question – has been the basic of one of the most powerful arguments against materialist (or objectivist) accounts of consciousness and/or mind. It had its most famous expression in Thomas Nagel's paper. 'What is it like to be a bat?' (*Philosophical Review* 83 (1974), 435–50). (Nagel generously acknowledges Sprigge's independent and prior discovery in *The View from Nowhere* (Oxford: Oxford University Press, 1986 p. 15). Nagel's argument against an objectivist (or materialist) theory of mind was that, however much we learned about the nervous system of a bat, we should still not know what it was like to *be* a bat. This argument has been taken up by many philosophers since, notably Frank Jackson and Howard Robinson, who have suggested thought-experiments to bring out the essential point of this argument; for example, imagining a blind 23rd-century superscientist who knew all there was about the physiology of vision. The latter would still not know what it was like to see, what the experience of light was like.

The discussion of Nagel's paper subsequently became rather muddled when Tye, and others, argued that what the blind superscientist was deprived of was not additional (objective) knowledge – so the materialist account of the world was, after all, complete. This, however, was to argue past Nagel's point: objective knowledge always falls short of subjective awareness of 'what it is like to be' a bat, or whatever. It is not additional (objective) facts that are required to bridge the gap between the materialist world-picture and the subjective viewpoint. The being of a material object is captured in objective and exhaustive knowledge of its properties; this is not true of the being of a human being.

The Nagel–Jackson–Tye arguments are discussed in Raymond Tallis, 'A Critique of Tye's The Subjective Qualities of Experience', *Philosophical Investigations*, 12 (3) (1989), 217–22; and Raymond Tallis, *The Explicit Animal* (London: Macmillan, 1991), pp. 149–55. I argue that Tye and others had missed the point of Nagel's argument; but I also wonder whether Nagel himself did also to some extent.

9. Most of what we are is unchosen by us; this is the background of 'facticity' (to use Sartre's term) against which we make our choices and choose 'what to be'. We are obliged to live out a body with certain properties, limitations and parameters; to be a person who has – or has to reject – this cultural heritage; to be a child born of this family, located in such and such a place in society. And yet this facticity is not purely contingent in the sense of being accidents 'about' me. When I bang my shin, it is no mere accident that it is I who suffer this pain. It has, and feels to have, a deep necessity. In short, there is an acquired necessity: once I am, I am this thing (defined in terms of the inescapables)and the things that happen to this thing are quasi-necessary.

Hazel Barnes succinctly defines facticity in the key to Sartre's terminology appended to her excellent translation of *Being and Nothingness: an Essay on Phenomenological Ontology* (London: Methuen, 1957):

> The For-Itself's necessary connection with the In-itself, hence with the world and its own past. It is what allows us to say that the For-Itself *is* or *exists*. The facticity of freedom is the fact that freedom is not able not to be free.

10. The post-Hegelian conceptualisation of a consciousness, or a conscious being, as 'a for-itself' is particularly associated with the Sartre of *Being and Nothingness*. Sartre contrasted unconscious Being ('Being-in-itself') with conscious being ('Being-for-itself'). These terms correspond roughly to Hegel's *an-sich* and *für-sich*. There was a third category, also derived from Hegel's sense of the essential human being coming to himself through acknowledgement by others: 'being-for-others'.

11. The fundamental question triggered by the formula *cogito ergo sum* is not whether it is a necessary truth – in other words, whether it can be accepted without question – but what it is a truth of or about. Whether, ultimately, it is true about something or nothing; whether it is true as a tautology, in

which case empty; or whether it makes a substantive point. Another reading of it is as a *demonstration* or – like Moore's famous proof of the existence of external reality to be executed by raising first one hand and then another – merely a *recipe* for a demonstration of a truism.

12. It is difficult to speak of 'it' with reference to the non-existent. All one has is a phrase 'the non-existent' which has sense but, by definition, no reference. At best its reference is to a class or category – a curiously empty category, the category of emptiness.

   I am reminded of the discussion that followed the recent Church of England pronouncement that Hell did not exist as a positive state: Hell, rather, was simply 'total annihilation of being'. According to the Dean of Lichfield Cathedral, this was no soft option for sinners since it meant 'being distant from, or having one's back turned on the love of God'. In other words, suffering would come not from positive assaults but from the privative torture of losing out on the joy of union with God. This is, of course, absurd. If one does not exist, one cannot have one's back turned on anything and one cannot be far from Him, any more than one can be near to Him. Nor can one suffer a state of privation – or any state, positive or negative.

   Indeed – and this is the relevant point here – once one is annihilated one does not have a particular portion of nothingness to call one's own, to call oneself. There is no such thing as *my* non-being. There may be *his* non-being which exists only for others. If nothingness has labelled quarters, sectors or spots that correspond to particular non-beings, they exist only in third-person discourse, not in reality. There is in extra-linguistic reality nothing corresponding to my non-being, your non-being, the non-being of a dead cat, the non-being of Atlantis, the non-being of a unicorn, etc. Non-being, in short, is not tacked down to owners, or to extra-linguistic referents that are also possessors of nothingness. There is nothing, and there never will be, something corresponding to 'my non-being'.

   Nor – *pace* the Dean of Lichfield – is non-being a state suffered by anyone. When I die, I shall not change from being a particular someone to being a particular no one. The nothing that I shall revert to will not have my label on it: I won't be *a* particular nothing, but dissolve without residue into the Not that exists only as a general limit to what is.

13. My astonishment that I exist connects with another astonishment – that I am this (rather than something else) – as follows. This second astonishment is based on my knowing, or knowing of, beings other than myself – other people, other non-human existents. Some of those other beings are beings that existed in the past and are no longer. That I might not be this [being] is linked with the intuition that I might not have been at all via beings that once existed and are no longer. I shall return to this in the main text.

14. Roland Barthes, *The Elements of Semiology* (translated by Annette Lavers and Colin Smith, London: Cape, 1967), p. 22.

15. This may immediately suggest another reason for damping down astonishment at my existing: if I did not exist, then 'I' would lack any referent (in my mouth) – it would, by definition, be unuttered by me; or it would lack

the referent necessary to sustain my astonishment at *my* existence. My existence is necessary for any expression of astonishment at my existence to have meaning, to count as a valid proposition, expression or speech act. (These three are, importantly, not the same.)

This point has been made by linguists who, while they distinguish between correct and successful reference, believe that this distinction cannot be maintained in the case of personal pronouns such as 'I'. For example, John Lyons, in his profound and illuminating chapter on 'Deixis, Space and Time', in *Semantics*, Volume 2 (Cambridge University Press, 1977):

> the distinction between correct and successful reference ... cannot seriously be drawn in relation to first-person pronouns. The speaker will correctly and successfully refer to himself by means of the pronoun 'I' in English under normal conditions (i.e. in situations other than those in which he acts as an interpreter or spokesman for somebody else) only if he is performing a particular deictic role. It is his performance of this role, and not the truth of any presupposed identifying proposition which determines the correct reference of 'I'.
>
> (p. 645)

16. Lyons, ibid., p. 643. If we go all the way and consider the referent of 'I' to be the speaker of the token 'I' at the moment of uttering that token, 'I' is in danger of becoming a self-reflexive token as follows:

   a) 'I' refers to the speaker at the moment of uttering the token 'I';
   b) that part of the speaker at the moment of uttering 'I' that is relevant to determining the referent of 'I' does not include all (or, necessarily, any part or, of his body). The relevant part of the speaker-moment is the act of emission of the token.
   c) The act of emission of the utterance-token has many elements that are irrelevant to its meaning and the utterance-token itself has many physical features that are irrelevant to its meaning.
   d) When all these irrelevant features are stripped off, we are left with a pure token-emission which, essentially, is inseparable from the assumption of a place in a grammatical sequence.
   e) Under such an interpretation, 'I' refers to this assumption of a place in the grammatical sequence.

By this means, the existential self-reflexivity of 'I' drifts to token-reflexivity.

This, I suspect, is how post-Saussurean thinkers eliminate the extra-linguistic context even from discourse, from utterances, that achieve reference deictically. However, the performative nature of speech-acts, and of the use of 'I' (as set out by Lyons above) forbids this last step. As Lyons points out, 'Deixis, in general, sets limits upon the possibility of decontextualisation; and person-deixis ... introduces an ineradicable subjectivity into the semantic structure of natural languages' (ibid., p. 646). Two minutes' reflection upon this would have saved the intellectual community many person-centuries of barking up the wrong Sequola under the leadership of Jacques Derrida and his followers.

17. The steps by which post-Saussurean writers such as Benveniste make the 'I' purely intra-linguistic (as part of a their general programme of trying to demonstrate that language 'speaks us' (as opposed to our speaking language) and that its referent is itself are critically analysed in Raymond Tallis, *In Defence of Realism* (Edward Arnold: London, 1988), Chapter 5, 'Realism and the Subject'; and *Enemies of Hope* (London: Macmillan, 1997), Chapter 8, 'The Linguistic Unconscious: Saussure and the Post-Saussureans'.

18. This is perhaps to adopt too uncritically J.S. Mills' view that proper names do not have senses, that they are meaningless marks that have denotation without connotation. John Searle (in *Speech Acts*, Cambridge University Press, 1969) has criticised this position forcefully. In Section 7.2 'Proper Names', he convincingly argues that not even proper names permit reference entirely without predication – 'for to do so would be to violate the principle of identification, without conformity to which we cannot refer at all' (p. 174). Nevertheless, the reference of such names is only thinly buttered with sense.

19. David Hume, *A Treatise of Human Nature*, Book I, Part 4, 'Of Personal Identity'.

20. As Sprigge (op. cit.) noted: 'Actually, there are also very great difficulties in imagining what it is like being oneself.'

21. I am not entirely sure of that. When I am deeply asleep or profoundly comatose I am unaware of my body as such (though in sleep it may assert itself indirectly through its influence on my dreams).

22. This not-quite-possessive relation to one's body is explored by Marcel. The following passage (Marcel, op. cit., p. 91) is very much to the point:

> it seems to me that corporeity ... is involved in having – just as corporeity implies what we may call historicity. A body is a history, or more accurately it is the outcome, the fixation of a history. I cannot therefore say that I have a body, at least not properly speaking, but the mysterious relation uniting me to my body is at the foundation of all my powers of having.

23. And we shall encounter the difficulty of reconciling the feeling of a unitary, unbroken 'I' – the 'I' as a non-composite simple – with the fact that I am distributed over, associated with, deposited in, responsible for, various parts of my body, over situations, preoccupations, duties, sensations, feelings, etc. Kant solved this by postulating a cognitive subject which was an active unitary consciousness known, not by introspection or observation, but by a 'transcendental' deduction. As Peter Rickman has put it, 'there is knowledge and this is a necessary condition of its possibility' ('From Hermeneutics to Deconstruction: the Epistemology of Interpretation', *International Studies in Philosophy*, XXVII: 2). The problem, however, is that of relating this unitary subject to the actual person, to the apparent seat of particular needs, impulses, sensations, projects, feelings, etc. and to the influence upon him or her of physiological, psychological, social and historical factors. This has preoccupied many post-Kantian thinkers, as Rickman points out:

This concept [the transcendental cognitive subject] has been attacked and challenged by major thinkers throughout the 19th century because of the supposed scandal that this cognitive subject should not be confused or identified with the empirical subject, the flesh and blood human being who – obviously related to the cognitive subject – acquires knowledge. Kierkegaard emphasized the intertwining of man's intellectual emotional and volitional life, Marx and his followers insisted that man's thinking is rooted in his practical activity of shaping his environment by work within social organizations. Nietzsche stressed that man was an animal whose instincts colored even his highest thought processes. Dilthey complained – as he looked at the history of epistemology culminating in Kant – that 'no blood flowed in the veins of the cognitive subject'. (p. 77)

24. Evolutionists and biologists of consciousness (criticised in my *The Explicit Animal* (London: Macmillan, 1991) and in Chapter 1 of the present volume) live inside this tautology. The assumptions that we get the world wrong at our peril, that the imperatives of survival demand that we tap into how things really are, that the forces of selection will have shaped living organisms into devices for revealing the truth about natural reality have more flaws than is pleasant to tease out. Suffice it to say that there is no evolutionary reason: a) why there should be consciousness at all; b) nor, consequently, why there should be a category of explicit truth; nor c) why the organism could not live in a state of adaptive falsehood or inhabit a world where objects, including organisms, are, as in Kant, to some extent the internal accusatives of consciousness.

25. To put this another way: consciousness of being an x is not simply an uncovering of a pre-existing x, of x 'coming to itself'.

26. I owe this formulation to Frederick Olafson, 'The Unity of Heidegger's Thought', in *The Cambridge Companion to Heidegger,* edited by Charles B. Guignon (Cambridge: Cambridge University Press, 1993), p. 100.

27. This is discussed in Raymond Tallis, *Enemies of Hope: a Critique of Contemporary Pessimism* (London: Macmillan, 1997), pp. 383–5.

28. Octavio Paz, *On Poets and Others* (translated by Michael Schmidt, London: Paladin, 1992), p. 171.

29. It is discussed in Raymond Tallis, *Newton's Sleep* (London: Macmillan, 1995).

30. For a discussion of this tension, see Raymond Tallis, 'Metaphysics and Gossip: Notes Towards a Manifesto for a Novel of the Future', in *Theorrhoea and After* (London: Macmillan, 1999).

31. H.J. Blackham, 'Gabriel Marcel', *Six Existentialist Thinkers* (London: Routledge and Kegan Paul, 1952), p. 67.

5
On the Edge of Certainty

It is so difficult to find the *beginning*
Or, better: it is difficult to begin at the beginning.
And not try to go further back

I

(1)

In December 1949, after several months of illness, Wittgenstein was discovered to have cancer of the prostate gland. At the time of diagnosis secondary deposits were already present in his spine, so there was no hope of cure. A palliative treatment in the form of hormones, however, had recently become available and he was started on Stilboestrol. For the next thirteen or fourteen months, while he was 'letting the hormones do their work'[1] he found himself quite unable to think:

> My mind's completely dead. This is not a complaint, for I don't really suffer from it. I know that life must have an end once and that mental life can cease before the rest does.[2]

His inability to think during this period is not altogether surprising. For a real thinker, thought is not merely a response to what others have said and written, but has endogenous roots; it takes its rise from a region, neither entirely sensual nor wholly verbal, where articulate consciousness merges with bodily awareness. In a profound intellectual impulse, the urge towards clarity and the perspicuous view is inseparable from an ache for sharper self-presence. The sense that the world has a deeper, secret meaning to yield up – which transforms technical problems into matters of the utmost personal urgency and makes the thinker willing to suffer and to protract the intolerable tensions of inconclusion, to cultivate active uncertainty – originates in an excitement, an agitation, a curiosity, that may borrow some energy from sexual desire. In the absence of pain, nausea, malaise, fear or confusion, certain disease states may displace the thinker from his familiar self and deepen the active dislocation that makes original thought possible. A treatment such as hormone therapy, however, must switch off the springs of delight and consequently the creative astonishment that formulates itself into questions and the intuition of possible answers. Linked to the world, presented to himself, through the mediation of an alien body, he may cease to think.

If it is not too difficult to understand how Stilboestrol rendered Wittgenstein's mind infertile, it is hard to accept his claim that he did not *suffer* from this loss of intellectual libido, that he accepted it as easily as he implied in his letter to Norman Malcolm. Did he really not mourn a lost self-taste or the vanished drama of intellectual tension and its resolution? Surely he felt empty when so much of his essential self had dissolved into vagueness, absence, generality? Surely he resented the perpetual sea-fog intervening between him and himself, the permanent mist over the mirror of self-articulation? Or was he already only half-alive, buried beneath both hope and despair and reconciled to the ending of himself?

There is, of course, no way of answering these questions with certainty. One writer, not always regarded as reliable, speaks of Wittgenstein's 'almost constant' depression during the last years.[3] Anyway, in February 1951, when it was obvious that his illness was beyond even palliation, he stopped taking the hormone tablets. His ability to think at his accustomed depth returned soon after. On 16 April, thirteen days before his death, he wrote to one of his ex-pupils:

> An extraordinary thing happened to me. About a month ago I suddenly found myself in the right frame of mind for doing philosophy. I had been *absolutely* certain that I'd never again be able to do it ... Of course, so far I've only worked for about five weeks and it may be all over by tomorrow, but it bucks me up a lot now.[4]

His physical well-being had returned:

> ... apart from a certain weakness which has constant ups and downs I'm feeling very well these days.[5]

To Mrs Bevan (the wife of his GP, in whose house he was living and dying), he said:

I'm going to work now as I've never worked before!⁶

The final period of thought lasted just under seven weeks. Its fruits comprise over half of the posthumously published volume titled *On Certainty*, compiled by two of his ex-pupils.⁷

On 10 March, he noted:

Not all corrections of our views are on the same level.⁸

This seemingly banal observation inaugurates an intense, polyphonic, obsessional meditation on topics that had engaged him for most of his thinking life. During these seven weeks he was 'apparently in the best of spirits';⁹ and the pages of *On Certainty* bear out von Wright's claim that 'as late as two days before his death he wrote down thoughts that are equal to the best he produced'.

The poignancy of the philosophical quest in of *On Certainty* is heightened by scattered autobiographical reflections. They are not given paragraph numbers and are severely cordoned off in square brackets. On the same day as his jubilant letter to Norman Malcolm, he observed:

[I do philosophy now like an old woman who is always mislaying something and having to look for it again: now her spectacles, now her keys.]¹⁰

Four weeks earlier he had written:

[I believe it might interest a philosopher, one who can think himself, to read my notes. For even if I have hit the mark only rarely, he would recognise what targets I had been ceaselessly aiming at.]¹¹

And on 5 April, he reflects sadly:

[Here there is still a big gap in my thinking. And I doubt whether it will be filled now.]¹²

The final entry, No. 676, was dated 27 April 1951 – the day he lost consciousness and two days before his death.

(2)

Immediately after the melancholy remark about 'the big gap' in his thinking is an entry which gives succinct expression to something that had from the outset lain at the heart of his philosophical views, attitudes, styles and inconclusions. It summarises his entire philosophical struggle; and illuminates why philosophy should have been so much more of a *struggle* for him than for others much less gifted than himself:

> It is so difficult to find the beginning. Or better, it is difficult to begin at the *beginning*. And not try to go further back.[13]

This was the burdensome insight he had lived with – or inside of – since he had first come to philosophy.

The traditional itinerary of the Western European philosopher was given its classical form by Descartes who set out in his *Meditations* from total doubt and thought he had ended at absolute certainty. Universal doubt, Descartes claimed,

> delivers us from every kind of prejudice, and sets out for us a very simple way by which the mind may detach itself from the senses ... and makes it impossible for us ever to doubt those things which we have once discovered to be true.[14]

Philosophy begins with the cultivation of a radical scepticism trained upon the deepest presuppositions and habitual assumptions of everyday life. Nothing is immune from this doubt – not even the belief that there is an 'outside' world independent of my mind, or that I am sitting here at my desk writing. Everything that can be questioned, everything that is known with less than total certainty, is burnt away until there remains only that which cannot be doubted without self-contradiction. When the demolition job is complete, the unassailable truths that remain form the basis for reconstruction. The philosopher builds upon the self-evidently given, the primitive, the axiomatic, unpacking a new world by means of impeccable arguments constrained by an iron logic. This new world is either a radically revised, 'truer' world than the old one; or – more commonly – the old, unchanged everyday world with its foundations, its truth, made explicit. The philosopher passes through doubt to certainty; and his scepticism, which destroys mere prejudice, clears the way for 'absolute' or 'true' knowledge.

The legitimacy of the recovered certainty on the far side of doubt had often been challenged since Descartes. 'Scepticism', David Hume observed, 'is a malady which can never be radically cured but must return upon us every moment, however we may chase it away.'[15] And

F.H. Bradley had sardonically characterised the metaphysician's attempt to place his world picture upon a firmer footing as 'the finding of bad reasons for what we believe upon instinct'.[16] Once radical doubt has been admitted, things can never again be the same again. No 'thinking certainty' can feel as secure as the unthinking certainty destroyed by critical reflection. Wittgenstein's originality lay not in his scepticism about the happy ending of the philosophical journey but in his questioning the validity of the doubts from which it set out. It was not merely the solutions philosophers found to their problems that he regarded as questionable but the problems themselves.

Like Kierkegaard – whom he deeply admired ('Kierkegaard was by far the most profound thinker of the last century'),[17] though he found him too 'long-winded' – he considered most philosophical questions to be inadmissible on existential grounds. Philosophical doubting was largely a charade – a matter of 'writing *de omnibus disputandum* and at the same time being as credulous existentially as the most sensuous of men'.[18] And he was influenced by Moore who found it absurd that a man should doubt (or worse, deny) the reality of space and time while confidently planning to have his breakfast before his dinner and to eat it in one place rather than another. But it was his dissent from traditional philosophy on logico-linguistic grounds that gave rise to some of his most original and interesting and once notorious contributions to twentieth-century philosophical debate.

You cannot, he said, really ask most philosophical questions since they cannot be formulated without suspending the conditions in which utterances make sense. If, for example, there were any real doubts about whether or not there was an outside world, then this could not be *discussed*.

> Scepticism is not irrefutable, but obviously nonsensical, when it tries to raise doubts where no questions can be asked.
>
> For a doubt can exist only where a question exists, a question only where an answer exists, and an answer only where something *can be said*.[19]

The conspicuous unanswerability of many philosophical questions is, therefore, merely the obverse of their overlooked unaskability. To reach as far back as the places where most philosophical discussion starts out is to go too far back. For a proposition or an utterance to be true (or even false) it must make sense. Only when an utterance meets sense-conditions – so that it can have meaning and secure reference – can it have truth-conditions and be either true or false.

> Most of the propositions and questions to be found in philosophical works are not false but nonsensical ... [They] arise from the failure to understand the logic of our language ...[20]

In *Tractatus*, the grounds for denying sense-conditions to most philosophical questions and answers are linguistic rather than existential – 'the failure to understand the logic of our language'. Philosophical questions

> belong to the same class as the question whether the good is more or less identical than the beautiful.[21]

In later years, however, logical and linguistic objections to traditional philosophy became interwoven in a more complex way with existential dissent. It was no longer sufficient to assert that many propositions of philosophy often contravened 'the *logic* of our language' and transgressed the boundaries of the sayable. For there is no single logic of language: the limits of the sayable are not internally determined, functions of the intrinsic properties of language. What is sayable cannot be inferred from the general features of the relationship between signs (or propositions) and the objects (or situations) that they signify (or propose). The meaningfulness of particular utterances is determined less by whether or not they have a particular structure (so that they are logical pictures of the reality they speak of) than by the customary use to which their component signs and their combinations have been put. It is not only the *structure* of an utterance that determines whether it is meaningful but the context in which it is uttered. Sense-conditions are existential as well as logico-linguistic:

> A proposition has meaning only in the stream of life.[22]

Life and language cannot readily be extricated from one another. Contrary to what had been implied in *Tractatus*, everyday speech does not have a formal symbolic system (with an unsayable grammar) at its heart; rather, it is composed of an indefinite number of heterogeneous language-games that serve the purposes of the moment.

Language has an enormous number of grammatical rules; there cannot be a single *philosophical* grammar describing the fundamental features, the logic, of language. Moreover, all its grammars are local: no grammar can be complete without reference to the differential existential settings in which language is used. The existential conditions that make utterances intelligible are inevitably local; so no universalising or philosophical grammar is possible. Philosophical discourse is often senseless, not because it contravenes 'the logic of our language', but because it uproots expressions from the specific contexts in which they have meaning and so deprives them of the existential conditions for complete sense.

To ask the question 'What time is it?' is to participate in a particular language-game which is deeply rooted in a certain form of life – our own. To ask the apparently similar question 'What is Time?' is to remove 'time' from the settings that give it a completed sense – rather like asking 'What is five o'clock on the sun?'[23]

Failure to recognise that the meaning of words is inseparable from the local contexts in which they are usually used also results in the error of confusing grammar with ontology; of inferring, for example, from the fact that the word 'time' is a noun in the question 'What time is it?', that 'time' refers to a 'substance' or a 'thing' or a 'medium'. Much philosophy consists in taking words and utterances out of the contexts in which they are usually used – and make sense – and subjecting them to abnormal scrutiny. Drawing ontological conclusions from accidents of grammar is in some respects analogous to studying the moves in football to determine the Laws of Motion.

Philosophers are especially prone to draw invalid universal conclusions from local grammar because they tend to concentrate upon a handful of utterances that have a particular kind of structure.

A picture held us captive. And we could not get out of it, for it lay in our language and language seemed to repeat it to us inexorably.[24]

The interplay of existential and linguistic grounds for Wittgenstein's objection to conventional philosophy is vividly expressed in his assertion that

Philosophical problems arise when language goes on holiday.

The confusions which occupy us arise when language is like an engine idling, not when it is doing work.[25]

(3)

Wittgenstein's repudiation of traditional philosophy had nothing to do with the easy scorn of the non-philosopher who has never been touched by the mystery of the world. Nor was it the shallow and lazy irrationalism of a man pleased to point to the limitations of logical thought as a pretext for turning his back on the rigours of hard thinking. He lacked neither the amazement which is the precondition of true philosophy nor the intellectual willpower to pursue an argument or a train of thought over hours, days, weeks, years ... As Russell said of him:

> He has the theoretical passion very strongly ... He doesn't want to prove this or that, but to find out how things are. It *hurts* him not to know.[26]

'It *hurts* him not to know'. If he was so consistently an original thinker, it was because he was one of those rare spirits possessed of the strength of mind to begin each day's thinking as if the world had not already been thought about the day – or the millennium – before. He refused to become a mere echo or imitation of himself; to decline in response to the pressures to publish from a thinker into a journalist; to freewheel through middle age on the intellectual momentum generated by the terrors and appetites of his youth. Nothing, therefore, could have been more unjust than Russell's diagnosis of the posthumously published *Philosophical Investigations* as the work of 'a man who is tired of thinking'. He never tired of thinking and his objection to traditional philosophy and its attempts to reconstruct a world razed by doubt were not shallowly anti-philosophical. They were deeply philosophical: they gave birth to much of what was most original in his thought.

Nevertheless, he knew that philosophical doubt was perfectly justified: the intelligibility of the world is incomplete, its structure and meaning only partly revealed and its purpose (if any) concealed from us; there are contradictions at the heart of consciousness itself; and we cannot even identify with certainty which things we are entitled to be certain of. At every level, in every direction, in every dimension, the sense of the world is incomplete, provisional. Wittgenstein never ceased to feel this and to suffer from a correspondingly fierce appetite for certainty. He knew the vertigo of the metaphysical moment, the panic-stricken hunger for absolute knowledge. And yet he could not ignore the implicit critique that ordinary life and ordinary discourse applied to the profound doubts and revolutionary conclusions of such moments.

My *life* consists in my being content to accept many things.[27]

His entire philosophical life was discoloured by an unresolved conflict between valid *felt* doubts (which opened on to astonishment) and the inadmissibility of most expressions of those doubts and (*a fortiori*) of expressed solutions to those doubts. Philosophical doubt cannot be made public without self-contradiction. I may genuinely *feel* as if I am now dreaming; but I cannot seriously *debate* it publicly. Philosophy that begins with the possibility that 'it might all be a dream' or that 'I may be deceived in my belief that there is a world outside of me' – indeed, uses it as an official or traditional starting point – begins too far back, outside of the existential sense-conditions of language. Philosophy that starts out from universal doubt must, at the very least, doubt its own intelligibility. Its making its questions a matter for public debate must undermine its authenticity.

He was held in stasis by the conflict between the doubts that moved him to grapple with philosophical problems and his perception that most philosophical debate took place outside of the conditions in which any utterance could have sense. For him there was no escape from metaphysical vertigo into the community of discussion. In his early youth, he at least had the hope of breaking that solitude with those whose intellectual powers he respected – Frege, Russell, Moore. But that hope evaporated. Frege steadfastly pursued this thoughts into a labyrinth of technicalities: he was a mathematician rather than a philosopher and gave the philosophy of language – and his attempt to reduce language to the status of mathematics by means of a logical calculus – priority over epistemology. Even when Russell pointed out the contradictions in his system, Frege did not yield to the epistemological temptation. He died a heartbroken technician, shipwrecked on the Russell paradox, but determined not to draw its ontological conclusions. Russell himself remained brilliant and prolific long after he had suffered what Wittgenstein considered to be 'a loss of problems'. Russell's quickness, lucidity and fluency seemed to him the mark of a fundamental shallowness; and the latter, exasperated by Wittgenstein's refusal to deal with conventional philosophical problems in the direct manner to which he was accustomed, described the later Wittgenstein as a man 'tired of thinking'. Moore, who was closest to sharing his second-order scepticism, confessed to never having suffered from philosophical problems in the first place:

I do not think that the world or the sciences would ever have suggested to me any philosophical problems. What has suggested problems to me is things which other philosophers have said about the world or about natural sciences.[28]

Moore's second-order scepticism, superficially akin to Wittgenstein's, was inseparable from the almost child-like honesty that struck all who knew him, including Wittgenstein. But it was also part of his second-order (though not second-rate) philosophical impulse. Nothing could have been more alien to a man possessed by the philosophical daemon than Moore's admission that it was not the world that prompted him to philosophise but philosophy books. Of the other thinkers whom he could respect as equals or near-equals, Sraffa was an economist who, like Keynes, turned his incomparable intellect upon philosophical matters only as a kind of recreation; while F.P. Ramsay, who had sought out Wittgenstein in Austria and had been one of the earliest admirers as well as co-translator of *Tractatus*, had died of leukaemia at the age of twenty-six in the year of Wittgenstein's return to Cambridge.

(4)

Almost, but not quite, paralysed by the conflict between felt doubt and the inadmissibility of philosophical discussion, he continued to tread a path between philosophy and anti-philosophy. Sometimes in total physical isolation, mentally in almost constant solitude, he moved away from the positions of his peers and contemporaries and yet was reluctant to turn back to expound his views to them in the systematic way that they expected of a philosopher. This was in part because he could not systematise his views:

After several attempts to weld my results together into such a whole, I realized that I should never succeed. My thoughts were soon crippled if I tried to force them on in any single direction against their natural inclination.[29]

Behind this incapacity was a stubborn refusal to order his thoughts along conventional curricular lines or around standard problems. And behind this again was a heroic scrupulousness – a refusal to abandon thinking to himself in order to think to or for others. His list of completed works, of thought-objects for public consumption – one short book published in his thirties, a brief article in his forties – was absurd for an academic; next to Russell's torrent of books it is almost laughable. And yet the posthumously published evidence of his unceasing activity makes it clear that the scantiness of his bibliography was the direct result of his valuing the process of thinking over mere products of thoughts. Like Valéry, he was intensely conscious of the opposition between the latter and the awareness necessary for true thought; of how one has to stop thinking at the deepest level in order to arrange one's thoughts into something that can be published, to turn them into an item in one's bibliography. With a scrupulousness rare even amongst great thinkers, he did not allow himself to be diverted from the pursuit of truth by a wish to *make* something – to build a book, an *oeuvre*, a reputation. He lived perpetually in his current account and did not permit himself the luxury of a deposit account – a body of published work – to fatten or to insulate his self-esteem.

He never ceased thinking to and for himself and yet it seems as if the dreamed of dialogue and someone with whom he might engage in discussion as an equal. His later books and notebooks contain snatches of dialogue and, though both voices are always his, they suggest that if he was not tired of thinking he was tired of being condemned to think always to himself. He could not find anyone amongst his few peers to mend his mind to the peculiar grain of his thought or to respond to the unremitting urgency of his approach to philosophical problems. And with others he so dominated any discussion that it became effectively a monologue: he grew impatient as they toiled over ground he had already covered. Moreover, to differ from him, to fail to understand him, was to be wilfully stupid, to show hostility. He could not tolerate those who did not, like him, think continuously, the 'tourists' who were not really troubled by the problems and thought about philosophy only when they talked about it. A philosopher was 'one who can think for himself'.[30] In the end he had to settle for disciples recruited from amongst pupils who accorded their teacher the status of a prophet. Inevitably he had (in the words of one of them) an 'inhibiting effect':[31]

> I feared his judgement and admired in silence: I accepted that most of what he said was beyond my then comprehension but hoped that some day understanding might dawn ... I was ... diffident about myself and my opinions and nervous of making an ass of myself in the rarefied atmosphere in which I now found myself, and I had already burned my fingers.[32]

Wittgenstein was uneasy with this authority, especially as the nervous awe with which he was held was at least as much a product of his failure as a man (his impatience, his intolerance) as of his power as a thinker.

He suspected that he was a bad teacher; and by all the usual criteria he was. He induced panic in his pupils so that they could not think in his presence and tended to ape his intellectual mannerisms in his absence. And yet he may have been a bad teacher of philosophy for good philosophical reasons; for to teach philosophy is to take one step deeper into the pragmatic self-refutation that is almost inescapable in philosophical discussion. If a teacher is someone who is senior to his pupils not only in years and office but also in virtue of the knowledge, experience, wisdom, maturity he has to impart to them, then the idea of a teacher of philosophy is absurd: how can one be 'senior' to another in the matter of raising, holding, handling, resolving or doubting the legitimacy of our belief in the existence of an external world? How can one *seriously* entertain the possibility that the whole of one's life may be a dream while at the same time engaging unquestioningly in organising tutorials (tutorials in which to doubt the outside world), planning timetables, devising curricula, assessing pupils – involving oneself in all the paraphernalia of the pedagogic enterprise? What would be an appropriate way to discipline a pupil who failed to attend a seminar in which 'our knowledge of external reality' had been subjected to critical and inconclusive examination? How can one commend a pupil's intellectual capabilities if they have been demonstrated in a discussion which failed to resolve doubts about our knowledge of other minds? From the metaphysical standpoint, all men are equal, none is more senior in knowledge than any other, there are no objective tors on the collective consciousness.

This may have been one of the many reasons why he did not give formal lectures. (Though there was also his disinclination to dismount from thought to put its products into conventional form or to engage in mere scholarship. He was unscholarly and unreliable as a reporter on other philosophers.) Instead, he thought out loud and (occasionally) engaged in dialogue. Since he had ceased to believe that he had solved any of the problems of philosophy by the time he had become a professional philosopher, he did not think that he had any *results* to impart. All he could offer was a method of philosophising that had developed out of his ceaseless dialogues with himself. His 'lectures' were an invitation to his pupils to engage with him in the process of thought. In practice, however, his impatience got the better of him and he cowed them out of thought into submissive silence, into abject pupilhood.

The conflict between the metaphysical equality implicit in the radical scepticism of philosophy and the hierarchical arrangement of individuals in a university reflected the conflict within him between his impulse to speak (to lay down the law, to assert the unassailability of his viewpoint, to dominate with monologues) and his conviction that, because they suspend the space in which utterances have sense, there is simply nothing to say about philosophical questions and certainly no experts available to answer them. Even *Tractatus* – the only book he published in his lifetime – was explicitly not a textbook:

> Perhaps this book will be understood only by someone who has himself already had the thoughts expressed in it – or at least similar thoughts. So it is not a text book. – Its purpose would be achieved if it gave pleasure to one person who read and understood it.[33]

In the posthumous *Philosophical Investigations*, one has the sense of overhearing Wittgenstein talking to himself; or of a dialogue between him and an ideal interlocutor whose absence made him tolerable and spared Wittgenstein the need to assert his authority. In this book, too, we are aware of being presented not with the products of thought but with the process of thought, with understanding developing through conflict with itself. He did not envisage his readers receiving his results as termini of the thought process:

> I should not like my writing to spare other people the trouble of thinking. But, if possible to stimulate someone to thoughts of his own.[34]

Nevertheless, the *Investigations* still implicitly carried the authority that accrues to something so thoroughly worked over. It is in the post-humously published notebooks that one has texts that are freest from being textbooks. And it is above all in *On Certainty* – especially in the last fifty pages or so where there is no hope of completion – that one gets the sense of being in the presence of a man truly thinking to himself, at ease in articulate self-presence, engaged in utterly free enquiry. The audience – real or imaginary – has attenuated to a faint ghost. In so far as there is an addressee, it is his equal, 'one who can think himself'.

[I believe it might interest a philosopher, one who can think himself, to read my notes. For even if I have hit the mark only rarely, he would recognise what targets I had been ceaselessly aiming at.][35]

Some to whom he could admit:

Here I am inclined to fight windmills because I cannot yet say the things I really want to say.[36]

(5)

To the end, however, he remained uneasy: hungering for the kind of truth and certainty that the older philosophers cultivated doubt in order to reach; while conscious that philosophical discourses were largely nonsensical. He still could not determine the sense-conditions that would make *expressed* philosophical doubts as legitimate as the felt doubts that prompted them.

In the pages of *On Certainty*, we see him coming to question even the second-order scepticism that countered philosophical doubt – to dissent from the 'robust common sense' that was Moore's characteristic stance. He was suspicious of Moore's protestation that he *knew* that there was an outside world because he knew these were his hands or that this was a tree. There is something dubious in asserting what is usually taken for granted (even if the assertion is intended to counter the absurdities of the sceptical position). It is 'like saying "Good morning" in the middle of a conversation'.[37]

I am sitting with a philosopher in the garden; he says again and again 'I know that is a tree', pointing to a tree that is near us. Someone else arrives and hears this, and I tell him: 'This fellow isn't insane. We are only doing philosophy'.[38]

And the illegitimacy of Moore's defending the common-sense certainties by saying 'I know there is a hand in front of me' goes deeper:

It is as if 'If know' did not tolerate a metaphysical emphasis.[39]

While there are sense-conditions for the assertion 'I know that there is a train from Cambridge to London at 5.00 pm', there are no such conditions for the assertion 'I know that there is a hand in front of me' intended to carry the metaphysical conclusion that there is an outside world. I cannot 'know' that there is a hand in front of me in the metaphysical sense or a world outside of me because I could not (accidentally) not *know* it; I could not be simply mistaken about it. I could imagine a situation in which I might be emphatic about my knowledge of train times – because it is easy to imagine doubt being cast upon it or even upon the likelihood of my being well informed on the matter. It is less easy to imagine reasons for others doubting my assertion that this is my hand, especially when the assertion is meant in a metaphysical sense. If an assertion is indubitable (and its indubitability is bound up with the metaphysical weight it is intended to carry), then it does not really count as a claim to knowledge, because I could scarcely be mistaken over it.

> Can one say 'Where there is no doubt there is no knowledge either?[40]

> Doesn't one need grounds for doubt?[41]

Where there are no such grounds, there can be no doubts – and hence no knowledge either.

The claim to certainty cannot, therefore, be made – or it cannot take the form of a claim to certain knowledge. When Moore says 'I know that that is a tree' he is mistaken in thinking that his absence of doubt is based upon certain knowledge. He is merely brushing away the grounds for doubt:

> I really want to say that a language game is possible only if one trusts something (I did not say 'can trust something').[42]

> If I wanted to doubt whether this was my hand, how could I avoid doubting whether the word 'hand' has any meaning?[43]

> To say of man, in Moore's sense, that he *knows* something; that what he says is therefore unconditionally the truth seems wrong to me – It is the truth only inasmuch as it is an unmoving foundation of his language-games.[44]

Moore, by countering the sceptical position with claims to have absolutely certain knowledge of at least some things, falls into the sceptical trap of overlooking that

> My *life* consists in my being content to accept many things.[45]

In other words, overlooking the existential grounds for rejecting the sceptical position. Moreover, doubt itself rests only upon what is beyond doubt:[46]

> A doubt that doubted everything would not be a doubt.[47]

So, even Moore's refusal to accept the validity of scepticism 'begins too far back'. Meeting the sceptics on their own dubious ground he is lured into poor arguments, mere protestation that 'of course' he knows that this is his hand, etc.

> What is the proof that I *know* something. Most certainly not my saying I know it.[48]

> And so, when writers enumerate all the things they *know*, that proves nothing whatever.[49]

Second-order scepticism – scepticism about the validity of philosophical scepticism – then, is going to be a much more complex and subtle position than a 'robust' or 'stubborn' defence of common sense, especially since metaphysical certainty seems to have little or nothing to do with the things that in practical daily life cannot be doubted:

> Why is there no doubt that I am called L.W.? It does not seem at all like something one could establish at once beyond doubt. One would not think that it is one of the indubitable truths.[50]

The existential and linguistic sense-conditions for admissible doubts, or for metaphysical certainty, prove impossible to define. But if it is not possible to determine what may be doubted, or known with certainty, there can be no way of knowing how or where to begin. This was 'the big gap in his thinking' which he noted so near to his death:

> Here there is still a big gap in my thinking. And I doubt whether it will be filled now.[51]

Unlike Moore, he could entertain the possibility that he had got everything wrong, that he had no basis for his common-sense confidence.

> Is my understanding only blindness to my own lack of understanding? It often seems so to me.[52]

But how was he to respond to that intuition and find the beginning from which to move forward? How to remove what he thought to be uncertain without transgressing common sense, to build only upon what had seemed irrefutable without talking nonsense? How to speak when he could no longer endure the silence he enjoined upon himself?

Again and again, he had felt the ground shift beneath his feet but this had not justified his questioning, in the traditional philosophical fashion the very existence of the ground. And now, in the last few days of his conscious existence, he continued his mental itinerary along the catwalk between philosophy and anti-philosophy, suspended above his own intuition of chaos in a superficially ordered world inhabited and run by people who knew nothing of that chaos and had no way of acknowledging it. To the last he struggled with his problem, his meta-problem and himself, fulfilling his vow

> that as long as I live and as often as my state of mind permits I will think about philosophical problems and try to write about them.[53]

(6)

He continued thinking and writing almost to the edge of his life, remained a consciousness still trying to make sense of itself as sense-lessness and coma approached. Even as he used the *Nachsommer* of his intellect to investigate the grounds of the confidence enjoyed by fluent, unsurprised daily awareness and to define the scope of legitimate doubt, he was encircled by many-layered uncertainty: he had no confidence in the value of his thoughts, or the direction they were taking; his mind did not know when it would cease to think ('it may well be all over by tomorrow');[54] and he did not know when he would cease to live.

There is an intense poignancy in the note that opens his last day's thought.

> We might speak of the fundamental principles of human enquiry.[55]

Yes, we might speak of them; but he knew now that if there were such principles they would elude him forever. His ceaseless endeavour to get to the bottom of things had resulted only in one short, systematic treatise, which he himself had rejected, and a huge wake of penetrating but scattered observations that scholars would comb over minutely for generations. The lure of complete but self-transparent understanding that had led him from mechanics to physics, from physics to mathematics and from the foundations of mathematics to philosophy had ended only in 'the big gap in his thinking' which he no longer believed would be filled. Again and again he had been deflected from the targets 'he was ceaselessly aiming at'. Between him and the fundamental questions lay language – language, without which there might not be such questions. And though he had once thought he had seen into the heart of language with a gaze before which the fundamental questions evaporated, he had subsequently come to understand that language had no heart – only an endless and unfolding surface upon which no perspicuous view was possible. And so he was twice removed from the fundamental principles; and yet ... these seven weeks had witnessed a kind of return to the mystery, to the riddle which, despite the anti-metaphysical stance of the author of *Tractatus* did, after all, exist.

He returned on this, his last day of thought, to the topics that had obsessed him over the previous weeks, the preceding decades.

> If someone believes he has flown from America to England in the last few days, then I believe, he cannot be making a mistake.
>
> And just the same if someone says that he is at this moment sitting at a table and writing.[56]

If my belief that I had flown America to England over the last few days had proved false, I could not be merely *mistaken*. Likewise, my belief that there is an external world, or that the world has existed for more than five minutes, or that others are not products of my imagination, could not turn out to be mere mistakes resulting from my happening to be ignorant of my own life – even allowing for the fact that, as he had said at the outset,

> Not all corrections of our views are on the same level.[57]

So it is odd, even perverse, for me to pretend to regard such beliefs as (mere) matters of knowledge. No experience, giving rise to information, could ever count as grounds for them or evidence against them. Indeed, it is probably wrong to described them as convictions at all, as if they could be something personal, something I hold, positions I have arrived at (as a result of experience): they are too fundamental. The framework, the presupposition for all knowledge, conviction, belief, they are hardly things I can be *merely certain* about. Even less can I be *uncertain* about them to the point of calling them into question.

> If I don't trust *this* evidence why should I trust any evidence?[58]

Nevertheless, there are seemingly fundamental things which can be doubted. As he had reflected a few weeks earlier:

> But what men consider reasonable or unreasonable alters. At certain periods men find reasonable what at other periods they found unreasonable. And vice versa.[59]

And now he writes:

> Is it not difficult to distinguish between the cases in which I cannot and those in which I can hardly be mistaken? Is it always clear to which kind a case belongs? I believe not.[60]

In the last few hours of his writing life, he admits to his uncertainty as to what can be – must be – regarded as unshakeably certain. It is no longer clear to him where empirical fact ends and the rules of grammar or metaphysical frameworks begin. There starts to emerge a third-order scepticism which modifies his own radical critique of the philosopher's radical doubt. The boundaries of legitimate doubt are ill-defined; and so, correspondingly, are the boundaries of justified certainty. The balance between philosophical doubt and existential certainty begins to tip towards doubt ... But the movement is arrested:

> There are, however, certain types of cases in which I rightly say I cannot be making a mistake, and Moore has given a few examples of such cases ...[61]

However,

> I can enumerate various typical cases, but not give any common characteristic.[62]

The argument then takes another, astonishing, turn:

> And, even if in such cases I can't be mistaken, isn't it possible that I am drugged? And if I am and if the drug has taken away my

consciousness, then I am not now really talking and thinking. I cannot seriously suppose that I am at this moment dreaming. Someone who, dreaming, says 'I am dreaming', even if he speaks audibly in doing so, is no more right than if he said in his dream 'it is raining', while it was in fact raining. Even if his dream were actually connected with the noise of the rain.[63]

These remarks take the reflection of a month earlier –

The argument 'I may be dreaming' is senseless for this reason: if I am dreaming, this remark is being dreamed as well – and indeed it is also being dreamed that these words have any meaning[64]

abruptly, vertiginously, deeper.

The obvious target is the artificial doubt that had led Descartes by so many false steps to the 0, 0, 0, point of Cartesian philosophy:

At the same time I must remember that I am a man, and that consequently I am in the habit of sleeping, and in my dreams representing to myself the same things or sometimes even less probable things, than do those who are insane in their waking moments .... At this moment it does indeed seem to me that it is with the eyes awake that I am looking at this paper; that this head which I move is not asleep, that it is deliberately and of set purpose that I extend my hand and perceive it.... But in thinking over this I remind myself that on many occasions I have in sleep been deceived by similar illusions, and in dwelling carefully on this reflection I see so manifestly that there are no certain indications by which we may clearly distinguish wakefulness from sleep that I am lost in astonishment. And my astonishment is such that it is almost capable of persuading me that I now dream.[65]

'*Almost* capable of persuading ...' In this respect, at least, Descartes was honest; but the rest of the paragraph is riddled with inauthenticity, with pragmatic self-refutation. We are asked to believe that the writer almost believes he is dreaming (to a degree sufficient to justify the doubt that sets his philosophy in motion); but since the writing is cast in the present tense, we must believe that he is capable of suspecting that he is dreaming and, at the same time, of communicating this suspicion. Wittgenstein has already pointed out that it is inadmissible to start by arguing 'I may be dreaming' because if I *am* dreaming when I say 'I may be dreaming' then my utterance lacks sense-conditions. So the proposal would have to be false for me to propose it. It cannot therefore be seriously entertained. And it certainly cannot be used to inaugurate a public debate. Even less can it be taken as the *traditional* starting point for philosophical discussion. Or, rather, there is something almost grotesque in the fact that it is.

'I cannot seriously suppose that I am at this moment dreaming'. Without a fully conscious communicative intent, my utterance would be merely a set of sounds: a material event, but not a speech-act. A dreamer cannot intend to communicate the fact that he is dreaming without moving outside of this dream state. And if 'we are close to waking when we dream that we are dreaming',[66] we must needs be wide awake to *assert* that we are dreaming – especially if we assert it with the explicit purpose of initiating a philosophical debate.

If it so happens that I *am* dreaming when I mutter 'I am dreaming', this does not make the sounds I produce count as a true statement. Before a vocalisation can qualify as a true statement, it has to be a statement; before it can be true, it has to make sense. A dreaming man mumbling 'I am dreaming' is no more making a true statement than a dictaphone located inside a corpse playing 'I am dead' is *someone* pronouncing himself dead. Nor would it be so even if the tape were a recording of the ex-man's own voice. The mere coincidence between a series of sounds and the truth-condition of the utterance that would use those sounds is not in itself sufficient to make the sounds a true statement because it is insufficient to make it a *statement*. (Failure to appreciate this point has played a large part in the recent proliferation of fallacious computer analogies in the theory of mind; if it had been understood, the thirty-year cul-de-sac of AI theories of mind, opening up at about the time of Wittgenstein's death, might have been avoided.)

(7)

The very last sentence he wrote takes his argument further, deeper:

> Even if his dream were actually connected with noise of the rain.[63]

Statement S may be about state of affairs A but a causal relationship between the occurrence of S and the occurrence of A is not in itself sufficient to make S be 'about' A; and *a fortiori* it is insufficient to make S a true statement of or about A. Without the mediation of a communicative intention (so that the sounds corresponding to S are being deliberately used to communicate 'that A'), S does not count as a statement; and as such it can neither be true nor false. The words coming from the speaker's mouth amount to a speech-act only if they are interpreted as such by someone else overhearing the words; and even then they amount only to an apparent speech-act. They become such only in another consciousness whose act of interpretation releases their potential meaning – a meaning that is, curiously, not actively meant by the producer of the words; a meaning that has a consumer but no producer; a meaning that is not meant.

This is analogous to the situation with natural signs where, for example, causes may signify their effects. Whereas I may infer from the clouds in the sky that it is probably about to rain, it does not follow from this that every cloud in the sky is a permanent statement to the effect that 'It is probably going to rain'. For this to be true (and for natural signs to be true statements of future or actual states of affair) the clouds would have to intend the inferences that are drawn from their presence; which, of course, they do not.

If states of affairs caused the statements that are 'about' then and thereby made those statements to be 'about them' and to be true, we would be witness to a curious convergence of causation and tautology, of causal and logical necessity. But Wittgenstein recognised (and this was what he was concerned to emphasise in this, his last written thought) that for an utterance to have sense, it must be explicitly meant. So the utterance 'I am dreaming' cannot make sense since, if true, it could not have an addressee and so could not be *meant*. In a dream there can be no one to talk to – not at least *about* the dream – so there can be no speech. The intrinsic properties of the utterance or even its relations – causal or otherwise – to that which a waking onlooker might regard it as 'being about' would be insufficient to fulfil the conditions for its having sense.

He had arrived back at the concerns that had occupied most of his philosophical life. And he recognised, perhaps, at last, precisely what was behind his twenty-five year quarrel with *Tractatus*. The author of *Tractatus* had believed, or wished to believe, or to prove, that the sense of a proposition and its meaning content could be guaranteed by a relationship between its structure and that of the state of affairs 'depicted' in it. A structural identity, a coincidence of logical forms, was sufficient to ensure that proposition P meant the state of affairs A. In this way the having of sense (by utterances) could be automated;

and the inexplicable acts of intention (of meaning) and comprehension (of meaning) could be bypassed. Meaning could be transmitted without its being explicitly meant or explicitly grasped. Not long after his return to philosophy, ten or more years after the publication of *Tractatus*, Wittgenstein came to the conclusion that the structure of a proposition was insufficient to determine its meaning even less to guarantee that it had a meaning. The same picture could be used to depict or illustrate different things; nothing in it could determine what it was a picture of – its intentionality. Structure was insufficient to fix, to generate fully determinate sense. The more radical conclusion of *Philosophical Investigations* was that a proposition had no intrinsic sense, being meaningful 'only in the stream of life'. He now touched the furthest point of the long journey from *Tractatus*, perhaps reaching in his last thoughts a mystery that he had intuited all his life: the irreducible mystery of explicitness (itself most explicit in speech) that is the consciousness of man – the explicit animal.

As he ended, the beginning was at last once more in sight and new horizons were opening up. Whether it was a beginning from which he could have moved forward, whether it opened on to a development in which his consciousness might have come closer to completing its own sense, moving from chequered doubt and certainty to the serenity of self-transparent mystery, is uncertain. We do not know what he might have written on 28 April 1951 because coma intervened. By 29 April he had re-entered the organic world from which the supreme explicitness, enjoyed or suffered by a philosopher of genius, had uniquely distanced him.

II

(1)

On the afternoon of 27 April, neither drugged nor dreaming, Wittgenstein took what proved to be his last walk. It was a cold, gusty day with spells of dazzling sunlight between the showers. So far as one can tell, he was alone as he made his way through the streets of a town in which, more than any other, he had worked out his destiny. In Cambridge, his inner chaos – that 'constant, indescribable and almost morbid state of excitement'[67] – had taken shape as the career of a philosopher; an external form part-willed, part-resisted but ultimately acquiesced in for lack of a more tolerable alternative.

A walk with Wittgenstein was 'very exhausting':

> He would walk in spurts, sometimes coming to a stop while he made some emphatic remark and looking into my eyes with his piercing gaze. Then he would walk rapidly for a few yards, then slow down, then speed up or come to a halt, and so on. And this uncertain ambulation was conjoined with the most exacting conversation![68]

His companions were not encouraged to relax. They were not at liberty to open themselves up to their non-verbal surroundings in order to contemplate the beauties of nature. They were caught up in the inner tensions of a man who almost from childhood had driven his intellect relentlessly. And that intellect had, equally relentlessly, driven him. From this inner pressure, it was hard to escape:

> Often he would rush off to a cinema immediately after the class ended. He insisted on sitting in the very first row of seats, so that the screen would occupy his entire field of vision ... He wished to become totally absorbed into the film no matter how trivial or artificial it was in order to free his mind temporarily from the philosophical thoughts that tortured and exhausted him.[69]

While the blaring crudity of the cinema might shout down or anaesthetise the lucid delirium of his thoughts, the spectacle of nature seemed unable to penetrate him:

> In his youth Ludwig showed great interest in technical things, unlike Paul (his brother) who was drawn overwhelmingly to nature by flowers, animals and landscapes.[70]

A walk was less an escape from philosophy than an occasion for peripatetic dialogue – with others or with himself. He could not lose himself in things that lay outside of his primary preoccupation unless he could actively engage them. He read widely in literature – for that required an interpretative response on his part: more words, more thoughts. He took a deep interest in architecture when he himself was occupied in building – and rebuilding – his sister's house. Music he could appreciate because the passivity it demanded was relieved by the analytic attention to structure that it invited; and because he could play or whistle or (in imagination) conduct it. I know of no record of his being interested in painting. It is not unreasonable to assume that the natural world lay at the distal end of his fierce scrutiny, prevented from entering him by the outward pressure of his unremitting self-awareness. He lacked that 'negative capability' which would have permitted him to dissolve, howsoever little, into the spring day surrounding the last walk of his life.

Spring can be seen as having four phases: the return of the songs; the return of the light; the return of the green; and finally the return of the heat. The last phase was late that year, as it always is. Although there had been a mild, sunny spell in mid-April, the weather from the 26th onwards was chilly, windy, showery. On the 29th there was a hail storm, brought to Cambridge by northerly winds emanating from a depression over Scandinavia. The light, of course, continued lengthening irrespective of the usual 'unreasonable' weather; and, although records of birdsong and greenery are not available, it may be assumed that blackbirds and thrushes were rejoicing in the chilly air with their carols and that everywhere the dehiscent buds were starting to blur the stark winter outlines of the Cambridge trees.

In his depression in the autumn of 1949 when the cancer was first diagnosed, he must often have woken early and heard the robins singing on the lawns and among the crisping leaves of Trinity College. Those chilly rills of sound could only have deepened the despair that haunts the intersolvent edges of thought, fatigue and sleep. The final period of thought had begun when birdsong had returned: the blackbirds were singing from their lodging places on the tops of the budding trees and on pinnacles of carved stone. It seems unlikely that their gleaming ribbons of song incising the April air could also slice through the fog-and-phlegm befuddled darkness and the endocrine glooms of the winter past. Unlikely that they had gladdened his heart as he struggled to formulate criteria by which to separate admissible from inadmissible doubt. Equally unlikely that they unpeeled the husk of summer memories as he walked towards Midsummer Common or along the Cam, brooding over something that someone had said about him or his work, attending to his body for signs of improvement or deterioration, or thinking in a moment of brilliant sunlight of the losses he was living beyond. For he had no such memories.

The South had never called him:

of this I am certain: that we are not here in order to have a good time.[71]

From his Catholic-Jewish-Protestant background he seems to have derived only a Calvinistic inability to relax; a guilty conviction that we are here to work and not to enjoy ourselves. (The iron will of his father – the great industrialist and patron of the arts – seems to have driven three of his brothers who had found it too burdensome to suicide.) Thought was not delight but labour and suffering, proof of a ruthless and unremitting integrity.

No, it was not the South but the North – the far North – that attracted him. In October 1913 he had left England to winter in the north of Norway, first in a farm and then in a yet more remote ski hut which he had built for himself, to concentrate on logic. There he passed his days 'between logic, whistling, going for walks and being depressed'.[72] He returned to Norway repeatedly, his last visit as late as autumn 1950. He scarcely found peace of mind there:

> Everyday I was tormented by a frightful Angst and by depression in turns and even in the intervals I was so exhausted that I wasn't able to think of doing abit of work. It's terrifying beyond all description the kinds of mental torment there can be! It wasn't until two days ago that I could hear the voice of reason over the howls of the dammed and I began to work again.[73]

> I often think I am going mad.[74]

> Sometimes things inside me are in such a ferment that I think I'm going mad: then the next day I am totally apathetic again.[75]

But at least he was spared the company of others:

> Being alone here does me no end of good and I do not think I could now bear life among people.[76]

There was perhaps a bitter satisfaction in the correspondence between the barren landscape of his mind, as he sought illumination in total darkness, and the glacial solitude of this dark and deserted Ultima Thule.

> If a blackbird could talk we should not understand him.[77]

No, the blackbird's song was unlikely to gladden his heart; or even, by reminding him that this might be his last spring, to sadden it either. As for the flowers, the leaves, the buds unclenching despite the chilly weather – it is doubtful whether he paid them much attention. He could not permit himself to become lost in looking. Compared with thought, sight – being irredeemably particular – is stupefaction. If he exhorted philosophers caught up in paradoxes not 'to think but to look' (as he did in *Philosophical Investigations*), he meant not to look at *things*, to break out of language into wordless reality, but simply to look and see how words were actually used rather than talking about them from within blind preconceptions. He himself could never have suspended his thoughts long enough to permit the seen to enter and possess him. True looking, pure seeing, requires a tranquillity and an ability to become passive; and this was beyond him. At a superficial level, the assertion in *Tractatus* that

The limits of my language mean the limits of my world[78]

might be interpreted as being less a description of how things are in general than an acknowledgement of his own imprisoned state; of the coextensiveness for him of wakefulness and words.

Upwelling words pressed back nature, sealed him off from the new-leafed spring: if he ever escaped his own voice down his senses it was into mind-cancelling banalities of the cinema screen and not into the electric yellow of the daffodils and the forsythia, the transfixed hail of the white-green buds, or the newly lengthened evenings and the mystery of the returned light.

(2)

On the night of 27 April 'he fell violently ill'.[79] Precisely what form this sudden deterioration took is not disclosed in Norman Malcolm's *Memoir*. There are many possibilities: haemorrhage due to the thrombocytopenia which may occur with widespread secondary cancer in the bones; a urinary tract infection giving rise to septicaemia and gram-negative shock; heart failure consequent upon a heart attack to which a period on Stilboestrol would have made him prone. He at first remained conscious, so that Dr Bevan was able to tell him that he did not have long to live. His response to this information was characteristic:

… he exclaimed 'Good!'[80]

Mrs Bevan stayed with him throughout the night.

There is no record of how he passed the hours that remained to him between his collapse and the loss of consciousness. It seems improbable that he should have prayed in any formal or conventional sense. Many years earlier, when he was a soldier moving (by choice) up to the front line, he had written:

To pray is to think about the meaning of life.[81]

In that sense of the word 'pray' he had never ceased praying since childhood. There are no reports of discussions about the possibility of a 'future life' or 'a next world'. As he had admitted to Drury a few weeks before:

Isn't it curious that, although I have not long to live, I never find myself thinking about 'a future life'. All my interest is still in this life and the writing I am still able to do.[82]

Yes, it was curious. There was a strange dissociation between the certainty and doubt that he was exploring in his thoughts and the vast uncertainty that encircled him. Perhaps his inability to address himself to the existential situation that was closing around him, the death that was moving towards him, poised to extinguish his thoughts and the ground on which they stood, was part of 'the big gap' in his thinking which he now doubted would ever be filled. His inability to connect his thoughts with his life – with the things that deeply disturbed him and still defined him however much he dedicated that life to the process of thought, was curiously a part of his unassailable integrity. He knew that the two – his thoughts, his life – were connected, but that the connection lay unimaginably deep. It was for the shallow philosophers, for Russell and Joad and their like, to move easily between technical discussion and the Wayside Pulpit.

When as a volunteer in the First World War, deliberately choosing the firing line, he had been close to death before, he had found it difficult to continue philosophising:

I've had time and quiet enough for working. But nothing stirs me. My material is far away from me. It is only death that gives life its meaning.

Only one thing is needed: to be able to contemplate whatever happens to one; *collect* oneself.[83]

Now that he was being pressed, involuntarily, to the firing line, he no longer, it seems, felt the need to collect himself, to gather up his consciousness into the kind of summarising reflexion, triggered by the nearness of death in battle, that had entered the repudiated *Tractatus*. He simply continued to reflect as often and as deeply on the topics that seemed to him most fruitful. His material was close to him.

His final weeks were not filled with theological discussion. As he had confided to his notebook in 1916:

> To believe in God means to understand the question about the meaning of life.
>
> To believe in God means to see that the facts of the world are not the end of the matter.[84]

This, rather than trying to address oneself to a chimera in which metaphysical and moral categories were inextricably fused. The essence of the religious sensibility lies in its appreciation that the sense of the world is open, indeterminate, provisional, and not rounded off, or completed in, or encompassed by, our everyday knowledge or understanding or even by the more general descriptions and interpretations of the scientist.

> It is not *how* things are in the world that is mystical, but *that* it exists.[85]

The inexplicable fact of the world's being there undermines the completeness of any attempted explanation of its specific character and properties. About the former, he was sure, there was nothing to say. Theology that aimed to define the mystery, to articulate the aesthetic miracle of the world's existence, to enclose it in the characteristics attributed to God, could not have meant anything to him. Moreover, he had already ruled out a death-bed conversion by revelation:

> An inner experience cannot show me that I know something.[86]

It seems probable, then, that in those hours between collapse and coma, while he was waiting for the world 'not to alter, but to come to an end'[87] there was no prayer, no discussion of a future life, no commending of his soul to God. (This last his friends performed for him after he had died – and one of them has 'been troubled ever since as to whether what we did then was right.'[88]) And yet, he seems to have awaited death without fear.

Fear in the face of death is the best sign of a false, a bad life.[89]

His end, like his father's was exemplary – free of pain as well as of fear.

In 1913, he sat by his father's death-bed and had written about the experience to Russell, the philosophical father he was soon to repudiate:

> My dear father died yesterday in the afternoon. He had the most beautiful death I can imagine; without the slightest pain and falling asleep like a child! I did not feel sad for a single moment during all the last hours, but most joyful and I think that this death was worth a whole life.[90]

And the wish he had expressed as a soldier over thirty years before:

> May I die a good death, attending myself. May I never lose myself[91]

seems to have been fulfilled. Just before losing consciousness, he said to Mrs Bevan:

> Tell them I've had a wonderful life![92]

And with this, his voice, his mind, and the language that was himself, his world, came to an end. The sense-condition of all utterances evaporated. He passed into coma, that most savage of all critiques of certainty. The explicit sense of the spoken word, the implicit unsayable sense manifested in his life, the gaps in sense that provoked him into thought and the senselessness intuited outside of sense, all went out. The inexpressible distances that his consciousness constituted and his language had stabilised imploded. He left behind only a wake of words: propositions that others would have to find sense in and utter for him. He was silent – with a silence that lay an immeasurable distance from which he enjoined upon others and tried to find without success within himself.

> Tell them I've had a wonderful life!

Norman Malcolm, who reported these last words, found them 'mysterious and strangely moving':

When I think of his profound pessimism, the intensity of his moral and mental suffering, the relentless way in which he drove his intellect, his need for love together with the harshness that repelled love, I am inclined to believe that his life was fiercely unhappy. Yet at the end he himself exclaimed that it has been 'Wonderful!'[93]

They were sad as well as 'mysterious and strangely moving'; for Wittgenstein's native language was German and he was talking to an English woman. The voice of this solitary man without wife or child or brother or sister, had ended in a language foreign to him. To utter your last words on earth in a foreign tongue and to someone whom a few months before you scarcely knew is to die far, far from childhood. But then anyone who has outlived his youth has lived long enough to have become remote from whatever as a child he had imagined himself becoming. He has lived long enough to lose sight of himself – although, in one sense, Wittgenstein had perhaps travelled less than most: he had kept faith with and close to more of himself than had the average man; there is a clear thread of tenacious self-adherence connecting the ten-year-old child who had astonished his family by constructing a sewing machine with the sixty-year-old philosopher bidding the world farewell.

There is no account of Wittgenstein's condition at the time of his last words. We are told only that he spoke them 'before losing consciousness'. Since his respiration is not reported, we do not know whether the sentence was gasped out or uttered without difficulty; whether it was articulated clearly or whether it was unclear what he actually said. We don't even know if his conscious state was such as to permit us to assume that the utterance had the necessary sense-conditions to carry a truth-value. The imagination provoked by these missing details reaches out to places where others, equally crucial, are lacking; until the utterance, uprooted from the stream of Malcolm's narrative, seems encircled by doubts, to reverberate in an enormous silence. For example: Was this an isolated remark? Had it been preceded by a long pause? Was it a response to question? Had he looked at Mrs Bevan as he uttered it? Was she holding his hand? What expression did he have on his face? Were there tears in his eyes or emotion in his voice? Had the dawn begun breaking and was there daylight on his face? Were the birds singing outside – reminding him of the spring and of the coming summer, the first one for sixty-two years he would not know? And whom did he mean by 'them'?

'By "them" he undoubtedly meant his close friends,' Malcolm assures us.[94] But who were they? Was anyone close to him? Were the close friends few or many? Mrs Bevan, at any rate, could not possibly have had any conception of the extension of 'them'. She may have been aware of a small, nearby, recent sector of them; but the further reaches – the far way, the long ago, the secret, the incidental, those many acquaintances (lost in the recesses of his failing consciousness or the corners of a devastated and changing Europe) in whose lives he had been an unparalleled occurrence – would have lain outside of her knowledge. The catchment area from which they were drawn spanned a nineteenth-century childhood in Vienna and a late middle age in postwar Cambridge. Friends and enemies had been made in Vienna, Salzburg, Linz, Berlin, Manchester, Cambridge, Skjolden, Cracow, Oltmutz, Monte Cassino, Schneeberg, London, Newcastle, Wicklow, Galway, Dublin, Ithaca, Oxford ... The reference of 'them' ranged over the eminent and the unknown, the ageing and the still young, the living and the dead. Did he believe, as he spoke, that his message, his concluding unphilosophical postscript, would percolate through the near-them to the middle-them and so to the far limits of the living them? And was there – among that widely scattered crowd (scattered both sides of the grave) of acquaintances, pupils, admirers, readers, colleagues, friends, adversaries, fellow soldiers, teachers and fellow-teachers, relatives, lovers – one person, a face, a voice, a heart that had once seemed like the wavering image of home, to whom above all this final statement was addressed?

Of one thing we can be certain (a cornerstone perhaps of the language-game): his final utterance was fashioned out of expired air. We are permitted, therefore, to imagine his body appropriating for the last time a portion of the formless atmosphere, giving it audibility as a cry sculpted by his larynx, his palate, his tongue, his teeth and lips and conferring sense upon it by his presence and his communicative intent. Thus was it spoken by the man and heard by the woman; and thence it passed, from lip to ear, along radiating lines of speakers and listeners until, in Norman Malcolm's *Memoir*, it reaches the printed page to be propagated in a thousand, ten thousand, hardbound and paperback copies and read decades after the sounds had faded, after that long night had passed and the mouth that had spoken it had dissolved in the rain.

This, then, was his final enactment of the mystery that he had devoted so much of his thoughts to elucidating; the mystery that had at some times seemed to intervene between him and The Mystery and at others had seemed itself the source of all mysteries, real and contrived: the mystery of verbal meaning. In his youth, this mystery had been hard-edged; as he grew older, it lost its sharp edges and melted into the larger, more elusive, less articulable mysteries of everyday life. How he had suffered as, in his middle years, the perspicuous view had escaped him and language had changed from the autonomous sign system of his earlier vision into a complex *instrument* that could not be extricated from the boundless rule-governed chaos of human sociality!

Perhaps it was appropriate, then, that his last utterance should have been precisely the kind of complex speech-act whose analysis would have been beyond the scope of the philosophical grammar of the *Tractatus*. Appropriate, too, that his last words should have been a command: 'Tell them ...' There could have been no more characteristic way for that small, spare man with 'deep, often fierce, eyes' to have closed his account with language.

Embedded in the command, however, was a statement:

I've had a wonderful life.

Was this a legitimate assertion? A permissible move in the language-game? Even *Tractatus* would have made short work of this: in order to evaluate our lives, we must step outside of them:

The sense of the world must lie outside the world.[95]

And since my world and my life are coterminous, the sense of my life must lie outside of it and, what is more, outside of my language. The value of my life is precisely one of those things that cannot be summed up and said. If it was strange that, in spite of his depression and guilt, his isolation and the ugly quarrels that had disfigured so many of his relationships with others, in spite of the unbearable tension of thought and his ultimate failure to arrive at a final illumination, his last utterance before dyspnoea or coma dictated silence should have been in praise of life, it was surely stranger still that he, of all men, should have chosen to end his life uttering words evaluating that life. His younger self, the author of *Tractatus*, who had touched death in his thoughts, would have judged the last statement of his final self, reaching death in his body, rather harshly. The conditions under which an utterance makes sense do not widen just because someone is dying – even if that someone is oneself.

In his defence, he could perhaps have cited another of the propositions of *Tractatus*:

Death is not an event in life: we do not live to experience death.[96]

Conclusions about life must be drawn by the living; after death, there is nothing to be said:

At death, the world does not alter but comes to an end.[97]

If we wait until the end to conclude, we shall have waited too long.

(4)

Had he ended, then, as he had lived, struggling against pragmatic self-refutation? Throughout his life he had longed to speak things that elsewhere he had established as belonging to the unsayable or meaningless. Sometimes he had spoken them: he had found it impossible to remain silent about the mystery of things that he denied himself the right to speak about. He longed for a general solution to the puzzling fact of being alive; and longed, too, to feel more deeply, more continuously, puzzled by it:

We find certain aspects of seeing puzzling because we do not find the whole business of seeing puzzling enough.[98]

Anything less than the forbidden metaphysical enquiry was too local, too superficial, in short too trivial, to have a legitimate claim on his thoughts and to answer to his needs. And so he remained arrested in indecision, in the borderland between two deeply conflicting views of life: as a problem to which there might at least be partial answers; and as an inviolable mystery which could be neither analysed nor explained – nor even spoken of. His mission was consequently in conflict with itself. Like Beckett's artist, Wittgenstein had lived inside

The expression that there is nothing to express, nothing with which to express, nothing from which to express, no power to express, no desire to express, together with the obligation to express.[99]

And the tireless thinker, who began each day's thinking as if the world had not been thought about the day, the millennium, before could have taken Molloy's conclusion as his motto:

I can't go on. I'll go on.[100]

Did he die, then, with self-contradiction on his lips? Did he say farewell to himself, and to the world, gripped by self-refutation? Writing in 1916, shortly he was taken prisoner in battle, he reflected:

The aesthetic miracle (*Wunder*) is that the world exists. That what exists does exists.[101]

And now, thirty-five years later, at death's edge, he did not say that his life had been happy, or that it had been worthwhile, or good, or even that it had made sense – only that it had been 'wonderful'. And on this, his younger self and his dying self, all his many conflicting selves, would have met in agreement. Seeing his life, reflected in the black mirror of death as an unaccountable fact, and the world as 'a limited whole',[102] what else could a truly profound man feel but the simple wonder that had visited him so rarely throughout his life but which had perhaps lain deeper than, and prompted, all else? Is it surprising that, knowing he had only a few hours or minutes to live, he should have been over-whelmed by astonishment at having been given such a self to live, such a world to live in? What else but wonder should he have felt (since he was not crushed by pain or drowning in nausea, malaise or confusion) on the threshold of unbeing, of the coma, of the death where the dialectic of speech and silence, doubt and certainty, would resolve itself?

(5)

And what of the beginning he had found so difficult to begin at? Was he to die, to end, without ever having reached it? A few weeks earlier, he had copied Faust's famous words into his notebook:

Im anfang war die Tat.[103]

In the beginning was the *Deed*. So, at the beginning, there is not philosophy with its puzzles, its problems, its first- and second- and third-order doubts. For the beginning was not the Word but the Deed – the deed that had brought about the strange fact of the world. And philosophy should begin not with doubt or certainty not with questions or disputations – they must come later. In the beginning, there must be astonishment – at the huge and beautiful fact of the world, at what the poet called 'the million-petalled fact of being here':[104]

There is nothing more wonderful than the *true* problems of philosophy.[105]

Philosophical problems are true when they are prompted by astonishment. To begin at the beginning (and not to begin too far back) means not to go further back than one's astonishment dictates or can penetrate.

Early in his career as a soldier, he had written:

Perhaps the nearness of death will bring some light.[106]

It seems it had. At the very limit of his life, when familiar, differentiated daylight had become the edge of undifferentiated eternity, where words were only the spindrift off breaking silence, he had glimpsed the strange truth that, to 'one who sees the world aright'[107] all lives that are not terrible are wonderful.

In the beginning was astonishment. And so it was with a cry of astonishment, of wonder, perhaps even of joy, that he passed over into silence.

On 29th April 1951 there died at Cambridge, England one of the greatest and most influential philosophers of our times, Ludwig Wittgenstein.[108]

Notes

1. Letter from Wittgenstein to M. O'C. Drury, quoted in *Ludwig Wittgenstein. Personal Recollections*, edited by Rhush Rees (Oxford: Blackwell, 1981).
2. Letter from Wittgenstein to Norman Malcolm, quoted in *Ludwig Wittgenstein. A Memoir* (Oxford University Press, 1958), p. 98.
3. William Warren Barkley III, *Wittgenstein* (London: Quartet Books, 1974), p. 130.
4. Letter to Normal Malcolm, 16 April, 1951, quoted in Malcolm, op. cit., p. 99
5. Malcolm, ibid., p. 100.
6. Malcolm, ibid., p. 100.
7. Ludwig Wittgenstein, *On Certainty*, edited by G.E.M. Anscombe and G.H. von Wright. Translated by Denis Paul and G.E.M. Anscombe (Oxford: Blackwell, 1974).
8. *On Certainty*, paragraph 300.
9. G.H. von Wright, *Ludwig Wittgenstein: a Biographical Sketch* (Oxford University Press, 1958), p. 18.
10. *On Certainty*, between paragraphs 532 and 533.

11. *On Certainty*, between paragraphs 387 and 388.
12. *On Certainty*, between paragraphs 470 and 471.
13. *On Certainty*, paragraph 471.
14. R. Descartes, *Meditations on First Philosophy*, translated by Elizabeth Haldane and G.R.T. Ross, in *The Philosophical Works of Descartes*, Volume 1 (Cambridge University Press, 1967).
15. David Hume, *A Treatise of Human Nature* (New York: Dolphin Books, 1961), p. 199.
16. Quoted in John Passmore, *A Hundred Years of Philosophy* (London: Penguin, 1968), p. 61.
17. Wittgenstein's remarks on Kierkegaard are quote in M. O'C. Drury's contribution to Rhees, op. cit., pp. 102–4.
18. S. Kierkegaard, *Concluding Unscientific Project*, translated by David Swenson and Walter Lowrie (Princeton University Press, 1944).
19. Ludwig Wittgenstein, *Tractatus Logico-Philosophicus*, translated by D.F. Pears and B.F. McGuinness (London: Routledge and Kegan Paul, 1963), 6.51.
20. Ibid., 4.003.
21. Ibid., 4.003
22. Quoted in Malcolm, op. cit., p. 93.
23. Ludwig Wittgenstein, *Philosophical Investigations*, edited and translated by G.E.M. Anscombe (Oxford: Blackwell, 1963), p. 111.
24. Ibid., p. 115.
25. Ibid., p. 132.
26. Quoted in Ronald Clark, *Bertrand Russell* (London: Penguin, 1975), p. 211.
27. *On Certainty*, paragraph 344.
28. G. E. Moore, *Autobiography*. Quoted in John Passmore. *A Hundred Years of Philosophy* (London: Penguin, 1968) p. 201.
29. Preface to Wittgenstein, *Philosophical Investigations*, op. cit.
30. *On Certainty*, between paragraphs 387 and 388.
31. Desmond Lee, quoted in Rhees, op. cit., p. 85.
32. John King, quoted in Rhees, ibid., p. 85.
33. Ludwig Wittgenstein, Preface to *Tractatus Logico-Philosophicus*, op. cit.
34. Ludwig Wittgenstein, Preface to *Philosophical Investigations*, op. cit.
35. *On Certainty*, between paragraphs 387 and 388.
36. *On Certainty*, paragraph 400.
37. *On Certainty*, paragraph 464.
38. *On Certainty*, paragraph 467.
39. *On Certainty*, paragraph 482.
40. *On Certainty*, paragraph 121.
41. *On Certainty*, paragraph 122.
42. *On Certainty*, paragraph 509.
43. *On Certainty*, paragraph 369.
44. *On Certainty*, paragraph 403.
45. *On Certainty*, paragraph 344.
46. *On Certainty*, paragraph 519.
47. *On Certainty*, paragraph 450.
48. *On Certainty*, paragraph 487.

Index

absolute idealism/idealists, 170
absolute truth, 19, 20, 56
abstract ideas, 77
abstract truths, 9
adaptive behaviour, 49; *see also*
    survival
agency, agents, 58, 127, 138, 158
aims, 83; *see also* goals
aletheia, 50, 68n
algorithms, 102
algorithms and grammar, 88
amnesia, 112
analytical truths, 11
anaphora, 47
Anglo-American analytical tradition,
    xiv
animality, 2, 5
animism, 73
anthropomorphism, 72, 81, 95, 99,
    103, 110, 146
anti-philosophy, 198, 205
appearance, 173
apperception, 144
arbitrariness, arbitrary signs, 47
Arithmetic-Logic Unit, 77
aseity, 11, 16, 45
astonishment, xi, 155, 156, 159, 160,
    162, 165–6, 168, 170, 185n, 186n,
    190, 197, 224
atomic theory, 23–4
atoms, 23, 100
Austin, J.L., 157
awareness, 3, 4, 7, 43–4, 93, 176; *see
    also* bodily awareness; self-awareness
awareness, unfocused, 7

Barnes, Hazel, 184n
Barthes, Roland, 166–7
Beckett, Samuel, 222–3
behaviour, 83, 86
behaviour, animal, 3
behaviour, grammar of, 89
behaviour, intelligent, 148

behaviour, rule-governed, 123
behaviourism, 84, 98
being, 164, 170-2
Being and Nothingness (Sartre), 179,
    184n
being-for-itself/being-in-itself, 161,
    184n
belief in God, 29, 217 (Wittgenstein)
beliefs, 85
Bell, David, 59, 69n
Benveniste, Emile, 187n
Bevan, Dr, 215
Bevan, Mrs, 190-1, 215, 218
binary digits, 100
biological epistemology, 66n
biological materialism, 2
biological naturalism, 108
biological theory of mind, xii
biology, explanation in, 26
bodily awareness, 156, 189
body, 156–9, 161–2, 171, and passim
Bohr, Niels, 21
Boole, George, 8
Bradley, F.H., 193
brain, 79–80, 81–2, 110, 117, 129,
    130, 144–5, 157, and passim
brain activity, 53, 131; *see also* neural
    activity
brain function, 90
brain processes, 53
brain states, 108
brain/mind barrier, 116 passim

calculations, 73, 75–80, 115
calculating machines, 77–9
Cartesian dualism, 152, 157, 182n
Cartesian epistemology, 152, 208
cash value of truth, 29
causal interaction theory, 132
causal theory of perception, 129
cerebral dysfunction, 130
certainty, 192, 203, 207
chaos, 205, 211, 221